Praise For *The Constellation Approach*

"The Constellation Approach: Finding Peace Through Your Family Lineage combines ancient wisdom traditions with contemporary family systems theory, and describes a radical reciprocal process of coming to wholeness… This guide book serves as a sacred blue print for coming to peace with our familial and ancestral legacies. [It's] an accessible and heart-felt explication of… the liberating experiential work done in the Constellation Approach."

Judy Tsafrir, MD
Adult and Child Psychiatrist and Psychoanalyst
Harvard Medical School

"The Constellation Approach is a jewel in the crown of Family Systems Constellations. This book is an excellent introduction to Family Constellations, but it far surpasses that purpose… [The Fausts'] work offers a spiritual practice, one which unfolds and strengthens with precision as it progresses. A work book, an engaging text, a meditation and a path of empowerment, this book is a treasure not only for facilitators of Family Constellations but all helping professionals."

Francesca Mason Boring, Family Constellation Facilitator
Author of *Connecting to our Ancestral Past—Healing through*
Family Constellations, Ceremony and Ritual

"To say that this type of engagement with the Family Energy Field is lifesaving is almost a rude understatement—I have never witnessed and personally experienced the healing power of anything coming close to this—not in Western Medicine or other forms of complementary medicine… To have a book describing the process and making it accessible to anyone interested in healing for themselves and others is a huge gift!"

Sabine R. O'Laughlin, MD

"The Constellation Approach offers great hope and possibility for our way of being with each other in the world. Jamy and Peter Faust have configured a path of healing that is profoundly relevant… Their work is simple yet complex, deep and far reaching, ancient, timeless and emergently imperative for healing and living in true community with all life. Beautiful and brilliant—a work that will influence many fields for years to come."

Sherry Pae
Dean of Advanced Studies, Barbara Brennan School of Healing

"Not just a book about theory but rather a practical guidebook that clearly guides the reader through a process of connecting to self, soul, and spirit. What emerges is a unique and powerful contribution to alleviate human suffering. The Constellation Approach... offers authentic assistance to make peace with the past, freeing us to reside in the present and generate a new peaceful future... I highly recommend [this book] to any fellow travelers on the path and as a very useful template for clinicians."

Ian Macnaughton, Ph.D.
Past President, British Columbia Association of Clinical Counselling
Author of *Embodying the Mind & Minding the Body* and *Body, Breath, & Consciousness*

"The Constellation Approach by Jamy and Peter Faust is a must read for anyone interested in Family Constellations from a spiritual perspective... It will certainly be required reading for all my future facilitator trainings."

Susan D. Ulfelder
Founder of Hellinger Institute of DC

"Jamy and Peter Faust have spent much of their lives exploring the vast landscape of healing modalities. Their study has taken them to many teachers, many ways. This book marks a moment of confluence for them as they introduce the Constellation Approach, a unique synthesis of and expansion upon the work of Bert Hellinger's Family Constellations and other perspectives. Their understanding is... both grounded and fresh."

Suzi Tucker
Family Constellations Facilitator/Presenter
Author of *Gather Enough Fireflies*

"The family is mankind's original social construct. It forms us, shapes us, and for better or worse, affects us throughout our entire life... "Multigenerational family therapy" has become a powerful new method for resolving our personal conflicts, and the Fausts' describe it beautifully in this fascinating new study that offers positive change for all of us."

Lynn A. Robinson
Author of *Divine Intuition: Your Inner Guide to Purpose, Peace and Prosperity*

"The Constellation Approach: Finding Peace through Your Family Lineage is a welcome and powerful contribution to the field of Family Constellations... Participation in The Constellation Approach Immersion Program with Jamy and Peter has expanded my compassion and appreciation for others, and brought me ease and a feeling of belonging. Their work has led me to a deeper sense of rootedness and reclaimed connection with my ancestral lineage."

Bruce Nayowith, MD

THE
CONSTELLATION APPROACH

Also by Jamy and Peter Faust

Poems of Love, Sex and God

THE
CONSTELLATION APPROACH

———— ✦✦✦ ————

Finding Peace Through Your
Family Lineage

JAMY AND PETER FAUST

REGENT PRESS
Berkeley, California

The Constellation Approach: Finding Peace Through Your Family Lineage

By Jamy and Peter Faust

Copyright © 2015 Jamy and Peter Faust

REGENT PRESS
Berkeley, California
www.regentpress.net | regentpress@mindspring.com

First Edition, 2015

Book design by Holly Moxley of Tracking Wonder Consultancy.

Cover artwork: Sandra Mayo, Finding Connection, original size: 18"x 24", medium: Monoprint-Collage, sandramayo.com

This book is available for special discounts for bulk purchases. For more information contact http://www. constellationapproach.com; office@constellationapproach.com

Library of Congress Cataloguing-in-Publication Data

Faust, Jamy and Peter Faust.

The Constellation Approach: finding peace / Jamy Faust and Peter Faust

Paperback:
ISBN 13: 978-1-58790-331-1
ISBN 10: 1-58790-331-8

E-Book:
ISBN 13: 978-1-58790-332-8
ISBN 10: 1-58790-332-6

Library of Congress Control Number: 2015952360

Printed in the United States of America

To our parents,
Robert Arthur Williams & Joan Margaret McNeil Williams Theriault
and
Edward Henry Faust & Joy Weldon Faust
and
To all families everywhere.

Contents

Foreword

We live in times of massive and irreversible global change. Accelerating destruction of the biosphere by the onslaught of petroleum-based industrial civilization is bringing about what evolutionary scientists call "the sixth extinction." Population pressures are combining with environmental degradation to create a "perfect storm" that threatens the foundations of the social order—even as feckless politicians squabble about protecting their parochial interest.

These rapid global changes demand that once-isolated fields be studied as multidimensional systems. Such a systemic approach, requires, for example that leaders in the fields of medicine and psychotherapy work together to forge new methods for healing and intervention. Psychotherapy can no longer be viewed as a special sort of private interaction between two individuals in a closed room, but necessarily involves consideration of the complex web of relations existing in families, across multiple generations and within communities.

This multidimensional perspective to approaching global challenges has given rise to a systemic approach to multigenerational family therapy. Numerous individuals have developed this approach over the past thirty or so years both in Europe and the United States. One of the most original and influential pioneers of the family systems approach is the German former priest and family therapist Bert Hellinger, who is one of the three main teachers whom The Constellation Approach founders Jamy and Peter Faust credit as contributing to their own unique approach. Perhaps because of his history as a missionary priest in South Africa, Hellinger discovered and taught that recognition of the spiritual reality of pre-birth and post-death *soul* consciousness—a kind of consciousness—can be accessed through simple perception, without verbal analysis, of the relative postures and positioning of bodies in space.

As Jamy and Peter Faust put it, there are certain "threads of consciousness" that connect family members regardless of time-space distances and regardless even of the boundaries of birth and death. It is here that we find in the Hellinger-influenced systemic approach the most radical departure from conventional individual or family systems therapists. The majority of family systems therapists, as well as most of the Western-educated public, still carry an almost instinctive distrust or resistance to any consideration, or even discussion of *soul*—the reality of what comes before conception/birth and after death. These are topics which cannot be reasonably discussed in any meetings or publications of therapists that adhere to the current professional paradigm.

My own work as a psychologist exploring different states and dimensions of consciousness in psychotherapy found a strong resonance with Hellinger's teachings, although I came to my work from a different direction and with a different methodology. In addition, the Fausts credit the body-oriented work of Barbara Brennan with subtle energy-fields as another of the sources of their uniquely synthesized Constellation Approach. All of these approaches, including Jamy and Peter's own application, recognize the primacy of perception over theory. The subtle energy-fields that both reflect and express our inner states can be felt and perceived, and as Hellinger continually emphasizes, his approach is phenomenological—i.e. based on perception not on theoretical speculations about inner complexes and the like.

I especially appreciate how Jamy and Peter incorporate in their Constellation Approach "statements of empowerment." "Statements of empowerment" are one of the strongest and most effective innovations that Hellinger introduced into the practice of family therapy. Most forms of therapy use various derivations or forms of questioning to elicit inner hidden feelings and perceptions in the client or patient. In the approach that Hellinger pioneered and that the Fausts use to great effect, the client may be asked or prompted to make what are called "statements or words of empowerment" to another member of their family system, or to that other member's "representative." The statements are empowering because they express the actual innermost truth of a situation or relationship from the perspective of *soul,* a perspective that never wavers from the truth, without defense or pretense.

Such statements of course cannot be faked. They must be true for that individual in that situation or relationship. It is part of the skill and intuitive insight of the therapist in those situations to find the statement that exactly expresses that truth. In the case descriptions included in this book, the reader will find several examples of individual clients relating how their empowerment statements liberated them from long-standing patterns of disconnect and negativity. Jamy and Peter are to be congratulated for their clear-sighted and warm-hearted presentation of this profound work of healing.

Ralph Metzner, Ph.D.
Professor Emeritus, California Institute of Integral Studies
Author of *The Unfolding Self* and *The Well of Remembrance*

An Introduction

Finding Peace through Your Family Lineage

One person can influence their family, one family can influence another, then another, then ten, one hundred, one thousand more, and the whole of humanity will benefit.

—Tenzin Gyatso, 14th Dalai Lama

There is a path that leads to inner peace. It is through your family lineage. Humanity's movement towards peace begins one person at a time, one family at a time. We each desire peace for ourselves, our species, and our planet. Our collective progression towards peace, though, begins with each one of us. It begins with our desire for peace and our willingness to embrace the spirits of our mothers and fathers to gain understanding and compassion.

In order to evolve your consciousness and experience inner peace, first acknowledge that peace begins in the home, with the self, and with your family lineage. Think of it this way: Each of us is the continuation of our respective mothers and fathers, of our respective family lineage, and all that has occurred by and to our ancestors. Many of our internal conflicts were handed to us in the form of unconscious beliefs. To begin a path towards peace, we need to look no further than the circumstances of our own birth to find the conflicts that have not been resolved. Our outer struggles as adults have roots in the conflicts of our developmental years and even the choices made before birth.

The journey towards peace is not easy, but what we are offering you is a distinct path that can help you navigate your way. The Constellation Approach (TCA) is a stirring journey towards reconciliation and wholeness that offers an array of means to face these great battles, and ultimately to make amends and come to peace. The Constellation Approach is also a lifelong process that deepens as it is practiced.

As human beings we are here to evolve our personal consciousness and contribute to the evolution of our family's consciousness. The steps we take ultimately contribute to the evolution of the vast pool of human consciousness. The Constellation Approach is a path to exploring your family lineage, experiencing your Soul nature, and coming to peace with the masculine and feminine energies within and all around you.

As a wife-husband team who has worked with hundreds of people with their familial relationships, we have noticed something. We've noticed that people come to us because they know that to arrive at lasting peace requires going beyond talk, analysis, and rehashing family stories. It requires moving into the Soul of their family lineage.

A Continuation of Healing Traditions

Like everyone, the two of us could say our spiritual journey began with our birth or perhaps, as we have come to believe, before our physical birth. After a decade each working as healers, our path began to crystallize when we discovered the teachings and philosophy of Bert Hellinger. Hellinger is an engaging German psychotherapist and philosopher who innovated the therapeutic method known as Family Constellations. Family Constellations reveal hidden dynamics in a family system or relationships so that conflicts can be acknowledged truthfully and healed. These dynamics typically span multiple generations. Hundreds of professional practitioners across the globe have applied Bert Hellinger's insights to a broad range of issues.

Our own experiences and trainings with Hellinger opened each of us up to a new path in our own healing and, ultimately, to helping our families and community. At first, we had no idea what we were getting into, but Hellinger's constellation method changed every aspect of our lives.

Our earlier education in healing began with Barbara Brennan, the renowned spiritual healer, physicist, and pioneer in the field of energy healing. Her work offered us the opportunity to observe the Human Energy Field and taught us how to see the healing process in a new way. She also gave us an energy-based framework to comprehend, facilitate, and ultimately teach what has evolved into the Constellation Approach. But it was Bert Hellinger, who later taught us about personal healing through the family lineage, and how to observe family members from a place of non-judgment. He showed us ways to enter the healing process through the frame of the Family Soul, enabling us to work within a larger energy template.

A third important influence on our healing work was the teachings of Dr. Ralph Metzner, a multi-talented psychotherapist, writer, poet, and researcher. Dr. Metzner is Professor Emeritus of Psychology at the California Institute of Integral Studies. When we began working with him, he shared his view of the journey of the human Soul and how it relates to the family we choose to be born into. He expanded our awareness of self immensely beyond the conscious mind into the level of Soul. Through those experiences of Soul consciousness, we were able to understand that Family Constellations not only offer a path to emotional and psychological healing but they also provide a lens into the Soul agreements that are made with parents, siblings, and ancestors. This awareness, once experienced and integrated, transcends the personality's attachments to pain and suffering, shedding new light on why events and circumstances may have occurred in our lives.

The Constellation Approach teachings braid together the seminal, innovative work of these three pivotal teachers—Hellinger, Brennan, and

Metzner—to whom we are deeply grateful. Hellinger has often described his work "phenomenological," meaning, "results can be observed [but one can't fully understand how it is happening]." This book, in part, is our attempt to explain, "*how* it is happening"—the movement that transpires in a Constellation, *how* healing occurs, and the necessary skills one needs in order to master this healing practice.

Other facilitators of Family Constellations have also contributed to our knowledge of this still-evolving practice. If there is one thing we have learned from observing the constellation practices of other facilitators, it is that the constellation method is a healing art of the highest degree. Each facilitator creates his or her unique healing style when administering this particular medicine for the Soul.

We are no different. Our Constellation Approach will help you find peace through your family lineage by emphasizing three distinct elements: an awareness of subtle energy, understanding larger energetic fields of influence on familial and lineage dynamics, and a focus on Soul Consciousness. Only when we move with Soul Consciousness, can we move towards deep peace.

What is a Constellation?

A Constellation is the placement of people or place-markers that depicts a relationship and/or situation in one's life. It can reflect inner feelings and images which are unknowingly carried, bringing new and different perspectives to light.

Imagine your family—extending through several generations—as a constellation. Each family member, alive and deceased, known and unknown, is a star of sorts. The relationships among those various stars create their own unique patterns and dynamics. You are who you are, in part, as a result of those dynamics. A Constellation within the Constellation Approach methodology draws from this analogy but also makes it concrete. We have described Constellations in detail throughout Chapters 3 and 4. We also have identified ten key kinds of Constellations that allow you to take this journey layer by layer. There is, for instance, a Mother's Lineage Constellation and a Father's Lineage Constellation. There is an Illness Constellation, and a War and Conflict Constellation. Part II and III of this book will guide you through each of these ten key Constellations:

- ≫ Family of Origin
- ≫ Father's Lineage
- ≫ Mother's Lineage
- ≫ Siblings
- ≫ Physical Disease and Mental Illness
- ≫ Death
- ≫ War and Conflict
- ≫ Immigration/Migration
- ≫ Religion
- ≫ Relationships

It's important to remember that healing is not theoretical. It is experiential. Your first-hand experience of a Constellation is instrumental for your healing and movement towards peace. One method, which this book guides you through, involves the use of figurines to represent various family members. In the pages ahead you will find direct instructions and exercises to facilitate your own Constellation experience.

A second way you can experience a Constellation is through our Constellation Approach seminars and our Immersion Program, which are outlined in the appendix. We have organized this program into ten modules in accordance with the ten key Constellations. During these live program events, a participant may be a Client who is actively working on an issue related to family. Through a carefully facilitated process, participants also become a part of the Constellations of other participants. A Constellation can be comprised of two to ten or more individuals, depending upon the nature of the Client's issue.

How to Use this Book

The book is divided into five parts. Part I orients you to the central tenets and concepts of the Family Constellation and Energy Field models that we use in the Constellation Approach. Because this process is nuanced and its effects emerge in a non-material sphere of energy fields and Soul Consciousness, it will help to have language for these new experiences. Part I will help you navigate this powerful process.

Parts II and III provide more direct experiences of each of the ten key Constellations. This section is divided into the ten Universal Themes that affect families regardless of social standing, ethnicity, or culture. At the end of these chapters you'll find sections labeled "Words of Empowerment" and "Reflections." These pages are designed to help you explore your personal relationship with these themes. They also offer you the opportunity to create a record of your family lineage and the facets that have had the most impact on your life. If you enter our Constellation Approach Immersion Program, these chapters will become essential guides to your experience. At the end of several chapters in Parts I, II, and III, you'll also find a section called "A Constellation Journeyer." These stories will help you recognize parts of your own journey in our experiences and those numerous people with whom we have worked.

Part IV invites you to extend your experience of Constellations into the realm of our shared Soul nature. This section reinforces the concepts that we are spiritual beings incarnated into human form with the distinct purpose of contributing to the evolution of the personal, familial, and the larger consciousness of humanity. We offer a variety of ways to practice Soul-level awareness by enhancing self-perception, your role within your family, and your current life within the world.

Part V offers the opportunity to practice and apply the Constellation Approach to your own family lineage. Here, the "Constellation Experiences" will guide you through detailed steps to set up your own Constellations for each of the Universal Themes presented in Parts II and III.

This book, the Constellation Approach seminars and Immersion Program are a direct result and reflection of our own journey of transformation. We offer this book as a tool to empower you, your loved ones, your friends—all of us—on our collective path towards peace.

We thank you for joining us as peacemakers and peacekeepers. May you journey to inner peace and may our efforts together heal, and lift the consciousness of humankind everywhere on the planet. Together.

—*Jamy & Peter*

Recognizing the sacred begins, quite simply, when we are interested in every detail of our lives.

—Chögyam Trungpa, Tibetan Buddhist meditation master

PART I

Acknowledging Our True Nature

Chapter 1

Remembering Who We Are

*I believe that to meet the challenges of our times, human beings will
have to develop a greater sense of universal responsibility. Each of us
must learn to work not just for oneself, one's own family or nation, but
for the benefit of all humankind. Universal responsibility is the key to
human survival. It is the best foundation for world peace.*

—Tenzin Gyatso, 14th Dalai Lama

It's easy and natural to get mired in our own conflicts. In fact, we often
identify ourselves with our conflicts. We forget who we are, but in reality, we
can disentangle ourselves from conflict by remembering our true nature. And
that deep remembering is part of what the Constellation Approach offers—a
way to awaken. It does not offer a system of personal psychotherapy or of
engaging in family therapy, but rather a path of discovering how the nature
of our Soul acts through us and our **Family Lineages**. Ultimately, we discover
how each family connects to a greater whole.

Following this simple, enriching path is not only a way to resolve our
personal conflicts. It also enables us to glimpse our Soul's purpose for this
life, for our family, and for humanity at large. In order to navigate this

journey, you may find it helpful to consider various ways of viewing your true nature. That's what this part offers—a sampling of perspectives that will help prime you for the Constellation journeys ahead.

On Conflict

We are not our conflicts. Resolving conflict begins with healing the unresolved strife each of us carries, often unconsciously. Much of our inner turmoil originates before birth; it begins with our mothers, fathers, grandparents, and passes from one generation to the next.

Every human being has the opportunity to be a peacemaker, a contributor to personal, familial, and societal peace though resolving our internal discord.

Everyone thinks of changing the world, no one thinks of changing themselves.

—Leo Tolstoy, novelist

In this sense, conflicts are the silver lining of our inheritance from our ancestral bloodlines. But if we do not heal the inner unrest with our own family—our mother, father and siblings—we carry it within ourselves and into the world. If we're in conflict (internal or external) with our mothers, we will eventually find ourselves in friction with women. The same happens with our fathers: if our discontentment is not healed, we will be at odds with men throughout our lives. Moreover, such unresolved conflicts create internal dissonance between the masculine and feminine aspects of ourselves. The pitched battles within us—sniper attacks on the opposing gender, running feuds with siblings, predictable patterns of gathering and losing resources—originated long before we were born in the actions, agreements and circumstances of our ancestors. In this lifetime, we either pass on these unresolved conflicts or contribute towards everlasting peace.

The Constellation Approach is an opportunity to discover true peace and happiness for ourselves, our families, and for those who will follow in our footsteps. The approach hinges on this simple view: Who we are and the conflicts we carry and aspire to resolve stem from our biological mother's and father's respective lineages. By exploring our parental bloodlines to uncover, understand, and integrate these conflicts, we can move forward with a sense of peace previously unknown to us.

If there is to be peace in the world,
There must be peace in the nations.
If there is to be peace in the nations,
There must be peace in the cities.
If there is to be peace in the cities,
There must be peace between neighbors.
If there is to be peace between neighbors,
There must be peace in the home.
If there is to be peace in the home,
There must be peace in the heart.

—Lao Tzu, Taoist philosopher

On Connection

To journey into our mother's and our father's respective lineages can be unnerving, to say the least. Such a process challenges some of our fundamental views of our individual self.

Many of us have grown up believing that to become a fully realized human being we must differentiate ourselves from our parents and "strike out" on our own. This cultural myth includes assumptions about free will, individuation, separation, and self-reliance—core beliefs of the self-realization movement. Yet, these tenets of emotional and psychological maturity have helped push modern civilization to the brink of disconnection from our ancestors. This urge to leave the nest, to break away from old beliefs that hold us in place, affects everyone regardless of social or economic circumstances. If we're lucky, we mature, and a new perspective forms. We gain appreciation for our parents, grandparents, and ancestors who have paved the way for us. If not, we stay stuck in the attitudes of blame and victimhood, which keep us small and fearful, and often lead to defensiveness towards others.

Many people spend whole lifetimes searching unconsciously for the meaning of why things happened in their lives or in their ancestors' lives. The answers to these questions remain elusive, or at best, rationalized on the mental plane of consciousness, but these "answers" and narratives do not bring peace within. On one hand, we feel free to do as we wish, to be different from those who have come before us. On the other hand, we are never truly free from the ancestral field in which we were born.

The particle is not separate from the field. The field determines everything. If you wish to understand the movement of the particle you must study and understand the field.

—Albert Einstein, physicist

We are merely a particle as Einstein tells us, part of an immense energy field that determines everything. Our movement, the direction of our life, the partners and careers we choose, even the illness and disease that occur in our lives are determined by this powerful field that influences us at the deepest levels of our unconscious being. If we want to truly know and understand ourselves, it is important to study and understand the influence of the Family Energy Field.

The Science of Behavioral Epigenetics

Part of who we are is genetic, but there is increasing evidence that our present behaviors stem from our ancestors' experiences. The science of behavioral epigenetics can shed light on our nuanced nature and prime us for the experience of a Constellation. Current scientific research on DNA transmission strongly suggests that our parents' and even grandparents' experiences influence the behavior of their offspring.

For instance, how might experiences such as abuse, trauma, or addiction affect the genetics of future offspring? Interestingly, traumatic experiences do leave molecular scars that adhere to our DNA—as cellular memories of our ancestors' lives. These scars mark the history of their lives but they also provide information about our own behavior—past, present, and future. What our parents, grandparents, and distant ancestors experienced in their lives literally creates an overlay on our DNA.

The Greek prefix *epi* means "over" or "outer." Behavioral epigenetics is beginning to prove that our behavioral traits—both our weaknesses, and our strengths—have their origins in our ancestral past. According to a recent article in *Discover Magazine*[1],

> Like silt deposited on the cogs of a finely tuned machine after the seawater of a tsunami recedes, our experiences, and those of our forbearers, are never gone, even if they have been forgotten. They become a part of us, a molecular residue holding fast to our genetic scaffolding. The DNA remains the same, but psychological and behavior tendencies are inherited. The mechanisms of behavioral epigenetics underlie not only deficits and weaknesses but the strengths and resilience that we inherit too.

We know that our DNA is the biological basis for our physical being, and that DNA testing now allows us to trace the migration of where we originated to who we are today. The Constellation Approach explores the possibility that these epi-overlays are, in part, our emotional inheritance from our ancestors.

The Eastern Medical Perspective of Congenital Essence

If we consider epigenetics alongside the Traditional Chinese Medicine view of Congenital Essence, we can gain even richer insight into our true nature. In the Taoist perspective on life and incarnation, we inherit parental energy from our birth parents that we cannot change, but we do have the opportunity, if we are aware, to transform it. This prenatal, pre-birth energy—all the energetic qualities

Our life is like a grain of sand
Blowing among others—
Touching and resting for a while
Moving through this universe
Exposed for all to see.
Take me, Oh great sea!
Carry me to some foreign land
Deposit me on a shore far away.
Let me have a taste of other earth,
Feel the wind of distant places
And the scent of tropic soil.
I face the fullness of this life
Yet forever will remain
Just a humble grain
From the beach where I was born.

—Jamy and Peter

---

1   Dan Hurley, "Grandmother's Experiences Leave a Mark on Your Genes," *Discover Magazine* (May 2013)

inherited from one's parents—is known as **Congenital Essence.**[2] It's the basis for our individual energy signature.

The Tao teaches that it is always up to the individual to accept fully what we inherit in order to cultivate our Congenital Essence for the highest good. With wisdom and understanding, we can utilize our inherited Congenital Essence to foster strengths and limit the effects of lesser qualities. Everyone receives aspects that are considered more or less desirable, the teachers of Traditional Chinese Medicine say.

Our very essence is derived from the qualities passed onto us though our incarnational journey, especially our Family Lineage. In the Constellation Approach, we work to accept fully what we have inherited and to consciously evolve those aspects for the better.

We all grow up with the weight of history on us. Our ancestors dwell in the attics of our brains as they do in the spiraling chains of knowledge hidden in every cell of our bodies.

—Shirley Abbott, author

The Hindu View of Samskaras

The Constellation Approach also complements the Hindu philosophical view of incarnation. According to this view, each of us has three distinct yet intertwined bodies of energy that guide our actions in our current lifetime: our father's and mother's energy signatures, and our own *samskaras*.

Samskaras are imprints or traces of past deeds and experiences (*karma*) involving ignorance, fear, attachments, afflictions, and ego-driven actions that each of us has accumulated over lifetimes. These impressions (*klesas*) are stored within the body-mind and may be carried from one lifetime to the next. But this cycle may be broken when the *samskaras* are realized.

Besides quieting the mind and gaining self-knowledge, another way to bring awareness to our *samskaras* is by approaching our Family Lineage with neither attachment nor repulsion, but rather equanimity. In this sense, The Constellation Approach process can guide us to attain lasting peace, or *brahma-nirvana*, much as ancient Hindu practices do.

---

2   Giovanni Mociocia, *The Foundations of Chinese Medicine* (New York: Churchill Livingstone, Inc., 1989)

The Mystical Principle of the Vesica Pisces

Something miraculous can occur in a Constellation when two willing participants come together with the simple intention of the highest good. Our view is that this sacred space, the Vesica Pisces, is the passageway that leads to experiencing our Soul nature. One of the most profound motifs of both ancient and modern times, the **Vesica Pisces** is shaped like an almond, and called a *mandorla*. It is created by two circles overlapping and has many representations including the Jesus fish, *Ichthys*, in the Christian tradition; the Ark of the Covenant in the Judaic; the Chalice Well at Glastonbury, England; the Goddess Venus; and the vaginal opening of female genitalia. The Vesica Pisces is considered a portal between heaven and earth. It symbolizes the joining of two, communion, to create a potent third energy, and therefore, is a source of immense power.

In Constellations, the **Vesica Pisces** is the sacred intersection of two overlapping Individual Energy Fields, represented by two figurines or by two participants. Within the Vesica Pisces, the auric field and the chakra system (Chapter 3) of each person play a vital role in the transformation of consciousness. As two or more participants in a Constellation move closer together, the field of information in the form of images and feelings intensifies. Few words are spoken. The emphasis is on silence. The rational mind is transcended and our personalities, though still present, seem to recede as we begin to recognize our shared Soul consciousness.

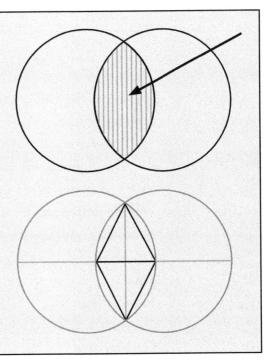

The Veil of Forgetting

Here's something useful to remember: All of us forget who we are. The Constellation Approach is a path that can help us to remember.

Between the above and below, heaven and earth, Spirit and matter, before and after, knowing and forgetting, there is a realm that has been called **The Veil of Forgetting**. The Veil is a barrier that protects us from knowing what we agreed to experience in this lifetime, with whom, and for what reasons. It's also the realm that each of us pass through during incarnation, when our consciousness shifts from Spirit to the form of Soul.

In Hindu and Buddhist mystical thought, a teaching used to help grasp this concept is conveyed through the symbol for *Om*. The symbol is divided into five sections: a dot, a curve, and three semi-circles. The upper single dot (*turiya* in Sanskirt) is the unmanifest, God Self, the Source of Creation, the Above, the All, the Pure Lands. The curved and horizontal line (*maya*) is the Veil of Forgetting, often referred to as the Veil of Illusion. It is the mist we pass through that erases our conscious memory of our incarnational choices.

Below the Veil of Forgetting are three manifest states of consciousness: wakefulness, deep sleep, and dreaming (*jugrat, sushupti,* and *swapna*). *Om*, pronounced A-U-M,[3] is the sacred sound that represents all manifested phenomenon. The *Om* symbol reminds us that we come from the  *noumenon*, the Source, the Above, the All, from Spirit. We originate from elsewhere as fully conscious beings and descend into consciousness, when we incase in human form. But in this process, we forget our reasons to incarnate.

As human beings we are Spirit consciousness existing as an individuated Soul in human form, with three ways to experience consciousness—waking, sleeping, and dreaming. On the purely biological level, each of us is alive

---

3   K. L. Seshagiri Rao and Kapil Kapoor, *Encyclopedia of Hinduism, Vol. II* (San Rafael: Mandala Publishing, 2013), 35-36.

because of our mothers and fathers. However, sustaining and nurturing our existence, and the quality of our life experience, are separate matters. First we have to arrive here to incarnate. Then, we can begin the gradual but thrilling process of waking up and remembering our true nature, and the reasons we chose this life.

The Constellation Approach helps lift the Veil of Forgetting and allows Soul awareness to occur. We begin to understand and comprehend events, circumstances, and relationships at the deepest level of our being.

We are not human beings having a spiritual experience; We are spiritual beings having a human experience.

—Pierre Teilhard de Chardin, Jesuit priest, philosopher

The idea that we are spiritual beings having a human experience may be difficult to comprehend, but it is a spiritual concept that has been taught and sought after since the beginning of our human journey. The major world religions teach us that we will return to the source of our creation. The practice of prayer, meditation, and right action, in words and deeds are common paths that lead to experiencing our Soul nature as enlightened beings before our physical death.

The Constellation Approach is a path of awakening and remembering why we have chosen to incarnate, why we have chosen our particular life path, and most importantly, why we have chosen the family into which we were born. Through our biological mother's and father's respective lineages, the path of parental bloodlines can be traced and explored into the unconscious realms where answers unavailable to the conscious mind—including the very reasons for our existence—await us. It is a path that helps us experience ourselves as spiritual beings—a way available to each of us.

Chapter 2

Three Perennial Questions

Each individual is different and unique, and has an individual purpose
for this particular incarnation. Your purpose and your longing walk
hand in hand through life. Your longing leads to your purpose.

—Barbara Brennan

You may have already begun to appreciate that you are not your conflicts and that your "nature" extends on a subtle energetic and Soul level beyond your immediate comprehension. But we want to also help ready your heart and Soul for the Constellation journey you will embark on.

The common yearning to experience and understand the reality of the Divine has been shared since the beginning of time. Whether we look back to Aldous Huxley's brave intellectual quest through an array of faiths in *The Perennial Philosophy* (1944)[4], or fast forward to Lipton and Bhaerman's *Spontaneous Evolution* (2009)[5], we see three recurring questions. Our journey begins with these same perennial questions:

---

4   Aldous Huxley, *The Perennial Philosophy* (New York: Harper Collins, 1944)
5   Bruce Lipton and Steve Braerman, *Spontaneous Evolution: Our Positive Future and a Way to Get There From* Here (New York: Hay House, 2009)

1. How did we get here?
2. Why are we here?
3. How shall we live our lives?

This chapter explores these perennial questions as a crucial starting point for self-exploration and for your journey towards peace with your family lineage. We believe they will help awaken your heart's desire to take this journey.

Question 1: How did we get here?

>> We chose to be here and chose the circumstances of our birth, including our parents.

>> We are consciousness that has come from elsewhere.

We all came into being through the **Doorway of Existence** made up of two halves—one half our father, the other our mother. Each person on earth, regardless of their specific circumstances after conception, is the result of the pairing of a human female life force (our biological mother) and a human male life force (our biological father). Who we are begins with them, and everything else that follows meets us on the other side of our own distinctive entrance into life.

First, we must open to the realization that we are more than mere flesh, bones, and brain. We are an amalgam of energies, a life force that coalesced and descended from the realm of Spirit into human form. We are Spirit as Soul. As Buddhist and Hindu philosophies teach, each one made a choice while in the Spirit realm, prior to incarnation, to descend into human form. We pass through the Veil of Forgetting and enter life through the combined ancestral, biological, genetic, DNA pairing of our parents. We got here through them. Were it not for the gift of life, we would not have the opportunity to awaken and remember our true nature.

This understanding gradually lifts us out of any sense of victimization. We begin to realize that what we experience in this lifetime, no matter how horrific, may have its beginnings in choices made before our human consciousness formed. In no way does this view diminish a true acknowledgement of the cruelty that humans habitually inflict upon each other. However, each of us has the potential to change habitual patterns that keep us from awakening our potential as Souls having a human experience.

Before you proceed to the second question, please contemplate our brief reflections on the first perennial question: *How did I get here?*

Contemplation

>> I came through a choice I made prior to birth.
>> That choice included my biological mother and father.
>> I am energy, a life force, consciousness that has traveled from another realm and now resides inside my physical body.
>> I am Spirit incarnated.

Contemplation is the purest of human action.

—Aristotle, philosopher, scientist

Question 2: Why are we here?

>> To evolve our personal consciousness.
>> To contribute to the evolution of our family consciousness.
>> To ultimately contribute to the collective consciousness of humanity.

Remember the Veil of Forgetting? The Constellation Approach is a practice that helps lift the Veil of Forgetting and stirs us from the unconscious state of not knowing. In that moment, we awaken and remember why we're here.

During a Constellation, we acknowledge our connection with other Souls in human form—particularly our parents, grandparents, and siblings. Our family, which includes everyone on both sides of our Family Lineage, is explored in order to reveal the purposes of our individual choice to incarnate. As each Soul connection is made, we gain insight into our Soul agreements with each other. We learn that our reasons for being here are directly related to choosing our specific parents and the lineage of their ancestral bloodlines.

We also begin to realize we are interconnected regardless of physical distance or emotional detachment. Each one of us is a drop of water within the ocean of civilization, separate yet connected. What affects one affects all.

The Divine came to me
One night in a dream,
She spoke of the
Possibility
Of Oneness,
Did I have the courage
To awaken,
Or would I continue
To sleep my
Life away?

— Peter

In the un-awakened state, one's sense of self is more individuated, insular, and self-centered. In an awakened state, our interconnectedness is illuminated at a level of awareness that causes us to think, feel, and eventually act differently towards others—especially our family.

In that moment when the Veil of Forgetting lifts, we glimpse our responsibility not only for ourselves, but for our family, which, in turn, contributes positively towards the Greater Consciousness of all. When we pursue such a path of awakening, particularly through facing the true origins of our life, a profound humility arises. We recognize at the deepest, cellular Soul Level that we are an extension of a very long ancestral line of human beings. We also become aware of the innate goodness that drives us consciously and unconsciously. At the very root of our humanity is the desire to move forward, to create and to cooperate. We want to help ourselves, those we love, and ultimately all human beings. This is the real meaning of evolution.

Desire

Desire is a crucial element in uncovering our true nature—that we are Souls in human form. Desire is essential for the forward progression of our evolution—to feel our goodness, our Divinity within as well as in others. This is the kind of deep desire that comes from yearning for a life less painful, more fulfilling, more whole. It's our heart's sometimes-hidden longing to come closer to our loved ones—those we have come into this life to be with, and to share all the ups and downs that life brings. It is the urge to reconcile, heal, understand, forgive, and find happiness and a lasting sense of peace. Desire is the key that turns the lock on the doorway of our existence, the *why we are here*.

Imagine standing at that doorway and asking yourself:

>> What is my desire?

>> What is my desire in relation to my father?

>> My desire in relation to my mother?

>> My desire in relation to my current relationship?

>> My desire in relation to a difficult event or circumstance in my life?

When the violin
Can forgive the past
It starts singing.
When the violin can forgive
Every wound caused by others
The heart begins
Singing

—Shams al-Din Hafiz,
Sufi mystic

According to Bert Hellinger, "peace begins in the Soul." In our experience, too, when our individual Soul comes to peace, the ripples are felt throughout our lives. The way we experience relationships improves, body tensions relax, and a process of profound transformation begins. Our frame of mind shifts to a more peaceful state. We also can't help thinking, feeling, and acting more compassionately towards the people and circumstances in our lives.

So, as you can see, the starting point for understanding *why we are here* is to acknowledge our Family of Origin, just as it is. Not how we wish it were different, but how it actually is at this particular moment in time. We also acknowledge that we are a contributing member to a vast body of knowledge that has accumulated through each and every single family member's life experience since humanity began. We are gatherers of information, like honeybees collecting pollen and returning to the hive, offering donations to our fellow creatures. Together we create substance that sustains the colony's life. Our pollen is our newly awakened consciousness, the ever-expanding knowledge we gain about ourselves in relation to our Family Lineage.

When learning to use a compass, first we are taught to stand still. In stillness we determine our particular orientation to the direction we desire. Our bodies, our thoughts, our sense of self, comprise our inner compass. The art of contemplation invites us to be still and determine which way our inner compass is facing.

Contemplate the second perennial question now: *Why are we here?* Why am I a member of my particular family? Consider these possible responses:

>> To evolve my personal consciousness.
>> To contribute to the evolution of my family consciousness.
>> To help advance the collective consciousness of humanity.

If you accept that the purpose of our human nature is the evolution of consciousness, you are ready to explore the third perennial question.

Eckhart Tolle, spiritual teacher and author, wrote, "Your inner purpose is to awaken. It is as simple as that. You share that purpose with every other human being on the planet—because it is the purpose of humanity."

Question 3: How shall we live our lives?

The Constellation Approach doesn't propose an answer to this third perennial question. Instead, it opens a pathway to living through our Soul. Each pathway is unique to us and us alone. No two Doorways of Existence are the same, and no two people, parents, families, or ancestral lineages are alike. Each is distinctive unto itself.

The answers for each person lie not on the surface of the conscious mind but deep in the unconscious where the Soul resides, beneath the functioning processes of our thinking mind. To get a glimpse of our Soul nature, we need to look beyond the physical sense of our self, past the brain's mental chatter, and through our emotional reactions to the varieties of people and events we have experienced. In this way, we can break through negative egoic structures into the healing expansiveness of Soul Consciousness.

Deep in the forested grove where your ancestral tree grows, along the trails of your parental bloodlines, your essential Soul nature is waiting to reveal itself. Every quest begins with the explorer's willingness to move forward. This journey is an exploration inward and back in time—to realms where we were not yet aware of our existence, before we were born on this magnificent planet.

Consider for a moment that the Doorway of Existence is behind you. On the other side grows your ancestral tree, full and strong. Every trail to this tree leads to knowing yourself more completely. You will see, think, and feel things that you have forgotten, some of them painful. But in the end, you will feel immensely better about yourself and the Family Lineage that you chose to be a part of in this lifetime. Many of you will be astonished by your newfound freedom. But no one can take this journey for us and we can't take another's place. Only *you* can turn around, take the key of your own desire and unlock the doorway of your existence.

Standing at the edge of the still water
It is into the depths I know I must go

My answers lie not on the surface
In the clear light of day

But down below
In the cold darkness where I cannot see

I fear leaving the shore
And immersing in the deep unknown

My fate awaits me
There beneath the water's stillness
Where I know I must go.

—Jamy

The Constellation Approach

A Constellation Journeyer
Lyn — One Woman's Loyalty

Lyn was bright, attractive, and self-sufficient. She moved away from the town where she was raised and overcame the addictive behavior that was prevalent in her Family Lineage. She yearned for a love that seemed to have eluded her through life. Like her father who had been married three times, Lyn was on her third marriage. She was not able to fully let her current husband in emotionally to experience the love she longed for. She felt there was something blocking her from fully expressing her love, accepting in her husband's love, and having the type of fulfilling relationship she knew was possible.

When Lyn set up her Constellation, she included Representatives for herself, her mother, father, her mother's parents, and her current husband. The Family Energy Field revealed that she was still caught between the energies of her mother and father who had divorced when she was three years old. Like two powerful magnets creating an overlapping field effect, Lyn was not able to break free of her lifelong loyalty to her mother, or move freely to embrace her father. She was stuck between their opposing energies that had not been fully resolved forty years after their divorce.

As Lyn faced her mother, the loyalty she felt towards her estrangement and pain began to shift. She was able to turn towards her father and let herself connect with him in a way that, as a child, she had never felt she had her mother's permission to do. The pattern of never being able to be happy in relationship (or happier than her mother) began to lift. She understood that her pattern of continually seeking better partners arose from her longing for a relationship with her father.

After a period of deep emotional catharsis Lyn began to brighten, feel lighter, and stand up taller. She moved slowly and deliberately to face the Representative of her current husband. She took one final look at her mother and father and walked slowly to her husband. With trepidation and tenderness, she allowed herself to be held in his arms. Lyn had been acting as a loyal child to the family history of her parents and grandparents: Her mother, who had been separated from her father at a young age, had struggled with maintaining loving relationships with men throughout her adult life. Lyn's grandmother had never fully recovered from the loss of her own marriage. Three generations of women—grandmother, mother, and daughter—had all been struggling to balance the scales of love and loss with the men in their lives.

Through the Constellation process, Lyn experienced viscerally the energy field that had held her in place. By acknowledging what had happened to the women in her maternal lineage, she recognized how her own life had been similar. By accepting that the ancestral pattern of loving and losing men had been passed on to her, she was free to let go of the pattern and make a different choice. But mental understanding alone was not enough for Lyn. She needed to realign in her energy body at the cellular level of her being. Her block was able to be removed by re-immersing into the Family Energy Field that created her unconscious loyalty to her mother and grandmother.

Since her Constellation, Lyn has reported that the tension she felt with both parents has lessened. She also described a new awakening of love and acceptance in her relationship with her husband—more than she imagined possible.

Chapter 3

How We are Connected

Our lives are not our own.
From womb to tomb we are bound to others,
Past and present.
And by each crime and every kindness
We birth our future.

—David Mitchell, novelist

The purpose of these opening chapters is designed to help you appreciate how multi-layered and multi-dimensional "you" are. The more willing you are to explore your multi-stranded nature; the more open you will be to the experiential components of The Constellation Approach. What differentiates our approach from other Family Constellation practices is our emphasis on an awareness of subtle energy bodies and the larger energetic fields of influence on an individual, and our focus on Soul Consciousness. In our view, the self is more than biological matter and psychological biography. We perceive the self as an energetic vehicle of consciousness seeking wholeness and balance. Consciousness surrounds us in layered fields of energy that are affected by nonphysical interaction as well as touch.

TCA recognizes these four fields of energy during a Constellation:

Individual

Family

Participant

Ancestral

Each layer nests within the other from the smallest (individual) to the largest (ancestral). During a Constellation, awareness of these fields establishes the landscape for the journey. If each of us is to move towards peace with our respective family lineages, we must recognize our self in these different fields of energy.

Constellation Energy Fields

The first is our **Individual Energy Field,** comprised of the **auric field** and the **chakra system**. The auric field surrounds us, extending approximately the arm's length of our body in 360 degrees. Within our auric field are seven chakras that function like invisible vortices gathering and transmitting knowledge and energy concerning our life's experience and surroundings. Their purpose is to keep the spiritual, mental, emotional, and physical health of our body in balance.

Located in the regions of the pelvis, solar plexus, heart, throat, and head, the seven chakras correspond to underlying organs and expand to create the auric field that surrounds the body in the front, rear, above, and below. Chakras are said "to reflect how the unified consciousness of humanity (the immortal human being or the Soul), is divided to manage different aspects of earthly life (body, instinct, vital energy, deeper emotions, communication, an overview of life or contact to God)."[6]

During a Constellation, the Client's Individual Energy Field becomes more engaged as he/she sets up, moves through, resolves, and reconciles

---

6   Peter C, Rogers, *Ultimate Truth, Book 1* (Bloomington: AuthorHouse, 2009), 38

with his/her family. Each family is its own unique Constellation of beings. Just like stars, no two are alike and every family has its own gravitational force in which ancestors orbit.

Imagine concentric circles that begin with the individual, then parents and siblings. The grandparents and their siblings come next, then great grandparents, each generation extending further outward and into the Spirit realms. We call this the **Family Energy Field**. (Bert Hellinger describes it similarly as the Family Soul).

The Family Energy Field serves as the basis for exploring our relationships and finding solutions to unresolved issues. The Field is the body of consciousness that is created when setting up a Constellation. It is specific to the Client and offers a unique representation of the family. No two are exactly alike.

When we realize that we are deeply connected to our Family Lineage, and that neither time nor distance can alter that, we begin to discover the complexities of our family's past and our unique place within our Family Lineage. The **Participant Energy Field** describes the field of individuals who are present and willing to support the Constellation process as the Client and Representatives open to their unconscious. They act as the holding container and witnesses to the process. Finally, the **Ancestral Energy Field** is the powerful spiritual presence that is the guiding force behind the healing. Through meditation, prayer, and invocation at the beginning of our seminars and programs, we ask for this presence and for the permission of our ancestors to help us with our work.

> *May all mothers and sons be reconciled.*
> *May all mothers and daughters be reconciled.*
> *May all fathers and sons be reconciled.*
> *May all fathers and daughters be reconciled.*
> *May all sisters and brothers be reconciled.*
> *May all husbands and wives be reconciled.*
> *May all partners and lovers be reconciled.*
> *May all family members be reconciled...*
>
> —Jack Kornfield,
> Vipasanna Buddhism teacher

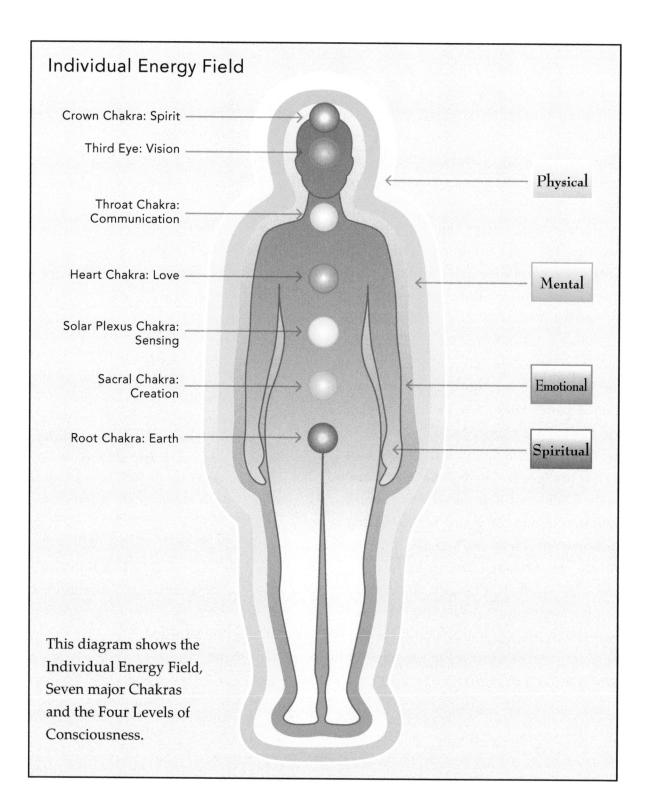

Individual Energy Field

Crown Chakra: Spirit

Third Eye: Vision

Physical

Throat Chakra:
Communication

Heart Chakra: Love

Mental

Solar Plexus Chakra:
Sensing

Sacral Chakra:
Creation

Emotional

Root Chakra: Earth

Spiritual

This diagram shows the
Individual Energy Field,
Seven major Chakras
and the Four Levels of
Consciousness.

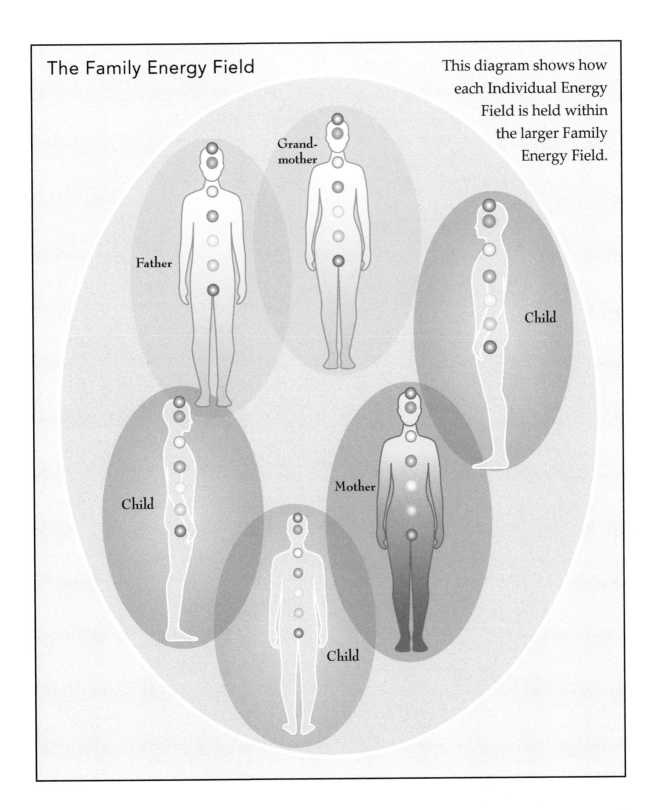

The Family Energy Field

This diagram shows how each Individual Energy Field is held within the larger Family Energy Field.

Grand-mother

Father

Child

Child

Mother

Child

Moving into the Vesica Pisces

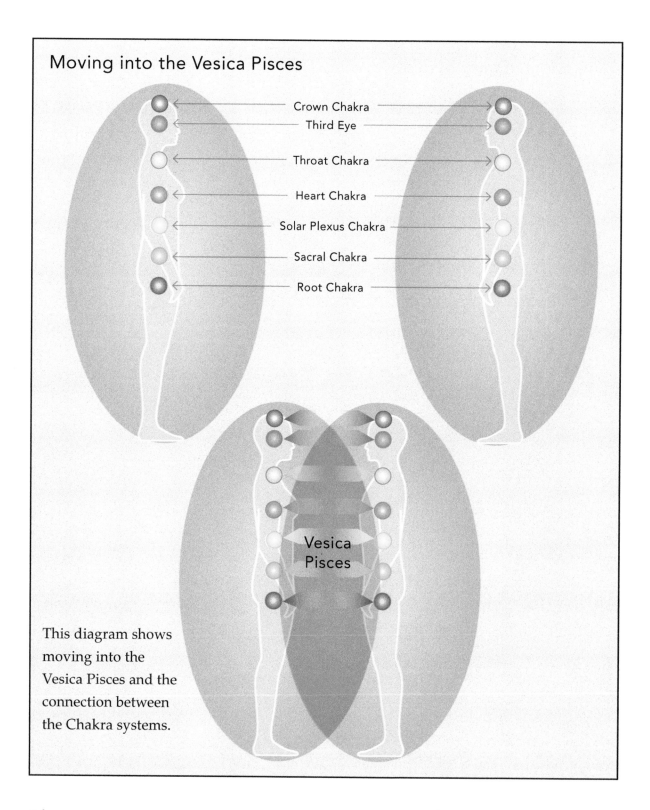

Crown Chakra
Third Eye
Throat Chakra
Heart Chakra
Solar Plexus Chakra
Sacral Chakra
Root Chakra

Vesica
Pisces

This diagram shows
moving into the
Vesica Pisces and the
connection between
the Chakra systems.

The Constellation Approach

Strands of Awareness—Ten Universal Themes

Imagine a rope comprised of three cords: One cord is you, the second cord and the third cord is your mother and father respectively. The cords are distinctive and separate unto themselves; intertwined, they create one solid piece of rope. Upon closer examination, the cords are created from individual strands. More subtly, threads of fiber make up each strand. Threads form a strand. Strands make a cord. Three separate cords create the rope. The rope, extending back in time, is solid, twisted tightly. The present moment, your place, is near the unbraided end.

Recognizing that we are the continuation of consciousness that began with our mothers, fathers, and our own pre-incarnational choices, we can examine the larger strands within these three cords. The Constellation Approach identifies these ten central **Strands of Awareness** as Universal Themes that are inherent of families everywhere on the planet:

1. Family of Origin

2. Father's Lineage

3. Mother's Lineage

4. Siblings

5. Physical Disease and Mental Illness

6. Death

7. War and Conflict

8. Immigration/Migration

9. Religion

10. Relationships

As you will discover in Part II, each theme provides the basis for a distinct Constellation that you can experience as part of your journey towards peace.

We believe it's our shared responsibility to continue to braid, passing on our respective contributions to the next generation.

Threads of Consciousness

Consider this: Embedded within each Universal Theme are finer and finer nuances of human experience. By slowly unraveling the Ten Strands through TCA, you will become more aware of these individual **Threads of Consciousness.** Attitudes, beliefs, and patterns regarding money and sexuality are prime examples that every family and individual inherits from the previous generation. These examples of Threads of Consciousness are non-personal, yet they affect each of us personally. They are woven into the cords of our being waiting to be examined.

Each Constellation offers the opportunity to bring to awareness the threads unique to our own heredity, and hence, the ability to make different choices. Because consciousness is interconnected, person-to-person, individual to family, family to community, community to society, society to civilization, and civilization to humanity, the effect of one person raising his/ her consciousness contributes to the positive evolution of all.

Some Threads of Consciousness

• sexuality	• body image	• shame
• money	• pride	• betrayal
• violence	• humility	• dignity
• separation	• patience	• belonging
• loss	• courage	• abandonment
• addiction	• generosity	• prejudice
• service	• kindness	• intimacy
• abuse	• tolerance	• rejection
• suicide	• charity	• isolation
• poverty	• devotion	• discrimination

Everyone in each generation contributes to the evolution of consciousness in a particular way. Through awakening to the awareness that Threads of Consciousness exist, we gain the ability to make different choices.

Levels of Consciousness

Levels of Consciousness are not linear or hierarchical but rather intersecting, permeating, and affecting all aspects of our being. In the Constellation Approach there is a progression through these four Levels of Consciousness: Physical, Mental, Emotional, and Spiritual. Each of us inhabits these Levels of Consciousness like layers of clothing, one on top of the other. The outermost layer is the Physical. It primarily comprises the senses—sight, hearing, taste, and touch. The Mental Level of Consciousness houses our thoughts, ideas, and beliefs of the situations and people in our life. Beneath the Mental resides the Emotional Level of Consciousness—where we experience feelings in reaction to what occurs externally in our environment. At the deepest internal level is our Spiritual Consciousness. This is the level where Soul Consciousness resides. It allows the expansive ability to comprehend the complexities of life. Imagine a pyramid with the base as the Spiritual Level of Consciousness. From this broad base of consciousness each level is added to create our individual pyramidal self.

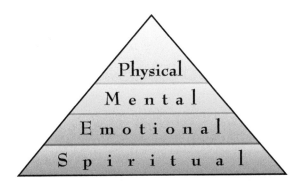

Life is experienced through our emotions, thoughts, and physical sensations. These three layers inform and supply us with useful information but not the complete picture. In order to have the broadest perspective on any given situation or relationship with another human being, we need to engage the Spiritual Level of our consciousness.

In a Constellation, you experience the Levels of Consciousness as the following:

1. **Mental**—The interview process, the starting place of a Constellation. The Client presents facts and their conscious understanding of an issue.

2. **Physical**—Naming and placing Representatives (participants who stand in to represent family members) within the Constellation. Seeing, hearing, noticing bodily responses to the Family Energy Field begins here.

3. **Emotional**—Feelings arise in relation to the Representatives in the Constellation. Deeper emotional reactions happen when Representatives come into closer proximity to each other within the Family Energy Field.

4. **Spiritual**—The Veil of Forgetting momentarily lifts, allowing Soul recognition to happen as knowing and remembering. The essence of the Soul's experience and understanding of this lifetime is illuminated.

A Constellation begins with the facts and story as it is understood at the Mental Level of Consciousness. As we move towards Soul Consciousness, the process progresses from verbal and engaged to more stillness. In Emotional and Spiritual Consciousness, most information is transmitted between the Client and the Representatives in quiet. When we reach the Spirit level, the Soul peers out from a deeply conscious internal space within our being. Since thoughts and feelings blur over time, the Constellation Approach helps us to clear and align the Levels of Consciousness. Like overlapping lenses, if one is out of true focus, we can't see clearly into the next level.

Often, our tears are the glass cleaner. They act to wipe away the smudge of hurt we still hold in our Emotional Consciousness. By clearing and wiping away our old—and sometimes ancient—feelings, we are able to reach the higher emotional states of appreciation, love, and devotion that exist in the depths of our Soul. As the lenses clear, we can perceive our Soul nature. From this Level of Consciousness, we can view the other(s) without the distortions of judgment or emotional pain. During a Constellation, a completely different view and perception of our life situations and relationships becomes possible. We simply travel into the depths of our consciousness to reach the Soul. Change and healing can then begin at the level of personal consciousness, ripple into family consciousness, and eventually affect the collective consciousness of humanity.

The Four Levels of Consciousness

This diagram shows the transition from the Physical to the Spiritual Level of Consciousness.

Spiritual Emotional Mental Physical   Physical Mental Emotional Spiritual

Physical Spiritual Emotional Mental   Mental Emotional Spiritual Physical

Mental Physical Spiritual Emotional   Emotional Spiritual Physical Mental

Emotional Mental Physical Spiritual   Spiritual Physical Mental Emotional

Human Nature—Soul Nature

This diagram shows the shift from Human Nature to Soul Nature through the Levels of Consciousness and the Vesica Pisces.

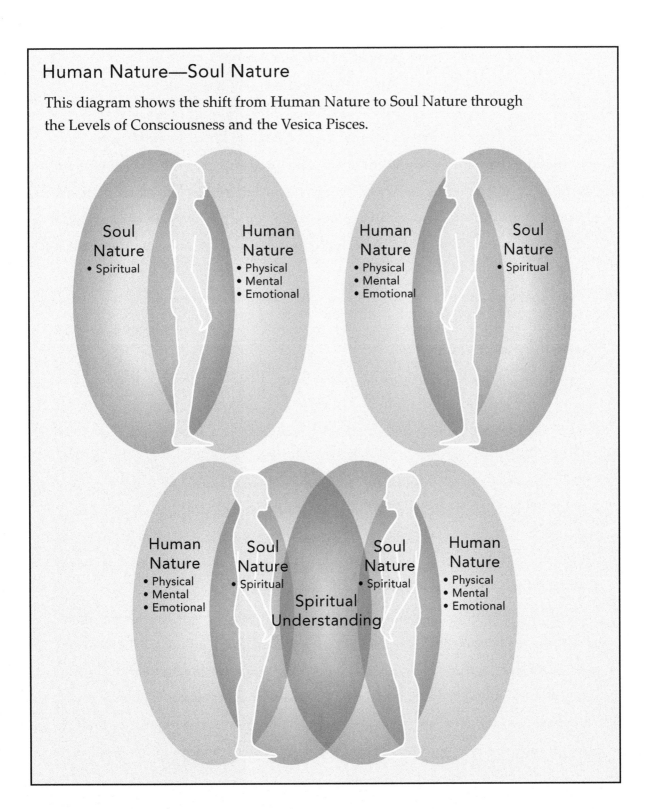

A Constellation Journeyer
Peter — An Unexpected Awareness

In my Family Lineage, one Universal Theme was my father's "handicap." That was the language of the time, his time, and my time growing up as his son. My father contracted polio when he was six months old. The shadow of his physical limitations hung over all aspects of our family life like an ever-present companion in our household. As a boy I felt the loss of not having a father who could throw a ball or teach me how to ride a bicycle. In a Constellation, following the strand of physical disease, I was able to unravel and reach into the deeper levels of the Threads of Consciousness that come from having Edward Henry Faust as my father.

In my Constellation, standing across from Representatives for my father and for the "handicap" of polio, I instantly became aware of the judgments I held for my father. Acknowledging that I had seen him as somehow less than a father brought waves of shame that dropped me to my knees. I saw before me the two-halved man: One side under-developed, skin loose, small muscles, bones visible, the effects of a body ravaged by polio; the other side a normal, strong man's body. Half was not good enough to get a good-paying job in those days, or to throw a ball with his son. I had judged my father the way the world saw him, as less-than, not good enough, as not man enough.

The memories, images, and feelings that moved though the levels of my awareness eventually brought me into a space where I could see beyond his physical body. The process of acknowledging my father, for who he was, not the way I wished he had been, led me into the realm of acceptance. This process of accepting my father helped me to release the judgments and shame, and allow me to finally see him for the teachings he had given me through his handicap.

I remembered his extreme patience and his methodical way of explaining and teaching me things that he could not physically do himself. I remembered how together we could accomplish what he couldn't do alone. I saw how he passed on to me his love of reading, writing, and learning. Most of all, I received fully in that brief moment what he had taught me about dignity.

Present before me was no longer the handicapped father I had as a child. Here stood a Soul that chose to learn difficult lessons through his body. I instantly understood, by being in silence and looking deeply into the eyes of the Representative for my father's Spirit, that he chose to experience shame and transform it into dignity. My father had lived every day of his life since infancy with his handicap. Out of that life he had developed a type of pride and dignity that can only be learned through an aversion. In that moment the internal image I held of my father was completely transformed. I no longer pitied or felt sorry for him. Instead, I felt the most amazing feelings of pride and gratitude towards Edward Henry Faust for being my father. I wept with appreciation for him. I knew deep in my Soul that I had agreed to be his son and he to be my father in this lifetime.

———————— ◆◆◆ ————————

Chapter 4

The Constellation Approach

I see my roots in my father, my mother, my grandfathers,
my grandmothers and all my ancestors.
I know I am only the continuation of this ancestral lineage.

—Thich Nhat Hanh, Zen Buddhist monk

Our particular view of our family is often limited by our understanding—colored by personal judgments, projections, and misconceived perceptions. The Constellation Approach allows us to expand our perception of life as a whole, rather than remain fixated on isolated incidents of wounding and pain. By viewing family situations with a wider lens, we can gain insights into root causes of issues, like why certain family members are shut out or not spoken of, as well as how and why behavioral patterns repeat, often unconsciously, from one generation to the next.

Our greatest joy as founders and teachers of The Constellation Approach is to facilitate Constellations. Each of us also facilitates Constellations for individuals by using figurines (to be explained in Parts II and V). These latter exercises are powerful tools of self-exploration, but they are not a substitute for working with a trained TCA Facilitator, attending a live seminar, or participating in our Immersion Program. With figurines, one must engage in active imagination and be open to receiving insights on one's own. But working with a trained Facilitator or attending a live Constellation allows you to be guided carefully through the Constellation process. The benefits of being part of a Constellation made up of live Representatives can only be experienced directly. Nonetheless, we invite you to take the journey with us using figurines, while hoping that one day soon you will participate in a live Constellation.

In the pages that follow, we explain how a live Constellation works—from the various roles participants play and the practices involved in each Constellation, to the four Phases of a Constellation and how they align with the Levels of Consciousness discussed earlier. This will prepare you to cross the threshold and begin your journey.

Roles and Practices in a Constellation

A Constellation is led by a **Facilitator** who guides the process from beginning to end. In addition to the Facilitator, there are three additional **roles** in a Constellation: the **Client** is the person who is actively working on an issue; the **Representatives**, as their name implies, represent family members or important people in the Client's life; and **Meta-representatives** stand in for non-personal energies such as an illness, family religion, or ancestral homeland.

As you may have already sensed, a Constellation operates at subtle, powerful energetic levels. Because of these nuanced dynamics, it is essential that before we begin a Constellation all Participants and Facilitators agree to engage in specific Constellation Approach practices. We share these practices below in the hope that as you read through Parts II and V, you also will agree to them. Like any practices, they require just that—practice. So, be kind to yourself if you find yourself forgetting one of them along the way.

Suspending Moral Judgment

In The Constellation Approach, as in all Family Constellation practices, it is imperative to **Suspend Moral Judgment**—to pause, postpone, or interrupt our usual way of perceiving. Morals derive from what our beliefs, society, and culture value as "good" or "honorable." Yet the act of deciding whether someone or something is good or bad, right or wrong, limits how far we can explore the realms of consciousness and the Soul because judgments act as a barrier to a greater perception of reality. To Suspend Moral Judgment is to open to larger levels of awareness and understanding. Each of us has had an experience of failure, of being hurt or wronged in the past. Can you think of a time later in life, when that pain or failure turned out to have been a blessing? When we Suspend Moral Judgement in a Constellation, we cultivate the ability to recognize the blessings that have emerged in our lives in the aftermath of hurtful or traumatic events.

Exploring our Family Lineage without judgment provides the opportunity to uncover secrets and investigate the lost and unexplained, what we previously knew as simply good or bad. These are the very things that bind us together as a family. When we look with open eyes, mind, and heart—Suspending our Moral Judgment—we are capable of letting go of what no longer serves our personal growth. Most importantly, we gather strength from a more meaningful and conscious connection to our Family Lineage. This strength feeds the Soul's development. The psychic energy we previously used to distance ourselves from our family is re-channeled into more productive efforts towards reconciliation and wholeness. This is the healing power and medicine of Suspending Moral Judgment.

Words of Empowerment

The second practice we use in TCA, called **Words of Empowerment,** refers to particular words or sentences spoken aloud in a focused, succinct manner by the Client or Representatives to one another during a Constellation. These are also described as "Statements of Empowerment" or "Solution Sentences" by Family Constellation facilitators. Words of Empowerment usually begin with "I" or "You" to establish self-responsibility or direct communication. A child might say to her mother, "You are the right mother for me." A father might say to his child, "I will take care of this; you are free to go." Or, to someone who has died and is terribly missed, "I will hold a place for you in my heart."

Such affirmations hold enormous energy for healing our deep emotional pain. When words are spoken with genuine respect and truth, a resonance or vibration is felt within all Representatives as well as the larger group. Words of Empowerment may be said to one or more Representatives. When the right Words of Empowerment are spoken there is a shift in emotion, often resulting in tears, as the Client's heart opens.

Acknowledging, Accepting and Agreeing

The third practice that's central to TCA: **acknowledge**, **accept**, and **agree**. These three simple words are at the very foundation of the Constellation Approach and used to shift perception and guide you through the process.

To acknowledge is associated with the Mental Level of Consciousness, the mind, the third eye, and crown chakra. It's the first phase of a Constellation.

I acknowledge you as my father.

You begin with a simple statement of truth: This person is my father. No one can have two biological fathers. To acknowledge a fact aloud assists you in moving to the Emotional Level of Consciousness.

To accept is more difficult than to acknowledge because accepting brings up the duality of choice. Accepting is associated with feelings, emotions, the heart chakra. This is the second phase of a Constellation.

I accept you as my mother.

When we **accept**, we wrestle with all the complicated and conflicted feelings that come with the acceptance process. We have to digest both the difficult and the pleasant aspects of our relationship with the other.

As Eckhart Tolle has written, "Acceptance looks like a passive state, but in reality it brings something entirely new into the world. That peace, a subtle energy vibration, is consciousness."

To agree is all-inclusive. It leaves nothing out. **Agreeing** is associated with the deepest level of our consciousness, our Soul. To agree is the final phase of a Constellation and can be felt at all levels of our being, through the entire auric field, to the essence of our core.

I agree to all that has happened between us in this lifetime.

This simple word can change everything in our perspective on life, relationships, and any number of far-reaching experiences we have faced. When we can fully agree to what has transpired in our Family Lineage, we are far more likely to move beyond our emotional attachments to the past, into the fullness of our own goodness and Divinity.

Resistance

Prior to moving to the level of Soul Consciousness, there is a natural hesitation, on the part of our personality—a **resistance** to change. Becoming aware of and moving through our resistance is another practice in TCA. This step forward occurs at the **Egoic Level**.

The ego is part of our consciousness that keeps us secure in our beliefs. Resistance is our ego taking a pause—catching its breath and centering, so to speak—prior to the profound change that we sense is about to occur. The ego acts like a diver pausing at the edge before leaving the security of the platform and leaping into the unknown.

Our thoughts and feelings up to this moment in time are about to be transcended. Intuition tells us that we are about to experience something potentially different, causing us to resist the unknown. Any true healing and enlightening requires that we move past our resistance and open our hearts and minds to a new reality. Resistance is normal and should be understood as a marker in the process of awakening.

Sometimes letting go is an act of far greater power than defending or hanging on.

—Eckhart Tolle

In a TCA seminar, the Client, Facilitator, and Representatives have agreed to enter into the unknown where the mysterious healing potential of a Constellation can take place. When we permit ourselves to let go of preconceived ideas, opinions, or formulas and to surrender, our perception intensifies, the unknown becomes known, and a deeper truth is found. The next step for healing appears. Mystery.

Family Constellations are a truly mystical experience particularly when witnessed live. There are two **phenomenological** effects inherent to the practice of Constellations that sometimes happen immediately, which reinforce the mystery of this practice. The first is when Representatives receive information and feelings about the people they represent that they could not have possibly known. "How did you know that? Or "That is exactly how they would of responded" are common reactions to Representatives in Constellations.

The second is when people who are not present in the room are affected. Numerous times, we have witnessed a person reporting that they received a call or message during a Constellation, or soon after it ended, from a loved one who was represented. It is uncanny how the healing energy seems to travel from the Family Energy Field almost immediately to effect positive change.

Phases of a Constellation

There are **four phases** in a Constellation, and each corresponds to a different Level of Consciousness, the various energy fields, time, and bodily sensations. Ordinarily, a Constellation progresses from the Client issue phase to the Spirit-Mind phase.

The **first phase** begins with a brief interview process that engages the Mental Level of Consciousness, during which the Client and the Facilitator determine a core issue to work on in the Constellation. A presenting issue might be related to the Client's perceived conflict with his mother or it might be related to a Client's loss of her brother in childhood.

Next, the Client places the Representatives—silently and intuitively - in particular positions around the Constellation working area within the seminar space. Imagine for a moment arranging participants you have chosen as Representatives of your sister in relation to, say, your deceased aunt or in relation to your chronically ill father. Then, the Client begins to observe his/

her Family Energy Field. From the Mental Level of Consciousness, the Client **acknowledges** what is being presented. Like a lighthouse illuminating night, the ocean of Constellations offer clarity, vision, and surprising moments of enlightenment. By expanding consciousness, Constellations increase our depth perception and reveal what was previously hidden from our view. They also increase our ability to see more of what has always been there but was obscured by a variety of factors.

The **second phase** of a Constellation involves movement on the Physical and Emotional Levels of consciousness. The Client begins to move through the Family Energy Field. He or she looks more closely at Representatives, often deeply into their eyes. Verbal communication is replaced in the second phase with specific Words of Empowerment chosen by the Facilitator to help the Client transition from the Mental to the Emotional Level. As the heart center engages, the story begins to recede. Only what is present in the form of thoughts, images, and feelings is relevant. The Facilitator follows the physical and emotional cues of the Client as well as the Representatives to see where a shift is needed in order to create balance in the family. All energetic systems seek a state of balance to be healthy. Both individuals and groups have an unconscious desire to achieve a state of equilibrium. In TCA, the Facilitator helps bring imbalances to the forefront in order to restore equilibrium through awareness, insight and resolution.

A Constellation Journeyer
Clair — Four Generations

Clair was in her early forties when she came for help concerning the feeling of separation she felt with her mother, and that she was beginning to experience between herself and her two daughters. During the interview process she revealed that her mother had been estranged from her own mother (Clair's grandmother) in early childhood.

Clair chose Representatives for herself, her mother, and grandmother. She placed the Representative for her grandmother several yards away and with her back turned to Clair's mother. This suggested that the grandmother was focused on something from the past and was not available to her daughter (Clair's mother). An additional Representative for the great-grandmother was placed in view of the grandmother. Soon thereafter, all three women began to cry and slowly began moving towards one another to embrace.

Clair was stunned. She didn't know anything about her great-grandmother or what had happened in her life, but watching the three preceding generations of mothers and daughters holding each other, touched her deeply.

The Representative for Clair helped her to enter the Constellation then sat down. The great-grandmother, grandmother and mother turned to face Clair. Upon sensing relief and love emanating from the Representatives, she burst open in waves of sadness, then joy. Clair understood that the separation she felt with her mother began two generations earlier. The women were placed in a line each resting their backs into their mother's bodies. She could feel the distance beginning to heal within her. Clair felt serene as she allowed the sense of separation to be replaced by a feeling of connection with her mother's lineage.

It is common in Constellations for the Facilitator to move certain Representatives to different positions in relation to each other and ask how the new positions affect them. Often their responses reflect an uncanny resemblance to the Client's family situation. When the "right" positioning is found, there is visible relief and relaxation on the part of the Representatives as well as the Client. This reflects a restoration of equilibrium, as a more complete picture of the family system begins to take shape. The Client may gain insight, know intuitively their next step, feel resolved, or come to peace with the issue they have presented. Most importantly, the Client **accepts** what has occurred, often meeting the very edge of his or her resistance at the Egoic Level.

In the **third phase,** the Client moves through the ego's resistance to enter Soul Level Consciousness where knowledge in the form of feelings, thoughts, and images is transmitted almost instantly. This third phase creates what in Sanskrit is called *anandamayakosha,* a bliss state of consciousness. In this state, we are absent of any judgment or criticism of those represented, or what has occurred. The Veil of Forgetting lifts, the heart center opens, and Soul agreements for this lifetime are remembered. The Client re-cognizes—sees again—the family member involved for who they really are in their Soul nature.

In some instances, we immediately understand why things transpired in our family as they have. Clear answers to some of life's biggest questions may arise, such as why I am the son or daughter of this parent, why certain illnesses presented in my life, and most importantly, why I chose to be incarnated into my Family Lineage. At the Soul Level of Consciousness it becomes possible to agree without hesitation; we feel freer and no longer held captive by the past. We gain insight into how we might live our life in relation to the family we actually have, to our loved ones. Along with a deep appreciation for our Family Lineage, we experience a humble willingness to contribute to the evolution of our family's consciousness. Moreover, Constellations at the Soul Level provide a precious opportunity to understand *why we are here,* enabling us to fulfill our Soul agreements.

The **fourth phase** usually begins with an alignment of all the Levels of Consciousness—as a deeply felt experience. This alignment may cause a transmission through the room, like a gentle shock wave that can be felt by each person who is in tune with the Constellation. This is the **Spirit-Mind phase**. During this phase, those in attendance often feel as if a powerful shared blessing has been bestowed upon them.

Ours is the time that knows
No bounds.
When we enter this space
All is forgotten and forgiven
Only love, only life.

This moment flushes out
The wounds of the past
To leave our hearts
Open, supple, ready to receive
Like never before.
We are endless,
We are one,
In this boundless time

— Peter

Phases of a Constellation

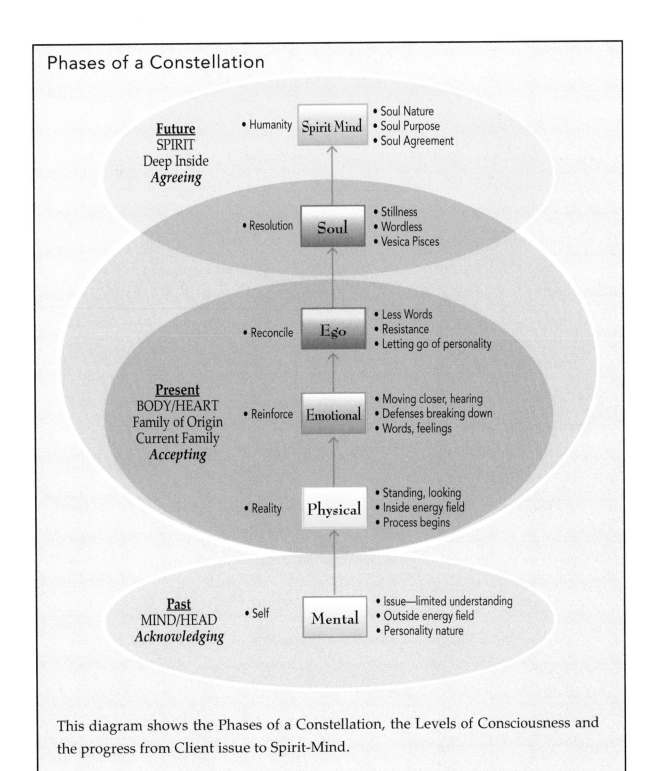

This diagram shows the Phases of a Constellation, the Levels of Consciousness and the progress from Client issue to Spirit-Mind.

A Constellation Journeyer
Anna — Appreciating Marriage

Anna felt a deep spiritual connection with the man she married from the first moment they met. Yet, she and her husband had an intense marriage that ultimately left her feeling inferior as a person, but even more so, as a woman. She eventually left the marriage and spent the next thirty years living independently, but very much following a spiritual path of inquiry.

At age sixty Anna was ready to try again. In her private Constellation session concerning her pursuit of a new partnership, she examined her relationship with her first husband. Feelings of love and loss washed over her—loss for what did not materialize between them, and love for what they had shared. As the Emotional state of consciousness shifted into the Spiritual state of Soul recognition with her husband, Anna began to understand other aspects of her marriage. She recognized that her husband represented the outwardly successful and highly spiritual male that she felt she could never measure up to. She vowed never to put herself in that type of relationship again.

In Peter's quiet office as Anna looked at a few wooden figurines representing herself, her first husband, and a potential partner (the past, present, and future), she dropped into Soul consciousness. Suddenly she realized that one of the underlying reasons for her marriage was to guide her to seek out a path of spiritual inquiry. Sitting in silence, a profound sense of gratefulness came over Anna. Past feelings of regret were replaced with an understanding that her marriage had been necessary in order to create the trajectory that allowed her to pursue her Soul's longing.

Crying softly, Anna became calmer and calmer as her mental state synthesized all the information coursing through her being. Her Emotional state was one of peace for all that had occurred in relation to her husband—beyond the personalities that had played out in their time together.

I also offered Anna Words of Empowerment to help solidify the healing and understanding she received though her constellation. She spoke these words with truth: "I see you now more clearly, dear husband." "Thank you for the time you spent with me." "I wish you well on your Soul's Journey." As Anna repeated these sentences, at first out loud and then internally, her four Levels of Consciousness aligned into a unified field. She could feel the tension and resistance that had accumulated in her pursuit of a new relationship melt away. Looking back at her life from her Soul's perspective, she felt deep gratitude for the last thirty years of her life, a life that she loved, and for the significant role he played in helping her pursue her own path of self-discovery. There were no regrets, doubts, or judgments, only appreciation for all her experiences that led her up to this present moment in time.

Without any prompting, she said several times aloud, "Thank you." To whom, or for what, only Anna knew. As we finished up the session, she added, "I feel ready to trust a man again."

PART II

Accepting Our Family As It Is

Dear Constellation Journeyer—

We begin the Constellation journey by pursuing the first Perennial Question—*how did I get here?* This question and Part II of *The Constellation Approach: Finding Peace through Your Family Lineage* will guide you through four foundational Strands of Awareness—Family of Origin, Father's Lineage, Mother's Lineage, and Siblings. At the end of each chapter you will be invited to include your personal journal reflections. You can turn to Part V to experience the respective Constellations using figurines.

These four Constellations are called **Systemic Constellations**. Systemic Constellations are those that originate with the Family of Origin or current primary relationships that include husbands, wives, partners, children, grandparents, grandchildren, step-children. The system is observed to determine if and where there is imbalance. These Systemic Constellations involve a step-by-step process that works trans-generationally from the oldest generation towards the current.

Ultimately, in exploring our own energetic and Soul origins in relation to our Family of Origin, we come to accept that we chose the circumstances of our birth, including our parents.

May you come to greater acceptance on your path towards peace with your Family Lineage.

—Jamy & Peter

Chapter 5

Our Family of Origin

The family is one of nature's masterpieces.

—George Santayana, philosopher

We begin our journey with the most foundational of all Constellations—the Family of Origin Constellation. A Family of Origin Constellation can be thought of as a Soul-remembering ritual. It creates an opportunity for us to acknowledge all of the members of our family. The Constellation simultaneously connects us to the Family Energy Field and with those who have agreed to accompany us on our life's journey. Likes and dislikes aside, they are our bloodline. We belong to them and them to us. They are our tribe, our clan, an intimate circle of beings with the same genetic imprint.

The pathway that leads to a full experience of our Soul nature begins with our Family of Origin. This particular Constellation summons up our deepest yearning to belong; it also allows us to navigate and take our place in the continuous stream of consciousness that has flowed since the beginning of time through our Family Lineage.

A Family of Origin Constellation is the first step in unraveling the Strands of Awareness. It is a true 'gathering of souls'— of seeing, feeling, and accepting all the beings that make up our family and discovering where we fit among them. We begin to understand the Threads of Consciousness that bind us together.

Our Family of Origin includes our biological father and mother, our siblings, and both sets of grandparents. It does not matter if we knew them or not, the type of relationships we have or had, or if they are living or deceased. We simply recall their names, their homelands, their lives. As each member takes their appropriate place, the Constellation reveals the unspoken, and often, unconscious, bonds we share with our family. We begin to awaken to a deeper sense of belonging and connection. The finding peace process has begun as we stand present with our Family of Origin.

The Family Soul

Call it a clan, call it a network, call it a tribe, call it a family.
Whatever you call it, whoever you are, you need one.

—Jane Howard, journalist

To appreciate our place within our Family of Origin, let's contemplate for a moment the number of people who have actually contributed to our DNA beyond the great-grandparents that each of us have:

16 great-great-grandparents

32 great-great-great-grandparents

64 great-great-great-great-grandparents

128 great-great-great-great-great-grandparents

256 great-great-great-great-great-great-grandparents

512 great-great-great-great-great-great-great-grandparents

1024 great-great-great-great-great-great-great-great-grandparents

In 10 generations, we are connected to 2,046 ancestors!

It's humbling to consider the astonishing number of familial forbearers who have walked this path of life before us, living and dying. In the Constellation Approach, the **Family Soul** is the continuous stream of consciousness that travels along the masculine and feminine lineages into the Family Energy Field that eventually leads to us. Whether family members are aware of it or not, they are unconsciously directed by the Family Soul, much like a conductor directing an orchestra. The Family Soul may also include non-relatives who have had a significant impact on one of our family members—for example, a former wife who may have died or a perpetrator in a violent event that left a family member permanently injured. Constantly seeking and moving towards a state of balance, reconciliation, and peace over generations, the Family Soul is present with us at all times. Like the wind, we can feel it, yet its origins are long ago and very far away. When we let ourselves feel our deep, ancestral connection with our Family of Origin, we awaken to our own unique Soul nature—along with our Soul's choice to be part of this family lineage.[7]

Rings of Influence and Levels of Conscience

In our journey towards peace with our Family of Origin, it's important to understand that each of us is affected by influences on our Family of Origin's conscious and unconscious actions and beliefs. These **Rings of Influence** are similar to magnetic fields in the way they exert a pressure to stay within the sphere of the group. The Rings are comparable to the Sociogram,[8] which was described in the writings of Jacob Moreno, the founder of Psychodrama. According to Moreno, human beings are akin to an atom's nucleus, but larger electromagnetic forces such as family, religion, ethnicity, political affiliations, and congenital illness surround us and direct our movements.

---

7   Ralph Metzner, *The Life Cycle of the Human Soul* (Berkeley: Regent Press, 2011)

8   Paul Holmes, Marcia Karp, Michael Watson, eds., *Psychodrama Since Moreno* (New York: Routledge, 1994)

Like atoms, all organizing relationships develop rules, norms, beliefs, and taboos that bind the network together. This creates a system, a systemic order. Those who adhere belong to the group; those who don't are excluded. As a member within a system, we may feel superior, innocent, or most importantly, that we belong. Yet, to another system, bound by a different set of rules, norms, beliefs, and taboos, we may appear guilty, unreasonable, and excessive. None of us individually has the power to stop the effects of these systemic forces, yet we all bear some of the weight and consequence for the actions of the group to which we belong. These mighty Rings of Influence contribute to something considerable larger than us or our families. They serve the still-larger non-personal consciousness of country, society, and humanity.

After working with hundreds of families over many years, Bert Hellinger began to recognize these greater influences as something mysterious, often unconscious, unseen, yet ever-present—calling them the limits of conscience.[9]

We identify them as **four levels of conscience**—the personal, familial, collective, and that of the Spirit-Mind.

- **Individual conscience** relates to those to whom we feel connected—parents, siblings, partners, children, friends, relatives, and groups. This conscience has different standards for each of our different relationships: one for our relationship to our father, another for that with our mother, one for the church/temple, another for the workplace. The individual conscience is held within the family conscience and measured through feelings of guilt and innocence.
- **Family conscience** often remains unrecognized. We neither feel nor hear this conscience, but we experience its effects as passed from one generation to the next. The family conscience holds everyone's personal histories, different fates, and important life events. It's a system with order safeguarding the right of membership for all who

---

9   Bert Hellinger, *Love's Hidden Symmetry* (Phoenix: Zeig, Tucker & Co.) 1998

belong to the family. It protects the bonds between its members. Family conscience also plays out over generations. Examples of loyalty to the family conscience include the following: marrying within the religion, continuing a lineage of shipbuilders, repeating several generations of alcoholism, etc.

- **Collective conscience** or **Societal conscience**, as defined by sociologist Emile Durkheim, is the set of shared beliefs, ideas, and moral attitudes that operate as a unifying force within society. Like the family conscience, we can't feel or hear the collective conscience, yet it affects us each waking moment of our lives. The family conscience is considered part of the collective conscience. As an example of collective-conscience shifting, consider the evolution of Gay rights over the last several decades.

- **Spirit-Mind** guides us beyond the other realms of conscience. It requires great spiritual effort because it tears us away from obedience to the dictates of our family, religion, culture, and personal identity. It challenges us to leave behind what we have previously known. Indescribable and mysterious, the Spirit-Mind is unbound and free. It does not follow the laws of our individual or familial conscience. Marrying outside our race or nationality, refusing to go to war, or joining a revolution are a few of the ways in which we may follow the Spirit-Mind.

Guilt and Innocence—The Operating System of Conscience

In our journey towards acceptance with our Family of Origin, there is a curious tension between innocence and guilt when it comes to whether or not we "belong." Conscience is always functioning within us. But a clear or guilty conscience has little to do with good and evil, right and wrong, but rather how one's actions align within our systems of belief. Conversely, we can feel quite guilty for honoring our Soul consciousness when it deviates from what others expect of us. Each of us wants to belong. We need to feel the safety of social convention and predictability of order. These are fundamental needs. In order to have these needs met our conscience demands one need and forbids another.

When we belong there is a sense of **Innocence**. We are intimately included with a feeling of closeness, freedom, and being entitled. When we are conscientious and loyal with respect to social order, we feel innocent. **Guilt** happens when our belonging is endangered; it feels like exclusion or alienation. When what we give and what we receive aren't balanced, guilt feels like indebtedness, obligation, and resentment. When we deviate from the order of the group, guilt includes the fear of consequences or punishment.

The Many Faces and Mirrors of Love

The dream of innocence without guilt is an illusion.

—Bert Hellinger

In order to break away from restriction in our lives, we must feel our guilt. We can't remain feeling innocent and grow. For instance, a young man leaves his parents' home to rent his own apartment. Feelings of guilt ensue. This type of guilt is **True Guilt**, necessary in order to progress in life. But there is a difference between true guilt and **Guilty Feelings**—a repetitive cycle of emotional turmoil that keeps us stuck in unhealthy patterns. True Guilt is the price we pay in order to grow and move past the limiting conscience that would otherwise keep us attached to these patterns. When we hold guilt with dignity, truthfulness, and an honest sense of pride, we honor ourselves along with the truth of where we have come from. Constellations are a unique tool for helping us distinguish between these two types of guilt.

A Family of Origin Constellation exposes us to many layers of feelings related to love. Bert Hellinger introduced concepts of **Blind Love** and **Enlightened Love** that can help us on this part of our journey. Blind Love is the kind of love that compels us to follow along with an individual or group out of a desire to belong or an obligation that does not serve our highest good. This love reflects a limited view of our self and the other. In contrast, Enlightened Love allows for an expansive view of the other. We see the lessons they have taught us, the sacrifices they have made, and the real value of their contributions. We also experience Enlightened Love when we make choices in alignment with our highest good as well as that of others. This kind of love necessarily includes an element of True Guilt, as described above.

Family Entanglements

Entanglements stem from attitudes, feelings, and fates that belong to others, what psychiatrists Ivan Boszormenyi-Nagy and Geraldine Spark calls "invisible loyalties."[10] When we seek to discover why certain patterns have not changed in our lives, reasons often lie in an entanglement from our Family of Origin. A person who is having difficulty in a current relationship may find that there is something unresolved from either a past relationship or even between her/ his parents' relationship. The person may act in ways similar to how a mother acted towards a father; and that relationship, in turn, may reflect someone else in the Family Soul.

> *You can kiss your family … goodbye and put miles between you, but at the same time you carry them with you in your heart, your mind, your stomach, because you do not just live in a world but a world lives in you.*
>
> —Frederick Buechner, author

In a Family of Origin Constellation, entanglements are revealed through the physical positioning, direction and spacing, of family members. For example, a child may be standing between her/ his parents, or a man may be looking solely at his first wife. Also, when Representatives are questioned about how they feel their responses often reflect an entanglement, such as a daughter's overprotectiveness towards her father, or a mother's overprotectiveness in relation to her son. Entanglements are not judged as good or bad. Instead they show us where our love and loyalties lie. When we simply

---

10   Ivan Boszormenyi-Nagy and Geraldine Spark, *Invisible Loyalties* (New York: Harper & Row) 1974

observe them, they reveal a starting place for the dis-entangling process within the Constellation.

One of Bert Hellinger's core teachings on how to navigate these entanglements is called the **Orders of Love**. These are natural, organic patterns that, when followed, create harmony and peacefulness in families, but when out of alignment, create entanglement, tension, and difficulty finding any lasting peace among family members. The Orders of Love include the following: the **Order of Precedence**, the **Order of Inclusion**, and the **Order of Balance**.

The **Order of Precedence** means that whoever came first in a family takes the first place, and the others follow in order. The parents come first and then the children. An older brother or sister comes before his/her younger sibling. A first wife comes before a second. If there is not an honoring and respect for those who have come before us, there will be a dissonance that occurs between the respective parties. If the dissonance goes unresolved, it can be passed on from one generation to another—fathers to sons, mothers to daughters, siblings to siblings.

Regardless of their behavior, those individuals who came before us come first. It is because of them that we are here today. This is also why, in any form of teaching, it is important that we name and honor those from whom we have received our knowledge. Only this way, are we truly free to pass on what we have learned.

The **Order of Inclusion** holds that each member of a family belongs equally to the family and is respected in the same way, regardless of their personal qualities or particular actions. Their belonging to the family is independent from whether they are talented, feeble-minded, or physically attractive. It does not matter if they are handicapped or mentally ill, died at an early age, or committed suicide. Every person is included equally within the Family Soul.

The **Order of Balance** demonstrates that over generations of a Family Lineage the system will always seek out a state of equilibrium. Each of us contributes to achieving this state of balance in our own particular way. One sibling may be wealthy, another poor. Regardless of how difficult or even terrible a person's life situation may appear, the reasons may originate deep in the consciousness of Family Soul. This does not mean we should not help family members or turn our back on those less fortunate. It means we need to allow them their own life choices and respect them if we do offer assistance.

Fate versus Destiny

When we seek acceptance of our place among our Family of Origin, we must also accept our fate and destiny. According to Hellinger's Order of Balance, includes the concept that each person is entitled to her or his own fate. Our **Fate** includes all the things that have occurred in our life. Our **Destiny** is what we create from our fate. We also say the cards we have chosen are our fate and how we play those cards is our destiny. As Souls who have chosen this incarnation, we can seek the reasons for our choices in our Family Soul consciousness. It is important to remember that it is the highest form of respect to allow another their fate. This also frees us from any Entanglement we may have with that person.

With our fate comes the responsibility for our actions during our lifetime. When a family member does not take responsibility for their actions, later generations will often try to balance out ill effects passed down by their ancestors. Through the Constellation Approach we have many opportunities to take responsibility for our actions and thereby release the generations that follow us.

More About Words of Empowerment

Words of Empowerment are a core component of Constellations when spoken slowly, succinctly, with an open heart. They have an impact that can profoundly touch those speaking and receiving them. It is the intention that counts, not the exact words chosen. Like throwing a healing dart, Words of Empowerment attempt to hit the bull's eye deep in the center of the heart and Soul.

The Words of Empowerment serve three purposes—"the **3 R's:**" to echo **Reality**, to **Reinforce**, or to **Reconcile**.

Words to echo Reality reflect the facts.

e.g., You are my family.

Words Reinforce our relationship with our family. They open the heart and bring about an emotional response.

e.g., You are the only family I have. Or, you are the right family for me.

Words that Reconcile move us in the direction of peace and understanding. Through language of reconciliation we begin to feel our Soul connection with the other.

e.g., I agree to all that has happened between us, the good and the bad.

Acknowledging What Is

What can you do to promote world peace? Go home and love your family.

—Mother Teresa, Catholic nun

Another practice is the simple concept of **Acknowledging what is** (also the title of a book by Bert Hellinger) is the first step in every Constellation. It invites us to take into account all that has happened. By doing so, we can objectively observe what has occurred in our own life and the generations of ancestors who have preceded us, as well as the effects. We can perceive more clearly the continuation of life as it has flowed from generation to generation. We can witness experiences of all kinds without blame, judgment, or a posture of victimhood. No matter how difficult the circumstance, it is essential to honestly look at and face the truth of any situation, event, or relationship we have experienced or perhaps inherited. This act of acknowledgment will always help to heal and integrate us—and our families. Acknowledging What Is also enables us to make different choices.

Source to Spirit-Mind

Consciousness is the essence of all creation flowing into the collective conscience of humanity, and subdividing into races, nationalities, communities. Each group has its own form of collective conscience. The family conscience comes out of the collective. It has its particular sets of norms and rules based on the paternal and maternal Family Lineage from which it was created. The self (you) or the individual conscience is born from the family into which we incarnated.

As explained earlier, our individual conscience is directed by larger fields of conscience. But, as the Orders of Love become the guiding patterns for our choices, we begin to mature and individuate from our Family of Origin and move towards a healthier, more enriching life. The conscience of the Spirit-Mind also acts as a magnetic pull drawing us further along our life path.

It's always worth reminding ourselves that we come from the Source. We all wrestle with feelings of Guilt and Innocence, and move between Blind Love and Enlightened Love. Through exploring Levels of Conscience, we can discover our Soul nature and gradually contribute more and more to the evolution of consciousness, including weaving the braid of our Family Lineage.

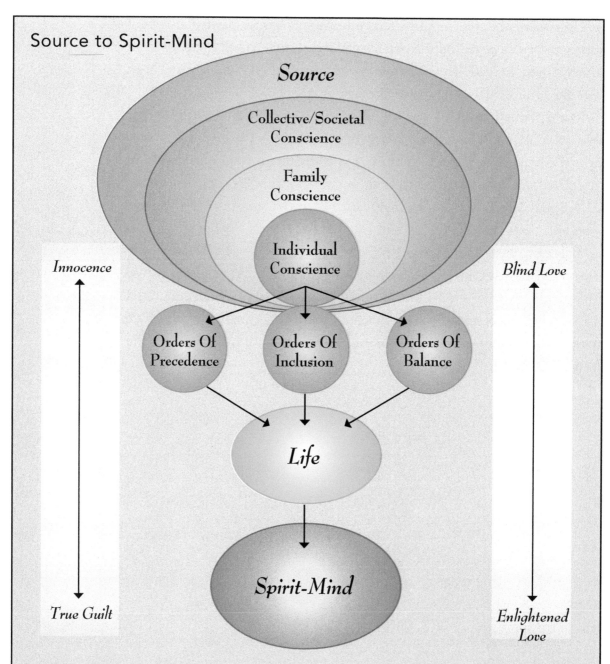

Source to Spirit-Mind

Source

Collective/Societal Conscience

Family Conscience

Individual Conscience

Innocence

Blind Love

Orders Of Precedence

Orders Of Inclusion

Orders Of Balance

Life

Spirit-Mind

True Guilt

Enlightened Love

This diagram shows the influential progression of the Levels of Conscience, the Orders of Love, and the effects of Guilt and Innocence as well as Blind and Enlightened Love as we emerge from Source and move through life guided by Spirit-Mind.

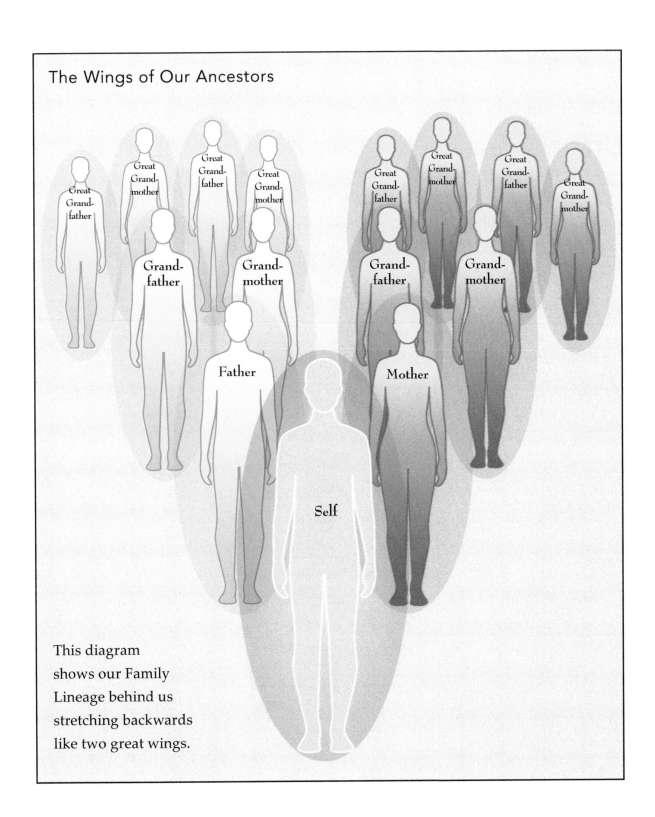

The Wings of Our Ancestors

Great Grand-father

Great Grand-mother

Great Grand-father

Great Grand-mother

Great Grand-father

Great Grand-mother

Great Grand-father

Great Grand-mother

Grand-father

Grand-mother

Grand-father

Grand-mother

Father

Mother

Self

This diagram shows our Family Lineage behind us stretching backwards like two great wings.

A Constellation Journeyer
Michelle — Returning Home

I left home when I was sixteen, escaping mental illness and physical abuse. After years of psychotherapy, thinking I had worked through my issues, I was surprised at the sheer terror I felt at the thought of facing my family in a Constellation. The compassion and support of the Facilitators and the group made it safe enough to try a Family Constellation. We were all there to face the difficult.

This proved to be a life-changing experience for me. I was able to stand with my family of origin, in all my previous feelings of being annihilated, but my fear was gone and replaced with a sense of peace and belonging. I felt I was back home. I realized I had been running from my family for the past forty-three years and now I could stop. It was freeing to be with my Family of Origin once again.

When I returned home from the weekend there was a package from my sister. It was, unusual to receive anything from her, especially if there was not a special occasion. It was an enameled butterfly box. I began to cry because butterflies were a favorite of my deceased grandmother, Mary, the only one in our family who I felt touched me lovingly. I deeply felt her presence in my life again, as if she had watched over my Constellation, and was now affirming the reconnection.

A Constellation Journeyer
Tracy Lawrence — The Second Time Around

After going through my Family of Origin Constellation the first time around, in the first year, I thought I had learned everything I needed to know and had felt all the feelings I could possibly feel: intense fear, resistance, deep sadness, and longing. I wondered what else could there possibly be for me? In my heart, I had reconciled myself with many of my family members. I felt peaceful.

I had an idea of what to expect the second time I did my Family of Origin Constellation but was surprised at the intensity of my emotions. My legs trembled nearly non-stop until the end of the Constellation. Similar to my first Constellation, I expressed tears of sadness, loss, and longing, but this time I also experienced tears of joy from feeling in my rightful place, in the right family for me. I was able to bow spontaneously in deep recognition and appreciation to my parents.

Insights kept coming for days after the Constellation. I now no longer feel like a victim and see a larger purpose for my life. I feel more grounded in my being as I walk this earth and can truly feel the support of all of my ancestors.

$$\longrightarrow \blacklozenge\blacklozenge\blacklozenge \longleftarrow$$

Words of Empowerment Practices

Here are some **Words of Empowerment** to practice reflecting reality, reinforcing, or reconciling with your Family of Origin.

Words that reflect reality:

I acknowledge that you are my family.

You are the only family I have.

I belong to you and you belong to me.

You are the family I chose.

Words that reinforce:

I accept all of you as my family.

You are the right family for me.

This is the right order.

You are where I come from.

Words of reconciliation:

I agree to all that has happened between us as family.

I agree to this order.

This is where I belong.

We belong together.

I both receive from and contribute to this family.

Notice how you feel when you find the 'right' words for your Family of Origin.

Reflections on Your Family of Origin[11]

>> I am _____ ,
(your full name)

the son/daughter of

_____
(your father's full name)

and

_____
(your mother's full name)

[If you were adopted complete the questions as best you can for both your Biological Family of Origin and your Adoptive Family.]

>> I am the grandson/granddaughter of *(your father's father and mother's full names)*:

_____ and _____

>> I am the grandson/granddaughter of *(your mother's father and mother's full names)*:

_____ and _____

Note: If you don't know their names, use "Great-Grandfather" or "Great-Grandmother

---

11   This exercise was inspired by Lisa B. Iversen, *Ancestral Blueprints: Revealing Invisible Truths in America's Soul* (Bellingham: Family Constellations West Publishing, 2009), p.77

>> I am the great grandson/great granddaughter of
(your grandfather's father and mother's names):

_____ and _____

_____ and _____

>> I am the great grandson/great granddaughter of
(your grandmother's father and mother's names):

_____ and _____

_____ and _____

>> I am brother/sister to *(their name(s); in birth order. If you have no siblings, note that as well.)*

_____   _____

_____   _____

_____   _____

>> The countries of origin that my ancestors come from are:

_____   _____

_____   _____

>> The religious or spiritual connections that my family held are:

_____   _____

_____   _____

Complete your reflections with the words:

"These are the family members and some of the facts of my Family of Origin, as I know them to be."

Chapter 6

Our Father's Lineage and Our Mother's Lineage

Because of you, I am.

—African Proverb

Many of the people we work with carry a host of unresolved feelings with one or both of their parents. Whether their parents were loving or not, present or absent, dead or alive, healthy or ill, sane or not, our clients often come to us not fully feeling at peace with their mother and / or father. How can we shift such deeply embedded *samskaras*—patterns that may have started before our existence and even before our mother's or father's existence?

To accept the truth of "Who am I?" starts with the Constellations of the Father's Lineage and the Mother's Lineage that follow. As stated previously, each of us is the result of the pairing of a human female life force (our biological mother) and a human male life force (our biological father). Who we are begins with them, and everything else that we encounter and experience on the other side of our own distinctive entrance into life.

Our Father's Lineage

Your father gives you many things in a lifetime... most of which you will not appreciate until way after he is gone.

—Linda Poindexter, writer

Accepting the masculine begins with the first man in our life—our biological father, the man who partnered with our mother and gave us the gift of life. We hold half of his DNA within our genetic makeup. Other men may have had great importance in our lives, such as a grandfather, uncle, or adoptive father who may have 'stepped in' for our father, who left, was excluded, or died. Any man may act as our father, yet for each of us, there is only one man who carries our bloodline.

Our Father's Lineage includes his grandparents, parents, siblings, as well as former wife/wives and children before coupling with our mother. Everyone is included.

Our experiences of all our male relationships are connected to the first, our birth father. A powerful bond to him exists regardless of the actual relationship we have or had with him—even if we never met him. Indeed, our ability to accept the father we have is directly related to our acceptance of all the males who appear in our lives—husbands, partners, brothers, sons, uncles, nephews, grandsons, male colleagues and friends.

Father's Lineage Constellations, like Family of Origin Constellations, are Soul-remembering rituals that name, claim, and recollect all who 'belong' to our father. Through our male lineage we can develop the capacity and skill to support ourselves and provide for others in the material world; to be structured, rational, and successful; and to protect ourselves and others. As we reconcile our attitudes of resentment, judgment, blame, guilt, or shame that we still may cling to in relation to our father, we begin to accept and feel at peace with the masculine. We are also able to claim or reclaim a sense of strength, fortitude and well-being as we tap into our Father's Lineage.

"Dear Father,

From you, I accept everything, all of it, with all the trimmings,
and at the full price that it cost you, and which it is costing me…

I take you as my father, and you can have me as your child.
You are for me the right one, and I am the right child for you…

I am happy that you have chosen Mother.
The two of you are the right ones for me. Only you!"

—Bert Hellinger[12]

Attitudes of Resentment and Judgment

In our fifty years' of combined experience working with individual clients, and groups, we have noticed certain recurring negative attitudes that are harbored toward parents. Two attitudes that frequently present in Father's Lineage Constellations are resentment and judgment. It is easy to judge our father for the things he has or hasn't done for us, but this judgement leads to resentment. The waters of his paternal life-giving energy can become poisoned and bitter, leading us to seek masculine nourishment elsewhere.

Since the post-WWII era it's been common for even the most dedicated father to be away from the family home for longer and longer periods of time. A common statement we hear is, "My father was a good provider but he was never home, or when he was there he was tired or unavailable."

Another form of resentment can stem from the rules, beliefs, or career paths fathers push children to follow. For example, "I

I shall no longer define myself as the son [daughter] of a father who couldn't or hasn't, wouldn't or wasn't.

—Cameron Conaway, martial artist, writer

---

12   Bert Hellinger, trans. by Ralph Metzner, *On Life and Other Paradoxes; Aphorisms and Little Stories from Bert Hellinger* (Phoenix: Zeig, Tucker & Theisen, Inc., 2002)

did this because my father wanted me to." But doing "it" for our father usually results in feelings of resentment later in life.

However, when we view our father in relation to his Family of Origin, particularly his father and grandfather, we begin to perceive him very differently. TCA can help shift our judgment and resentment to understanding, compassion, and a new depth of respect for what our father experienced in his life prior to our arrival. We're also able to acknowledge what he has done for us and the sacrifices he may have made on our behalf.

Three Healing Words

How do we shift those attitudes and patterns of resentment and judgment? In the Father's Lineage Constellation—and in *any* Constellation for that matter—we aim to create a new dialogue, a healing dialogue with a family member, present or not, alive or dead. This healing dialogue can open the doors to reconciliation and peace. Three powerful words, taught to us by Bert Hellinger, may be used in practically any Constellation but are especially potent in both the Father's and Mother's Lineage. The words, *please, thank you,* and *yes* are the basis for much of this healing dialogue.

When a father gives to his son, both laugh. When a son gives to his father, both cry.

—Sephardic Proverb

Please is said when we wish for something to change with a person with whom we are in relationship. This simple word has a quality of acknowledging what is.

Please, Father.

Thank you is an expression of appreciation and gratitude for what the other has done for us. It also reflects acknowledgment and acceptance.

Thank you, Dad.

Yes means that we have surrendered our egoic desires for how we wanted or expected things to be. It is an expression of full acknowledgement, acceptance, and agreement to all that has happened in relation to the other.

Yes, Papa!

These three simple words have enormous potential to help us recollect the Soul connections we have with each other.

Deepening the Words of Empowerment

There's another way to shift these deeply held attitudes that separate and keep us at a distance. It requires renewed focus, truthfulness and sincerity as we move through the Levels of Consciousness to eventually communicate from our Soul to our father or mother with Words of Empowerment.

When using Words of Empowerment, we are often encouraged to say the chosen word(s) three times. Behind every word or phrase spoken is a vibration of energy. Everyone knows the difference between heartfelt words and those that are merely parroted. With repetition, the words can be felt at ever deeper Levels of Consciousness. Initially, the spoken words usually come from a Mental Level of understanding, perhaps after being prompted by the Facilitator. With the second repetition, the words are felt at the Emotional Level of honesty. But a more complete healing is reached with the third repetition, which allows the energy to be carried to the Soul. In TCA, Words of Empowerment are spoken slowly to allow the energetic vibration to touch the heart and Soul of the one speaking as well as the one receiving.

Thanking our father generates an appreciation for all good things masculine.

At Peace with Strength & Fortitude

As you're coming to see TCA is an opportunity to shift from discord to peace. All of us feel the desire to be at peace with our mother and father. Peace is a state of strength. When we are at peace we are not diffusing our inner resources to wage battle or hold ourselves in a defensive position. Instead, the gates of our heart are open allowing feelings of acceptance to flow between us and our parents.

Peace naturally builds towards inner harmony and fortitude, continually increasing the longer we live without conflict, judgment or resentment in relation to our father. A peaceful heart and mind allow our own Inner Masculine[13] to flourish. We no longer expend energy keeping

---

13   The Inner Masculine and Inner Feminine are discussed in Part IV.

ourselves away from the life-enriching well of our paternal spring. Peace with our father brings feelings of appreciation and gratitude for his life and the life he passed on to us. Blame and victimhood are replaced with a sense of pride, belonging and connection.

No matter how many times we set up our Father's Constellation there is always more richness and strength to be received from him in the Vesica Pisces. With him at our back, we can feel strong, unafraid. And when we're at peace with our father, we begin to be at peace in the world.

Fathers

Not all are warriors
Some gentle and kind

Some missing a limb
Or part of their mind

Others rarely at home
Or difficult to reach

Seldom are they natural
But created over time

Unfairly, we expect more from them
Than they received from theirs.

—Peter

A Constellation Journeyer
Martina — Choosing Something Different

I have worked several Constellations with my father during the Immersion Program, and I know that each of them has brought me closer to this man who gave me life, molested me as a child, and who for most of my life didn't exist for me.

In my first Constellation I stood across the room from him and was offered the choice to walk towards him and come close enough to acknowledge him as my father. Simple as it sounds, that was perhaps the most daunting experience of my life. In that moment I recognized the element of choice in choosing something different with my father. Those fifteen-twenty feet in distance was a lifetime in healing for me, each step requiring more courage, strength, and a belief in a new possibility. I did make it across the room and so began my healing journey with my father and my male lineage. It took me several Constellations to get from acknowledgement, to acceptance, and finally to agreement. I often marveled at others who moved through these stages easily and effortlessly, and wondered why it took me so long. But I realize that in this work we heal in our own time, at our own pace.

I also began to see clearly the trans-generational pattern of abuse, and it changed my whole perspective on my life and my family. I recognized the greater contract—that my family chose this issue on a Soul level to transform. I came to accept that my Soul had also chosen this issue, had manifested this family who showed up and played it out perfectly, and that at the end of the day there were no victims, only willing participants in my family's healing legacy. We had all come together with perfection, each bringing our own piece for healing.

Words of Empowerment Practices

Here are some **Words of Empowerment** to practice reflecting reality, reinforcing or reconciling with your Father's Lineage.

Words that reflect reality:

You are the only father I have.

You are my father and I am your daughter/son.

I am your daughter/son and no one else's.

I acknowledge you as my father.

I belong to you and you belong to me.

Your blood runs through my veins.

Please Dad.

Because of you, I am.

Words that reinforce:

You are the right father for me.

I accept you as my father.

I accept all that has happened between us as father and son/daughter.

I paid a high price to have you as my father.

You paid a high price to have me as your son/daughter.

Yes, father.

Words of reconciliation:

I take you fully as my father with all the good and all the bad.

I agree to all that has happened between us.

Let us find another way, together.

When my time comes, we will meet again, Papa.

I leave it with you now, Dad.

Thank you, Father.

Notice how you feel when you find the 'right' words for your Father and his Lineage.

Reflections on Your Father's Lineage

Complete the following journal reflections concerning your Father and his Lineage. It is helpful to have a photo(s) of your Father and his Lineage as you do this.

>> I am _____ ,
>>>>> *(your full name)*

the son/daughter of

_____
(your father's full name)

>> He is the son of *(his father's full name)* and *(his mother's full name)*

_____ and _____

>> He came from a family of *(number of siblings)* _____ and his birth order is_____

>> He is the brother to *(name his siblings in birth order)*

_____   _____

_____   _____

_____   _____

>> He is/was husband to *(your mother's full name)* _____

>> Significant relationships prior to or after your mother *(their names)*

_____   _____

_____   _____

>> He is/was the father to *(the names of his children, including you, in birth order)*

_____   _____

_____   _____

_____   _____

>> He is/was the grandfather to *(the names of his grandchildren and great grandchildren in birth order)*

_____   _____

_____   _____

_____   _____

_____   _____

_____   _____

>> If he is deceased, what caused his death and when did it occur *(year)*?

_____

>> His age at death was _____ and my age at his death was _____ .

>> If your father is living, how many years do you sense you have left with him? _____

>> Is/was your father unresolved with any person or event?

_____

_____

>> Is/was your father trying to evolve any particular Threads of Consciousness that came from his lineage *(his father's or mother's)*?

_____

_____

>> I have the most difficulty accepting my father because

_____

_____

_____

>> I am most proud of my father because

_____

_____

_____

>> A trait that I carry from my father is

_____

_____

_____

>> The color of my father's eyes is _____

>> A Thread of Consciousness that I am trying to evolve in relation to my father or his lineage is

_____

_____

_____

Complete your reflections with the words:

"These are some of the facts of my Father's Lineage and his life as I know them to be."

Our Mother's Lineage

Mother is the name for God in the lips and hearts of little children.

—William Thackeray, novelist

Our mothers are portals to the world, to our very existence. Needless to say, accepting the feminine begins with acceptance of the first woman in our lives, our biological mother, she who carried us within her body as we grew from egg to infant. Half our DNA, the basis for our biological life form, is received from our mother. Together with our father, she gave us life.

We may have been mothered or raised by other females due to a variety of circumstances, but there is an unbreakable energetic Strand of Awareness that connects us with our biological mother; it is ever-present in our consciousness. Our Mother's Lineage includes her grandparents, parents, siblings, former husband / husbands, and children before joining with our father. As with the Father's Lineage, everyone is included.

All of our relationships, whether they're with a female or male, connect us to this first relationship with our birth mother—even if we never met her. To fully take in our mother means to accept the feminine as it manifests everywhere in our lives, including with our wives, partners, lovers, sisters, daughters, aunts, nieces, granddaughters, female colleagues, and friends. Conversely, to embrace the feminine, we must come to peace with our mother. Mother's Lineage Constellations, like the Family of Origin and Father's Lineage Constellations, are Soul-gathering rituals that bring together all who belong to our mother by naming and remembering them.

Through the feminine lineage we adopt ways of nurturing and caring for ourselves and our bodies. We learn how to maintain our home and environment, to be respectful of others, to be intuitive, to trust and to live from the heart. Whether she had horrible addictions, a mental illness, or was the best mother in the world, it doesn't matter—she is the only one we have. When we strengthen the connection to our mother and her lineage, the maternal source flows more fully into our lives. We are able to claim or reclaim a sense of interconnection with the earth, with nature, with our inner beauty and light, and are replenished by our maternal wellspring.

"Dear Mother,
From you, I accept everything, all of it, with all the trimmings,
and at the full price that you paid for it and that I too am paying
for it…

I take you as my mother, and you can have me as your child.
You are for me the right one, and I am the right child for you…
I am happy that you have chosen Father.
The two of you are the only ones for me. Only you!"

—Bert Hellinger[14]

Attitudes of Too-much and Not-enough-ness

In Mother's Lineage Constellations we have noticed common attitudinal patterns of disharmony. We identify a few of those patterns here in case they resonate with you. We have noticed that many Clients harbor judgments of their biological mother for being over-giving or under-giving, for being overly attentive or underly attentive—or 'too-much-ness' and 'not-enough-ness.' Depending upon the era in which you were born, your mother may have had to sacrifice her budding career to become a stay-at-home mom, or perhaps she adorned the Superwoman suit in an attempt to balance both. She may have been neglectful, overwhelmed, or controlling. Statements we often hear range from "My mother was depressed, so it was hard for me to leave

---

14   Bert Hellinger, trans. by Ralph Metzner, *On Life and Other Paradoxes; Aphorisms and Little Stories from Bert Hellinger* (Phoenix: Zeig, Tucker & Theisen, Inc., 2002)

her" to "She was involved in every aspect of my life; so I could not wait to get married."

Rejecting what our mother gave us as too much or not good enough deadens us. Wanting more than she could give halts our forward movement. Often, our sense of superiority or inferiority towards her manifests as harsh self-judgment and lack of self-care. When we can perceive our mother in relation to her Family of Origin, we're able to see her in a new way. Our rejection and wants are transformed into acceptance, fulfillment, and deep recognition of all that occurred for our mother before we arrived. We accept all that she has done for us—most especially carrying us within her body and giving birth to us.

> *Some mothers are kissing mothers and some are scolding mothers, but it is love just the same, and most mothers kiss and scold together.*
>
> —Pearl S. Buck, Pulitzer Prize writer

The Act of Bowing in TCA

How do we reconcile those complex feelings and conflicting attitudes with our mother? To accept the feminine means that we honor what is humble and reverential within ourselves. To accept the feminine within our Family Lineage means that we also honor the energetic patterns and relationships that have been passed onto us through her lineage. We respect and accept her ways and the traditions of her mother, grandmother, and great-grandmother. We carry on the traits that serve our growth and leave behind without anger or blame those that don't support the evolution of consciousness.

One way to accept the feminine is to bow. The practice of bowing has been used since ancient times as a way of showing respect or gratitude for someone or something that is deeply honored or admired. The **Act of Bowing** is used particularly with our parents. A bow may also be used to acknowledge a phenomenon or force greater than ourselves, such as a Representative for a congenital illness, an ancestral homeland, or even death.

Bowing in a Constellation is performed neither hastily nor with exaggerated slowness, but with a reverent and humble attitude. If one bows too quickly, it can feel casual or lack seriousness; bowing too slowly can feel pompous or disingenuous to receive. As a ritualistic movement it helps return us to our place within the Orders of Love: Precedence, Balance, and Inclusion.

Our mother came first. Because of her we are here today. Bowing to her acknowledges that she precedes us in life and paved the way. We are honoring the sacrifices she made so we could have our life. The Order of Balance is restored when we bow by lowering our bodies and releasing any feelings of authority towards our mother or father.

The Act of Bowing creates an opportunity to enter the sacred field of the Vesica Pisces and release ourselves from our attachments to judgment, superiority, resentment, or victimization. Bowing to another does not absolve them from responsibility for their behavior. Rather it helps us to release our attachment to wanting something to be different than it is or has been. The larger the resentment or judgments we hold, the greater the feelings of superiority—the lower and deeper we must bow.

TCA's Three Bows

There's three ways in which a bow may be enacted: lowering the head, bending at the waist and fully prostrate with the Representative standing before you. Each bow begins with sustained eye contact then by softly lowering your eyes and chin. This first position is the **Head Bow**. To enact, allow yourself to pause in this humble posture; relaxing, noticing your thoughts and feelings and taking a few full breaths. Next, raise your head and resume eye contact. This is a simple movement, yet a very powerful act. Performed with sincere intention, a successful bow will reveal your parents differently to you.

The eyes are the window to the Soul.

—Matthew 6:22-23

Next is the **Waist Bow.** Just like the head bow, it begins, for example, by connecting with a Representative for your mother, through sustained eye contact; then, slowly lowering your chin to your chest. By gently focusing your eyes on her feet, it helps the mind not to wander. Bending at the waist, bring your head lower than your heart. The ritual is completed by slowly returning upright and lifting your chin to connect with the eyes of your mother's Representative.

As you'll see in the diagrams to follow, the Head Bow engages the Third Eye and Throat Chakra. Lowering your eyes turns the focus inward while bending your chin can begin to break up energy blockages in the throat. The Waist Bow can open the Heart and Solar Plexus Chakra and align the Crown Chakra with the Heart Chakra of the Representative of your mother. This circular movement softens the emotional defenses and places you in a position of vulnerability—a prerequisite for deep healing.

Bowing to our mothers creates receptivity for all good things feminine.

The **Deep Bow** is with full prostration and the most respectful bow of the three. It can be a vulnerable posture that requires your full attention and intention during this precious and sacred work with your parent's Representative.

Continuing from the Waist Bow, kneel, and then lower your upper torso until your forehead touches the ground, arms extended. Your palms face upward in a gesture of openness, and willingness to receive. Breathe deeply, staying inwardly focused and surrendered to Soul consciousness. Finally, gently touch the feet of your mother's Representative. This modest act of reaching for and holding her feet allows a transmission of energy to flow between Souls. In TCA, we call this the **Ancestral Blessing**. It is a powerful experience for you as well as for the Representative.

After a period of time, you will sense a feeling of completion. Return to kneeling and raise your head with palms open. Once again, make eye contact with the Representative. Often, another wave of understanding and insight can happen without the need for verbal interaction. Conclude the Deep Bow by rising to your feet and looking into your mother's eyes. You may find yourself in the state of Enlightened Love—a love that the Soul recognizes and doesn't forget once re-membered.

Life is hard, mother hold me.

—Sioux Indian Prayer

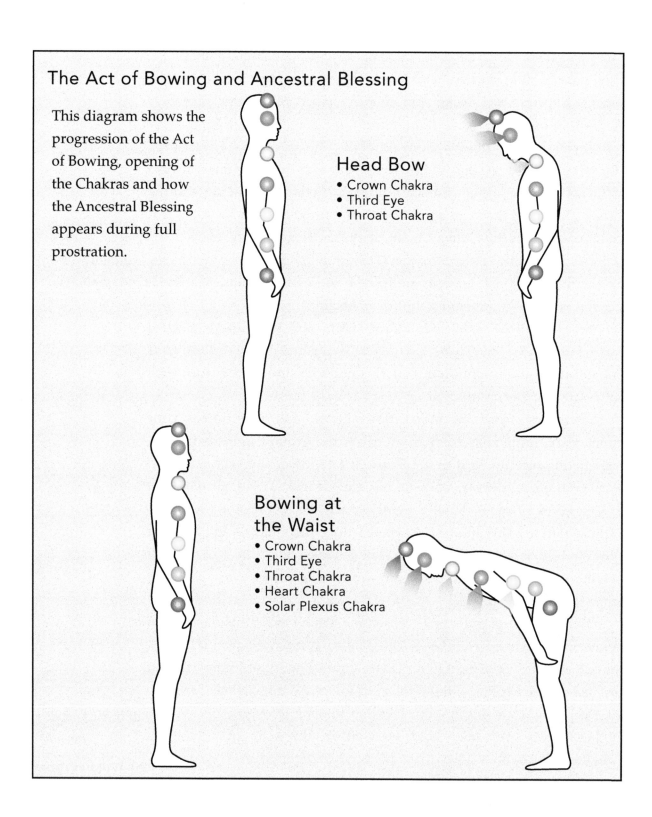

The Act of Bowing and Ancestral Blessing

This diagram shows the progression of the Act of Bowing, opening of the Chakras and how the Ancestral Blessing appears during full prostration.

Head Bow
- Crown Chakra
- Third Eye
- Throat Chakra

Bowing at the Waist
- Crown Chakra
- Third Eye
- Throat Chakra
- Heart Chakra
- Solar Plexus Chakra

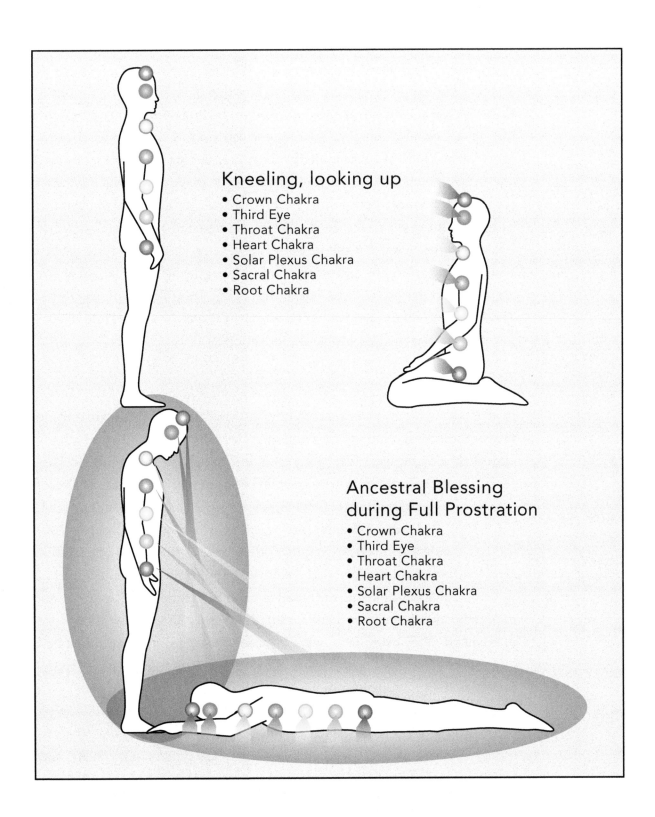

Kneeling, looking up
- Crown Chakra
- Third Eye
- Throat Chakra
- Heart Chakra
- Solar Plexus Chakra
- Sacral Chakra
- Root Chakra

Ancestral Blessing during Full Prostration
- Crown Chakra
- Third Eye
- Throat Chakra
- Heart Chakra
- Solar Plexus Chakra
- Sacral Chakra
- Root Chakra

The Bow and Aspects of Healing

The Bow corresponds with our Mental, Emotional, Egoic and Soul Levels of Consciousness, respectively, as well as with the Practices we move through during a Constellation. Eye contact corresponds to the first practice, or aspect of healing—we **acknowledge** the other. The act of lowering our eyes and bowing our head invites the second practice; we **accept** the other and what has transpired between us in this lifetime. Returning to eye contact completes the cycle. In the third practice, we **agree** to all that was and is in relation to the other and the power of his or her lineage. Healing occurs. The Veil of Illusion lifts and some of our Soul agreements are revealed. We are able to transcend attachment on the Egoic Level of our personalities. The Act of Bowing is a movement that expands our awareness into deeper Levels of Consciousness and Soul connections.

Tears

In all Constellations, tears are common, but especially when we are coming to accept the masculine and feminine energies moving through our Father's and Mother's Lineages. Tears are a great indicator to pay attention. In TCA we've identified two types of tears commonly shed: **Tears of Regret** and **Tears of Relief**. Tears of Regret precede Tears of Relief.

Never interrupt a person when they are crying. It is a most holy act best given space.

Tears of Regret are released when we confront a loss, connect with a deep longing, or face responsibility for our actions. These tears confirm that we have shifted from the Mental Level of Consciousness into the broader, more fluid Emotional Level. We are in touch with our feelings. Tears of Regret lubricate the hinges on the door to the heart. They carry away what has been missing or lost. Accompanied by feelings of sadness, they may manifest for some as a single tear from the corner of an eye, while for others they may flow for several minutes.

Tears of Relief flow after we break through our resistance to feeling regret. The sadness passes, and relief begins to stream through us and out our eyes. When we feel what we love in the very depths of our heart and Soul, we cry Tears of Relief. A child who has lost her or his mother too early in life will usually release Tears of Regret in a Constellation until she or he moves through resistance and is ready to reconnect with the Spirit of her or his mother. That desire for connection creates an opening for the Tears of Relief to flow. These tears feel completely different, bringing with them a sense of joy. The crying shifts and is often followed by a smile and the brightening of eyes, with little shyness. When the Client cries Tears of Relief, the auric field expands and he or she feels energized.

Those tears that burn your face

The salt cutting little rivers
As they run down your cheek

Don't be so quick
To wipe them away.

They remind you
Of things

You should
Not
Forget.

—Jamy and Peter

At Peace with Compassion and Fulfillment

The feeling of satisfaction begins when we accept and agree that what our mother gave us was enough. We see that she put forth her best, including resources we were not conscious of before entering the Vesica Pisces. Our mother helped prepare us for our lives in ways we can only understand by meeting her on the Soul Level. Being at peace with her enables a powerful transmission of consciousness. We experience a direct knowing that occurs through non-verbal communication and is bestowed upon us when we are at peace with her. We're also gradually enlightened as to the reasons for our mother's actions and behaviors.

Agreeing that our mother gave us enough frees us from the feelings of deprivation or smothering. As we step back from our wants, desires, criticism, and blame, we cultivate compassion for our mother as well as for ourselves. With our mother standing behind us, her Soul qualities of nurturing and loving-kindness flow into us, fill us, and move outward into all of the relationships in our lives. This compassion for our mother allows the wellspring of our Inner Feminine[15] to arise within our being. Her ways of inclusiveness, receptivity, and heart-centeredness naturally become part of our awakened state of consciousness.

TCA moves us through the barriers that separate us from the masculine and feminine in our Family Lineage, enabling us to tap into the pure, powerful, positive energies available to us through our mother and father.

Integrating the Constellation Process

All of us begin the Constellation process with ideas, feelings, and situational understanding that constitute our world view. More often than not Constellations turn our world view upside down, causing everything to settle in a different way. In TCA we call this 'the snow globe effect.' With this shifting of feelings, the process of transformation can begin.

The lasting effects of a Constellation take hold after the physical experience ends. It takes time to integrate our new awareness into the fabric of our being. Our mental framework has been stretched, and our spiritual comprehension broadened. The snowflakes in the globe need time to settle in a new way.

Once a Constellation is complete, we encourage participants not to add to the Client's experience. Additional input, regardless of how well intended, may actually take away from the effects the Client is feeling. We

---

15   The Inner Masculine and Inner Feminine are discussed in Part IV.

encourage Clients not to discuss their Constellation for three days because for the first few days following a session, we are in a state of reacting to what has transpired. The brain is trying to make sense of what can be an overwhelming emotional experience. If what occurred is over-analyzed, the effects become diluted. This **Three-Day Guideline** creates a safe container that allows the process of integration to continue without interruption.

After a few days, our body-mind moves from reaction into a state of Responding. The Levels of our Consciousness have had a chance to align and relax into their expanded state. We shift from a state of Blind Love into that of Enlightened Love wherein we respond differently to the people or events in our life that were addressed in the Constellation. The snow globe settles into a new pattern.

Bert Hellinger said, "A Constellation is medicine for the Soul." As with any remedy, it is important to let the dose take effect and to allow the body-mind to respond and heal at its own pace. Resembling a stone thrown in a pond, the impact of our work in TCA can be seen and felt immediately, but the ripple effects travel far and wide in our individual and family consciousness over time.

A Constellation Journeyer
Jamy — A Deep Bow

I was struck the first time I observed Bert Hellinger ask a Constellation Client to bow her head to her mother and offer these Words of Empowerment: "You are the big one. I am the little one." I'd learned about paying homage and respect for spiritual authority in my formative years through genuflecting before the main altar of my parish church. Further, I recognized deep reverence in the prostration bows that I practiced while living with a Tibetan Buddhist community during my twenties. But to bow to my mother, a gesture to let go of all that I still held about her—not to curtsy frivolously but to bow fully to her—I wasn't so sure.

I knew I could acknowledge and accept that she is my mother, but could I surrender the struggle and strain that still lingered between us? At first, I felt scared, excited, and then humbled. I called her to share that I would be teaching a piece about mothers that I'd like to practice with her: the act of bowing.

My mother arrived at my office as I had requested. In preparation for the bow, I asked her to stand a few feet before me. I looked clearly into her bright green eyes. My mother, Joan Margaret McNeil Flynn Williams Theriault, is a first-generation American. Her parents and their siblings immigrated to Boston from Nova Scotia, Canada, and inter-married. She is the third of five children, the latter two, stillborn. My mother was a young girl during the Great Depression, a teenager by the end of WWII, married and divorced by seventeen. At twenty-one, she gave birth to me and had six more children with my father. By forty-two, she was widowed, remarried, and began secretarial school. Her third husband died as she turned fifty-two, and she lost her fourth child at sixty-five. She is the grandmother to eight, great-grandmother to one. Despite all that she has experienced, my mother rarely takes "no" for an answer, knows the latest fashion and the current music, and talks to everyone without reserve.

Standing before this tiny white-haired Soul through whom I incarnated, moments of our life together flashed through my mind—as her confidante, best friend, partner in child-rearing alongside my disappointment, judgment, and criticism of wanting her to be different. Bowing my head tenderly, I felt sad for the hardships we shared. A letting go of something deep inside my heart persisted as I bent at the waist and knees. Fully prostrate upon the brown carpet, her white stocking feet beckoned me to reach out and touch them. Sensing the enormity of the woman who is my mother, my belly surged, and I began to cry. I could not control my emotions. Blame, rejection, and anger that I still harbored flooded my senses and released downward into the floor. I was relieved to finally give up my resistance as I agreed to my place as her daughter and child.

After what seemed like both nanoseconds and eons, unprompted she reached for my arms to help me up. I sat back on my haunches and looked into her eyes. "I love you, Ma," I said. Our eyes filled with tears as she replied, "I didn't know that."

Words of Empowerment Practices

Here are some **Words of Empowerment** to practice reflecting reality, reinforcing or reconciling with your Mother's Lineage.

Words that reflect reality:

You are the only mother I have.

You are my mother and I am your daughter/son.

I am your daughter/son and no one else's.

I acknowledge you as my mother.

I belong to you and you belong to me.

Your blood runs through my veins.

Please, Mom.

Because of you, I am.

Words that reinforce:

You are the only mother for me.

You are the right mother for me.

I accept you as my mother.

*I accept all that has happened between us as mother
and son/daughter.*

I paid a high price to have you as my mother.

You paid a high price to have me as your son/daughter.

Yes, Mother.

Words of reconciliation:

*I take you fully as my mother with all the good and
all the bad.*

I agree to all that has happened between us.

Let us find another way, together.

I leave it with you now, Mum.

I am thankful to have you as my mother.

I am thankful that we have each other.

Thank you, Momma.

Notice how you feel when you find the 'right' words for your Mother and her Lineage.

Reflections on Your Mother's Lineage

Complete the following journal reflections concerning your Mother and her Lineage. It is helpful to have a photo(s) of your Mother and her Lineage as you do this.

>> I am _____
(your full name)

the son/daughter of

_____
(your mother's full name)

>> She is the daughter of *(her father's full name)* and *(her mother's full name)*

_____ and _____

>> She came from a family of *(number of siblings)* _____ and her birth order is _____

>> She is the sister to *(name her siblings in birth order)*

_____   _____

_____   _____

_____   _____

>> She is/was wife to *(your father's full name)* _____

>> Significant relationships prior to or after your father *(their names)*

_____   _____

_____   _____

>> She is/was the mother to *(the names of her children, including you, in birth order)*

_____   _____

_____   _____

_____   _____

>> She is/was the grandmother to *(the names of her grandchildren and great grandchildren in birth order)*

_____   _____

_____   _____

_____   _____

_____   _____

_____   _____

>> If she is deceased, what caused her death and when did it occur *(year)*?

_____

>> Her age at death was _____ and my age at her death was _____

>> If your mother is living, how many years do you sense you have left with her? _____

>> Is/was your mother unresolved with any person or event?

_____

_____

>> Is/was your mother trying to evolve any particular Threads of Consciousness that came from her lineage *(her father's or mother's)*?

_____

_____

>> I have the most difficulty accepting my mother because

_____

_____

_____

>> I am most proud of my mother because

_____

_____

_____

>> A trait that I carry from my mother is

_____

_____

_____

>> The color of my mother's eyes is _____

>> A Thread of Consciousness that I'm trying to evolve in relation to my mother or her lineage is

_____

_____

_____

Complete your reflections with the words:

"These are some of the facts of my Mother's Lineage and her life as I know them to be."

Chapter 7

Our Siblings

I don't believe an accident of birth makes people sisters or brothers. It makes them siblings, gives them mutuality of parentage. Sisterhood and brotherhood is a condition people have to work at.

—Maya Angelou, poet, author

Our siblings are the only other persons to have entered through the same portal of our mother's body into life as we did. With similar genetic inheritance, energetic signature, and imprinting from the paternal and maternal ancestral lineages, there is no other human being who has the potential to know and understand us as our siblings do. Visual resemblance to each other may not be evident, yet for the Soul siblings recognize one another intensely.

The Soul's most intimate and shared experience is through birth to the same set of parents. Siblings enter through the identical Doorway of Existence. This mutual fate is an invisible bond linking us together. Sibling relations are among our first interactions with other human beings other than our parents. Developing and growing together, the connections we have with our brothers and sisters may range from cherished to antagonistic. We may have been each other's biggest cheerleader, closest ally, constant rival, or perhaps someone to imitate or signal about oncoming danger. Sibling relationships last longer than marriages and live on after our parents' death. During the course of a lifetime we drift in and out of association with our brothers and sisters to varying degrees. We pursue individual paths, following our Soul-longings, while remaining energetically tethered to a matching mother and father. Parents bring us together and perpetually link us throughout life. Through their aging and dying processes, they create new opportunities for us to reconnect and reaffirm our Sibling relationships.

As we age, having a sibling as a friend can be a great boon to our well-being. On the other hand, a sibling with whom we have an argumentative relationship or even feel indifferent about can strain our health. But not to cooperate with our siblings is, in the words of author Jeffrey Kluger, like "inheriting a thousand acres of fertile farmland and never planting it."[16]

We carry our sibling experiences into our friendships, partnerships, workplaces, and other daily involvements. Both the strong bonds and the unhealed places in our sibling relationships are reflected in the closeness or separateness we experience with those around us. Through the Sibling Constellation, we can explore the dualities of human nature — alliance, bonding, cooperation, companionship, loyalty, rapport, sharing, and warmth in conjunction with antagonism, competition, conflict, confrontation, distance, distrust, and rivalry.

In TCA, these dualities are aspects of the Threads of Consciousness that can be observed between siblings within the Family Energy Field. Most of us weave these threads into other relationships in varying degrees. In many of our associations outside our Family of Origin, we often search for connection, attempting to fill whatever feels missing with our siblings. Sibling Constellations allow us to witness our brothers and sisters in relation to their experience with our mother and father, an experience which is

---

16   Jeffrey Kluger, *The Sibling Effect: What the Bonds Among Brothers and Sisters Reveal About Us* (New York: Riverhead Books, 2011), 281.

often completely different from our own. Observing Representatives for our siblings gives us a new perspective and appreciation for our siblings who arrived before and were born after us.

In addition, Sibling Constellations can reveal repeated generational patterns such as estrangement between sisters, a son following a vocational path similar to another family member, or a family tendency of addiction. TCA highlights entanglements between siblings and other family members, begins the disentangling process, offers a way to heal past wounds with our siblings, and instills respect and understanding for each of our unique places within the Family Lineage. Each sibling is contributing to the family consciousness in certain ways often not evident on the surface. A Sibling Constellation brings these hidden ways to the surface so they can be understood, appreciated, willingly accepted and agreed upon.

In our sibling relationships—whether deeply intimate, faithful and trustworthy or mired in difficulty and drama—it is possible for us to heal ourselves and to evolve into true Soul friends as adults. This is what Sibling Constellations can offer us.

Parental Effects

As children, we first learn about relationship from our parents, just as they learned from theirs. We absorb their perceptions, attitudes, and viewpoints, and take in the emotional tone of how they relate towards their brothers and sisters. Our own sibling relationships reflect our parents' perspective, and we do our loyal best to reenact them as best we can. Wanting to please, to belong, to be loved, we imitate our parents by selecting or rejecting just as they did.

Our parents' siblings are our aunts and uncles. The relations our parents have or had with them to a large extent govern our experience as a niece or nephew. In time, we too assume roles as an aunt or uncle. The quality of our relationship with our own siblings usually determines our behavior, attitude, and rapport towards their children.

[Siblings] know one another's faults, virtues, catastrophes, mortifications, triumphs, rivalries, desires [and] ... have been banded together under pack codes and tribal laws.

—Rose Macaulay, writer

Similarly, our nieces or nephews may only grow close to us relative to the closeness they perceive we have with their parents. A niece/nephew may also attempt to bridge the conflict or separation between their aunts and uncles as well as their parents. Through their love and loyalty they attempt to bring the family back into the Orders of Precedence, Inclusion, and Balance.

Without Siblings

After our Father's Lineage and our Mother's Lineage, siblings are the third force that influences our Individual Energy Field. Whether our siblings are physically present or not, their energy inhabits the third quadrant of the Family of Origin. In fact, the absence of siblings can be as powerful a presence as having several. There is a Soul Agreement with the parents to be the only child, just as there is in having brothers and sisters. For individuals without siblings, it is important to look into the seemingly empty space to perceive how the absence of a brother or sister has served his or her evolution of consciousness.

Usually there will be a Representative placed for the 'non-sibling' to assist the Client through the process. Clients without siblings who have completed this Constellation often report a new understanding of the gift of being "the only one." Their feelings of missing something have been replaced by a sense of freedom and uniqueness. We have also observed that being an only child creates an inimitable relationship with her / his parents, often instilling values of equality and friendship early in life. The fate of having to be responsible only for oneself and not having to share can feel like a great relief when it's experienced without guilt.

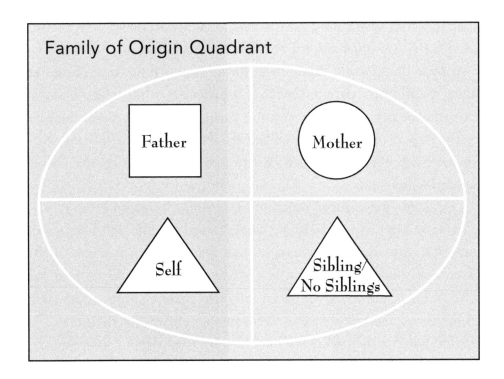

Family of Origin Quadrant

Father

Mother

Self

Sibling/
No Siblings

Adoption

Adoption represents a complex set of Soul Agreements between five individuals and two Family Lineages: the child, birth parents, and adoptive parents. It has a powerful impact on the Order of Balance, of giving and taking, loss and receiving for everyone involved. The birth parents give up their biological child, and the adoptive parents receive a child they would not have had. A person who is adopted usually loses their biological parents and their Family of Origin but receives a different life, a life that we believe they chose prior to incarnation to further their evolution of consciousness.

It is a delicate act of balance to stand in a Constellation between birth parents and adoptive parents, fully acknowledging each—accepting the biological parents for giving life and the adoptive parents for nurturing life. It takes tremendous courage for a person to face the fate of adoption and all that comes with that particular Soul Agreement. For any birth parent who gave up his or her child, the Constellation Approach creates a sacred container to transform guilt and shame, and to reconnect with the Soul of their child. The birth parent also has the opportunity to acknowledge the adoptive parents and thank them for doing what he or she could not. Equally, the adoptive parents bow in respect and gratitude to the biological parents for the privilege of raising and caring for a child not of their own ancestry. When any parties involved in adoption begin the process of acceptance and agreement, they start to move towards a greater sense of peace and wholeness.

A Constellation focused on adoption ordinarily includes the two sets of parents and the adoptive child. The biological parents stand on one side of the child; the adoptive parents on the other. The child stands slightly back so each person's eyes can be easily met. The process of resolution begins where it all started, between the birth parents. They acknowledge each other and the fact that they were unable to care for their child. The biological parents then acknowledge the adoptive parents, thanking them for raising their child. In return, the adoptive parents acknowledge and thank the biological parents for their part in the great mystery of birth, life, and the interconnectedness of their five Souls. Like a delicately balanced scale with one set of parents on either side, this practice helps to equalize the energies of both family lineages. Once the biological and adoptive parents have completed their parts in the Constellation, the adoptive child may begin the journey of consenting to his or her own fate which includes belonging to two families.

The Blended Family

Since blended households are often the norm today, an understanding of sibling relationships within a stepfamily deserves our attention. Before resolution with half- siblings (from one of birth parents) and step-siblings (from neither of one's birth parents) can begin, it is important to complete a Constellation first involving only biological siblings from the same parents. Working with the exact paternal and maternal lineages solidifies the Family Energy Field. When the Family of Origin energetic template is fully embodied, the complexities of a blended family can be explored more effectively. The strongest influences upon children or siblings come from those with whom they have the most biological connection. As Bert Hellinger says, "Biology dominates."

In TCA, when step-members of one family are placed with step-members of another, the Orders of Inclusion and Precedence are essential. Every member from both families is included in a Constellation of step-members and half-siblings. Those who left through separation, divorce, or death remain part of the family. New members are included and considered sequentially in the order they entered the Client's life, regardless of his or her age. When all individuals—father, mother, stepfather, stepmother, stepbrothers, stepsisters, and half-siblings—have been included in and the reality of the entire blended family is acknowledged, accepted, and agreed to, *as it is*, peace follows.

Soul and Spirit

In order to fully grasp the power of sibling relationships or any family relationship for that matter, it's essential to remember that we are spirit encased in human form. We are an individuated Soul who has chosen our life path with our Family of Origin and Ancestral Lineage. When we step into the Vesica Pisces with a Representative for our sibling, we can experience him/ her as a Soul and glimpse our Soul agreements with each other.

In TCA we use the terms **Soul** and **Spirit** to differentiate between embodied and disembodied consciousness, respectively.[17] When consciousness resides inside a physical body, we say that we have a Soul—meaning we possess Soul consciousness or have a Soul Nature. When an individual's physical body no longer exists, we say they are now in Spirit. Their consciousness, released from physical form, is free to wander in the

---

17   Daan van Kampenhout, *Images of the Soul: The Workings of the Soul in Shamanic Rituals and Family Constellations* (Heidelberg: Cari-Auer-Systeme Verlag, 2001), 65.

non-material planes of existence. There are many names for these places where Spirits live, depending on the tradition, Heaven, the Pure Lands, the Above, the Afterlife.

In our experience, the most permanent shifts in consciousness occur at the Soul Level through connecting with our ancestors' Spirits and our loved one's Souls. This is why in our TCA meditations we actively call on our ancestors' Spirits to support our work through mindfulness of the Ancestral Energy Field. As Representatives, we're acting as a temporary medium for the represented person's Spirit. As a Client, we are attempting to align our Human Nature with our Soul Nature so that we may embody new awareness at the Soul level of consciousness.

Soul is consciousness that resides inside our physical container. Spirit is consciousness that resides outside our physical container.

Healing as a Practice

All Constellations invite us to participate consciously in a practice of healing. If we wish to have healthier, more loving, more peaceful relationships with our siblings, we must be willing to enter into an experience that moves through time, revealing the unknown. Healing is a two-stage process that involves the past and the future. First, we begin by openly acknowledging our desire for change. Then, we actively work to shift our consciousness to create the change. For all of us, there are situations and relationships that weigh on our hearts and hinder our Soul nature. They prevent us from living fully, moving without fear towards what lies ahead.

In the first stage of healing, our perspective on our past begins to change. As we come to see our lives from the level of Soul, we create the possibility of a very different future.

In the second stage of healing, we put into practice the changes in consciousness that occurred during TCA—through thought, feeling, and action. New actions solidify the progression of our healing. Without them, we risk drifting back into resentment, blame, anger, or jealousy. It is up to each of us as individuals to keep alive the awareness that occurred during our Constellation. As Bert Hellinger often says at the end of a Constellation, "Now we leave it up to their Soul."

Think of a Constellation as opening a window and allowing the energies of reconciliation, peace, and love to flow abundantly into our lives. This Enlightened Love extends from our Ancestral Lineage to each one of us. It is ever-present, waiting for us to maintain and continue strengthening and deepening our connection through conscious practice.

The end of a Constellation is the beginning of a practice.

A Constellation Journeyer
Michaelene — Becoming a Sister

When I was eighteen months old, my five-week-old brother, Jeff, died of SIDS, Sudden Infant Death Syndrome. My brother Kevin was born two years later. Jeff's death left me with a fear that loving and feeling loved only meant that anyone I became close to would leave and there would be great pain and sorrow. This fear ran my relationship with Kevin. It created a desperate underlying theme of, "I can't get close to him because what if I lose him, too?"

But often, I also felt responsible for Kevin as if I had to be his "mother." We had a love/hate relationship growing up. We couldn't, most times, be in the same room with each other more than five minutes without arguing about something. In trying to curb my fear of losing him, I ended up distancing myself from him. That is, until I did my Constellation about our relationship.

As I sat in the chair to begin my Constellation, tears welled in my eyes and I felt relieved. I was no longer alone in my plight. My heart was melting, and I was overwhelmed with sadness as I looked around at each person in the group. I was fighting both the fear and love dwelling within me. It was all I could do to keep myself present. I had never felt so much love and support before. As the Representatives for my family members began to stand, I became aware of how deeply I loved them. I felt my loss even more. I knew I had to acknowledge my deep feeling of loss for Jeff. Until I could do this, I would be afraid of fully loving Kevin and taking him in. Jeff seemed to be the connection. He was our brother.

Seeing my Constellation set up was heartbreaking. The feeling of loss was palpable, especially when I looked at Jeff. Then, I realized I do have a brother who is very much present in my life. I understood in that moment that

I didn't have to be afraid. Maybe I could allow Kevin into my heart, too. As I was thinking this, the Facilitator placed a Representative for Kevin in my Constellation. I immediately began to sob. I missed him. I only wanted to let myself love him and to truly be his sister. Guilt and shame washed over me. As we held each other, I surrendered and felt genuine love for him as well as a desire to be his sister in a different way. My crying subsided; a calm came over me. The love between us became so real I believed I could touch it, wrap the both of us in it. It was lovely, the warmth and peace, a pure bliss. This "sibling love" was nothing like I had ever felt before. It was so comforting and strong. It was the depth of our Souls connecting.

This experience helped me to feel what it was to be a sister instead of a "mother" to Kevin, that he was in charge of his life and I was not responsible for him. I only had to love him. This was the turning point of our relationship. For the first time there was no fear, no pressure, and no more feeling alone. I had my brothers with me.

Words of Empowerment Practices

Here are some **Words of Empowerment** to practice reflecting reality, reinforcing, or reconciling with your Sibling(s).

Words that reflect reality:

You are my brother/sister and I am your brother/sister.

We are from the same mother and father.

I acknowledge you as my brother/sister.

You came before me. I came after you.

I came before you. You came after me.

We are different but we are blood.

Words that reinforce:

We belong to each other.

You are the right sister/brother for me.

I will always be your brother/sister and you will always be my brother/sister.

I accept you fully as my sister/brother, with all the good and all the bad.

I see you differently now brother/sister.

Please, brother/sister.

Words of reconciliation:

You are the only brother/sister I have.

You had it a little harder than me.

Let us leave this with them, and find another way together.

I agree to all that has happened between us in this lifetime, as brother and sister/ sisters/ brothers.

Leave this with me. It is mine to carry.

It is only us now. Mom and Dad have gone.

Thank you for being my brother/sister.

Notice how you feel when you find the 'right' words for your siblings.

Reflections on Your Siblings

Complete the following journal reflections concerning your Sibling(s) and their lives. It is helpful to have a photo(s) of your sibling(s) as you do this.

Siblings from same set of parents:

>> I am _____ ,
(your full name)

the sister/brother of *(your sibling(s) full name in birth order)*

_____   _____

_____   _____

_____   _____

>> We are the children of *(your father's full name)* and *(your mother's full name)*

_____ and _____

>> My birth order is _____ of _____

Step-siblings/half-siblings:

>> My step father's name is/was _____

>> My step-sibling(s)/half-sibling(s) from my step father are *(name sibling(s) in birth order)*

_____   _____

_____   _____

>> My Step-mother's name is/was _____

>> My step-sibling(s)/half-sibling(s) from my step mother are *(name sibling(s) in birth order)*

_____ _____

_____ _____

Adoption:

>> I was adopted at age _____ .

>> My biological Father's name is _____

>> My biological Mother's name is _____

>> My Adopted Father's name is _____

>> My Adopted Mother's name is _____

>> My adopted sibling(s)'s name is *(in birth order)*

_____ _____

_____ _____

Parents' Siblings:

>> My father's sibling(s)'s name is *(in birth order)*

_____ _____

_____ _____

>> Do any of your father's siblings have any special life circumstances such as a physical or mental disorder, veteran, death of a partner or child, addiction, serious accident, died early in life, been institutionalized, or other?

_____

_____

>> Are any of your father's siblings particularly important to you? *(Who and how?)*

_____

_____

_____

>> Is your father unresolved with any of his siblings? *(Who and why?)*

_____

_____

_____

_____

>> My mother's sibling(s)'s name is *(in birth order)*

_____   _____

_____   _____

>> Do any of your mother's siblings have any special life circumstances such as physical or mental disorder, veteran, death of a partner or child, addiction, serious accident, died early in life, institutionalization, or other?

_____

_____

>> Are any of your mother's siblings particularly important to you? *(Who and how?)*

_____

_____

_____

>> Is your mother unresolved with any of her siblings? *(Who and why?)*

_____

_____

_____

_____

Siblings:

>> If you have a deceased sibling(s), what caused their death and when did it occur *(year)*?

_____

_____

_____

>> Their age at death was _____ and my age at their death was _____

>> In which order do you sense your sibling(s) may die *(name in order, including yourself)*?

_____   _____

_____   _____

>> Do any of your siblings have any special life circumstances; such as a physical or mental disorder, veteran, death of a partner or child, addiction, serious accident, died early in life, institutionalization, or other?

_____

_____

_____

>> Is/was your sibling(s) unresolved with any person or event? *(Who, what and why?)*

_____

_____

_____

>> Is/was your sibling(s) trying to evolve any particular Threads of Consciousness that came from your family lineage *(your/their father's or mother's)*? Name the sibling and what thread of consciousness they are trying to evolve.

_____

_____

_____

>> I have the most difficulty accepting my sibling(s) because

_____

_____

_____

>> I am most proud of my sibling(s) because

_____

_____

_____

>> I am similar to my sibling(s) in these ways:

_____

_____

_____

>> The Thread of Consciousness that I am trying to evolve in relation to my sibling(s) or by not having any siblings is

_____

_____

_____

Complete your reflections with these words:

> *"These are some of the facts of my Siblings and their lives as I know them to be."*

If you have no biological, step, or adoptive siblings use these words:

> *"These are some of the facts of my Family Lineage of whom I am the only child."*

PART III

Accepting Our Family Influences As They Are

Dear Constellation Journeyer—

Our Constellation Journey takes us more deeply into the second Perennial Question: *Why am I here?* The purpose of Part III and the next series of Constellations are to help us experience how generations of factors in our Family Lineage have influenced both our Soul nature and our choices for being here this time around. On this part of the journey, we move beyond our immediate Family of Origin into Constellations that are called Phenomenological Constellations.

Phenomenological Constellations are a way of exploring phenomena that have had a large impact upon the family system or specifically on the Client. Examples include grave illness in the life of a family member, conflict causing a family or some members to migrate, lost pregnancy, serious accident, divorce, or an untimely death. In these Constellations, the particular phenomenon itself is placed in the Constellation by means of a Meta-Representative.

By moving through different forms of Constellations, we come to accept the greater and sometimes subtler influences that have shaped our Soul nature and purpose in tandem, with other Souls.

May you come to greater acceptance on your path towards peace with your Family Lineage.

—*Jamy & Peter*

Chapter 8

Physical Disease and Mental Illness

There is suffering.

—The First Noble Truth of Buddhism

Like loyal servants, physical disease and mental illness accompany many of us on our life's journey. If we do not suffer personally, it's not unusual for another family member to carry the burden of physical or mental distress. Either way, the phenomenon of disease and illness touches every Family Lineage in one form or another. Through the Constellation Approach, each generation can seize the opportunity to evolve their personal and familial consciousness in relation to both body and mind.

Regardless of the underlying circumstances, a Constellation allows us to explore our unconscious relationships to these non-personal energetic influences. TCA can assist in many ways by acknowledging what is, accepting fate, releasing entanglements, and most importantly with disease and illness receiving help from our ancestors.

The Unbidden Gift

Every disease and illness carries within it a gift. When realized, it shifts our perspective on suffering. From our students and clients, we've learned that the gift often comes in the form of a lesson long after the discomfort has passed. For one person, the lesson might be patience or kindness. For another, the gift might be learning the art of protecting and providing for a sibling less fortunate.

My illness has taught me something about the nature of humanity, love, brotherhood, and the relationships that I never understood, and probably never would have.

—Lee Atwater, political strategist

An ailment may propel us to strive and succeed in order to compensate for a lack in a specific physical or mental capacity. On the other hand, it is common among the elderly with declining health to finally allow themselves to receive the love and care they need after a lifetime of giving. Each disease or illness is unique in its effect and the gifts it brings. The interrelatedness of our Family Energy Field guarantees that what one family member absorbs will be felt and integrated by the others, each in his or her own way.

Physical disease prompts us to ask, Why did this particular 'guest' arrive in our lives? The disease becomes a teacher when we are open to the spiritual insights it can offer. The more severe the ailment or condition, the more likely it is that the source of the disease resides in our Ancestral Energy Field. Under these circumstances, the Disease and Illness Constellation allows us the best opportunities for insights and healing.

The realization that everyone is entitled to his or her own fate helps us to understand the most difficult situations from a larger perspective. We appreciate *why we are here*—and that we have chosen this life and its specific circumstances so that our consciousness can evolve. Sometimes a Soul will choose to incarnate with a mental illness to break an "ill" mindset that has been in the Family Lineage. He or she will literally "go crazy" to stop the illness from going forward into the next generation.

More often than not, severe mental illness is rooted in experiences of cruelty and abuse in previous generations.

In TCA we observe rather than judge these effects of Threads of Consciousness that linger from one generation to another. The process of tracing mental illness to a previous generation with similar conditions often reveals a path to disentanglement. An individual's suffering acts as both a gathering and stopping point for these negative energetic influences.

When viewed from a Soul perspective, we gain deep appreciation for the fate a loved one may have chosen so we do not have to suffer a similar fate. In some families we have observed, mental illness appears to be disbursed more evenly among a new generation. Instead of one person suffering on behalf of all, a few may carry varying degrees of mental illness. But viewed over generations it becomes apparent that the pattern is softening, lessening with each sequential generation.

How we treat our fellow human beings is another indicator of mental health. Viciousness, brutality, and harsh treatment in all its varied forms typically stem from mental or emotional imbalance. One sure measurement of the evolution of our mental and emotional consciousness is the degree to which we respect our fellow human beings as equal and worthy of fair treatment—the same treatment we've come to expect for ourselves.

In many ways, civilization has progressed in its collective state of mental health. Corporal punishment of children and students once considered the norm is now rightly viewed as abuse. Laws that protect against child labor, racial discrimination, religious intolerance, bias, and around sexual orientation represent strides in our individual, family, and societal mental health. From observing families through TCA, it's evident to us that the prejudices, opinions, and actions habitually projected on others have been changing from one generation to the next. We've witnessed not only an evolution of tolerance, but also inclusivity. It's important to remember that each Soul and every Family Lineage is responsible for its actions to others.

Dynamics of Disease and Illness
in The Constellation Approach

Illness is not a personal, individual phenomenon.

—Stephen Hausner, constellation facilitator

When working with either physical disease or mental/emotional illness in TCA, a Representative for the non-personal entity is placed in the Constellation. This Representative is referred to as a **Meta-representative**. In subsequent chapters there will be Meta-representatives used for phenomena such as death, countries of origin, and religions of ancestors.

If the disease or illness occurred in previous generations, the phenomenon is traced through the Family Lineage to its earliest known origin in the past. As described in Part II, a **Systemic Approach** Constellation traces such happenings through the family system. The process of healing then progresses trans-generationally to the Client of the current generation. If there is no known previous occurrence of the disease or illness in the Family Lineage, the Client works directly with the Meta-representative. This is also referred to as a **Phenomenological Approach** Constellation.

One method that has proven most effective in helping with the effects of disease and illness is to strengthen the energetic connections with the Ancestral Energy Field. This is particularly true if the disease or illness has its origins with either parent, grand- or great-grandparent. It's as if our ancestors with similar fates seem to want to support their offspring's health and wellness.

Three primary dynamics contribute to an Entanglement of disease or illness in a Family Lineage. A fourth dynamic, we believe, is karmic, having to do with an individual's *samskaras* from a previous life, which she or he chooses to balance in this lifetime. Each dynamic rests in the fundamental concept that everything we do stems from love and loyalty to our Family Lineage. What may appear as a difficult personal fate to the Soul is a deep commitment to the self, another, or the family.

The First Dynamic is illustrated by the phrase, "I'll be like you." In this case, the individual is imitating the characteristics of someone else in the family system. She or he has a similar disease or mental illness that keeps her or him connected to that person. This action is a form of love and loyalty towards the other. It is not uncommon for several people within a lineage to have the same disease. "I'll follow you" is another form of love and loyalty. This often shows up towards the end of a person's life or during a life-threatening disease. The individual is following a similar path to death.

The Second Dynamic stems from the Order of Inclusion— everyone has the right to belong. The phrase "I'll remember you" strongly signifies this type of energetic connection. When an ancestor suffered disease or illness, a member of the current generation may represent them with a similar malady. A family member who has been excluded will often be represented by another person living a comparable lifestyle—e.g., a tendency towards gambling or drinking alcohol. Releasing the Entanglement is accomplished through acknowledging and honoring the ancestor, then practicing consciously remembering the person in a different way.

My main memories of my father are of his illness.

—Daniel Day-Lewis, actor

The Third Dynamic, signified by the attitude "I'll do it for you," is a form of Blind Love. This Entanglement can be released when we remember that everyone is entitled to his or her own fate. Respecting individual fate is the very foundation of equality between Souls. Each person has chosen her or his life and its specific circumstances for reasons we cannot always fathom or understand. It is better to support another person with her or his fate than to play rescuer.

In other situations, a particular family member takes on a disease or illness for the entire Family Lineage. Such a situation often expresses itself as, "It is better that I suffer than you." This is a way to balance past deeds or contribute to the larger family consciousness. This member's fate is best acknowledged and honored by those who have had the fortune of not suffering as greatly. In these circumstances, a sister, for example, who has carried the Thread of Consciousness of addiction or schizophrenia allows the other siblings to have it a little easier.

The Fourth Dynamic, as we see it, is karmic and arises from an individual's *samskaras,* what they brought into this lifetime to evolve. *Samskaras* are impressions or traces of past deeds. The Order of Balance, across generations of time, is at play in Constellations involving this dynamic. Situations when a difficult disease or illness arises can be a form of this Order of Love—fate.

Since Soul consciousness is not limited by linear time, a Constellation can help a person develop a different perspective on her or his fate. As we become conscious of past experiences, the taking of responsibility for our actions lessens feelings of anguish. And, with this greater awareness, each of us is able to carry her or his burdens with a greater sense of honesty and self-respect.

Alcoholism and Addiction

Of the three dynamics described above that stem from the Family Lineage and contribute to Disease and Illness, the first two —"I'll be like you" and "I'll remember you in this way"— most often occur with alcoholism and addiction. These two types of Entanglements represent love and loyalty to someone in the Family Energy Field. A Client who drinks like his/her father or uses drugs like his/her mother is merely following in the footsteps of the person he or she loves. In many cases a loved one has gone missing from the Family Field; a father, mother, or grandparent has disappeared in some form. Drinking alcohol can be a way of searching for that person's Soul. Perhaps this is why liquor is referred to as "spirits"—drinking in excess may be a misguided attempt to transport oneself to the Spirit realm.

It can be very freeing when a client realizes that her or his behavior comes from an excess of love and loyalty. As the energetic re-connection is made on the Emotional and Spiritual Levels of Consciousness in the Vesica Pisces, more mindful choices become possible. A new channel of energy manifests connecting the Spiritual consciousness to the Emotional, which supports the Client in redirecting her or his decisions. When particular behavior no longer serves the Client, TCA can open up a different perspective on his or her relationship to loved ones. Blind Love can be transformed into Enlightened Love by choosing to be aligned with—or remember—the family member in a different way.

Moreover, Disease and Illness Constellations can be a powerful way to enlist our ancestors as allies on our path towards finding peace. We come to realize our intention is not only to recover from our personal ailment, but also to reclaim a healthier, more peaceful alliance with our Family Lineage.

A Constellation Journeyer
Rebecca — It is not my time

My hematologist looked at the scan and said, "It might be, but we have to watch it." I knew from the moment I heard those words that I had lymphoma. The cancer was in the mesentery wall of my abdomen, just like my mother's and father's cancer. Their illnesses ended where mine began.

My mother was diagnosed with lymphoma twenty-five years earlier, which started a journey with me at her side that lasted the next seven years. There were nights I wanted to take away her illness so she could live longer. I wished I could do this for her. My mom and I had been distant from each other except when I was a child and ill; when, she took care of me. Taking care of her gave us a chance to be close again. My dad was heartbroken when my mom passed. I believe he wished it was him and not her. My father passed a year and a half later, also from lymphoma in his abdomen. I think it was how my dad showed he loved her, dying of the same disease.

When I began my Constellation I could feel waves of emotions run through me. My maternal lineage was set up with three Representatives, three generations of women, each having died of cancer. When their names were called, I felt tightness in my chest along with all the fear that I had been carrying. I was afraid to see the truth and what might be revealed to me. I got a feeling that these women had held a tremendous amount of shame around where they were from and who they were. I began to get a sense that cancer represented the shame that our heritage brought to our family. We hid from our Southern heritage because of all the bad that came with it historically.

I thought, if I am not seen, I will die. I understood that in order to heal, I needed to ask my sister to see me as her little sister, not as the cancer I had been diagnosed with. I called for someone to represent my older sister, Jerri. As we stood before each other, I began to well up. I said to her, "Jerri, please see me." I kept repeating it, and on the fourth time our Souls connected through our eyes. I could feel her presence. I got a sense of peace from her. I knew that in that moment, we did not have to let our female lineage do the same thing over again, repeat history, and die from cancer.

I knew she saw me, not just the disease. It did not have to be the same way; I did not have to die like Mom. I had a chance to do it differently. I began to understand through looking at the Representative for cancer that there was a contract we had in our family: Through sickness we could learn to love.

Kneeling in front of my great-grandmother, grandmother, and mother, I realized how much strength they had. They did not want me to carry their burden. It was okay to turn and walk into my own life and lean on them for support. I felt I did not have to carry the cancer anymore, whatever the cancer represented. Before, the only way I felt I could have these women close to me was to be like them and carry their disease. Now I feel I do not have to die of cancer like they did. For the first time, I felt that I had them, that I was connected to them. Standing with them I could sense the pride of being a Southern woman. I wanted to claim who I was. I understood I did not have to use my cancer to get what I need—to be seen, to be recognized by my family.

Words of Empowerment Practices

Here are some **Words of Empowerment** to practice reflecting reality, reinforcing, or reconciling with the quiet and not-so quiet companions of Disease and Illness in your Family Lineage.

Words that reflect reality:

I see that this disease/illness is part of you.

You had this disease/illness and so do I.

We have the same disease/illness.

In this way, we are alike.

I acknowledge the price you have paid for carrying this disease/illness.

Said to a Meta-Representative:

You are a part of me.

I acknowledge you in my life.

Yes.

Words that reinforce:

I accept you as my brother/sister/father/mother and your disease/illness.

You have carried this disease/illness for all of us.

With this disease/illness standing with you, I see you a little differently.

Said to a Meta-Representative:

You have been part of our Family for a long time.

I accept you and the gifts that you have brought.

I accept the price I pay, having you in my life.

You are the right disease/illness for me.

Please.

Words of reconciliation:

I see now why this disease/illness has been part of your life.

I'll leave this disease/illness with you now.

Leave this disease/illness with me.

I'll remember you in a different way.

I respect and honor your fate.

Said to a Meta-Representative:

I agree to you (name disease/illness) and all that comes with it.

I will carry you (name disease/illness) a little differently now.

I will do something good with you (name disease/illness).

Thank you.

Notice how you feel when you find the 'right' words for the phenomenological disease and illness of your Family Lineage.

Reflections on Disease and Illness

Complete the following journal reflections concerning Disease and Illness in your Family Lineage.

Father's Lineage:

>> In my Father's Lineage, disease and illness were present in the form of

_____

_____

_____

>> Who carried the disease/illness?

_____

_____

_____

>> This disease or illness affected my father in the following ways:

_____

_____

_____

Mother's Lineage:

>> In my Mother's Lineage disease and illness were present in the form of

_____

_____

_____

>> Who carried the disease/illness?

_____

_____

_____

>> This disease or illness affected my mother in the following ways:

_____

_____

_____

Family of Origin:

>> The disease and illness that had the largest impact on my Family of Origin were

_____

_____

_____

>> Who carried the disease/illness?

_____

_____

_____

>> This disease or illness affected my family in the following ways:

_____

_____

_____

>> And me specifically in these ways:

_____

_____

_____

Current Family: (self, partner, children, adoptive, stepchildren, grandchildren, great grandchildren)

>> In my Current Family, illness and disease are present in the form of

_____

_____

_____

>> My partner's most pressing health issue is

_____

_____

_____

>> My children, grandchildren, great grandchildren currently carry these disease/ illness:

_____

_____

_____

Myself:

>> The disease and illness that I carry is

_____

_____

_____

>> How this disease or illness affects me is

_____

_____

_____

>> Currently, I have no disease or illness, but based on my awareness of the Family Energy Field, I am predisposed to

_____

_____

_____

≫ The disease/illness that I am most afraid of inheriting from my Family Lineage is____ because____.

_____

_____

_____

≫ The disease/illness that I am most afraid will be inherited by the next generation of my Family Lineage is___ because___.

_____

_____

_____

Complete your reflections with these words:

"These are some of the facts regarding Disease and Illness and my Family Lineage, as I know them to be."

Chapter 9

Death

There are those who do not realize that one day we all must die.
But those who do, settle their quarrels.

—The Dhammapada (Verse 6)

Inhale, life begins. Exhale, life ends. Through the simple act of breathing we practice dying from the moment we are born; yet, when death comes, we are rarely ready. Our connection with death is indescribably intimate and personal. It may come slowly, suddenly, violently, painfully, or in the most gentle and kind manner imaginable. And when someone we love dies, nothing remains the same. Often we want to turn away from the experience.

In our experience as TCA facilitators and teachers, acknowledging the dead—however death arrives is the best medicine for healing and moving towards peace. The Constellation Approach teaches us how to look at those in our Family Lineage who have died and the phenomenological influence of death on our lives. When the inevitability of death nears, a Constellation supports facing and accepting the changes that will come. After a death, a Constellation assists in integrating and agreeing to the fact that the one we loved is gone. When a loved one has died, and we who remain are at peace, a Constellation affirms and galvanizes the love between our Souls.

It can also support us in fully grieving a death; in healing any lingering feelings of guilt, resentment or blame; and coping with the difficulty of living when another has died. TCA is especially potent for those whose parent died before they were old enough to emotionally process the experience as well as for those who lost a sibling during childhood.

In the sections that follow we will distinguish between the Constellation Experience offered in Part V and participation in a Constellation using live Representatives. Exploring the effect of the phenomenological influence of Death reveals how death has affected our Family Lineage allowing us to practice reconciling with those who have passed. Paradoxically death severs the connection with the other, but a Constellation concerning death reconnects us with those we have lost.

The wounds of death are many and varied. The loss of a spouse or partner returns us to being single and might mean being a single parent, making life more difficult. The feeling of aloneness weighs heavily on our hearts. Prematurely losing a father or mother as a child or young adult can disconnect us from the energy of the masculine or feminine. We can even spend the rest of our life attempting the impossible, trying to fill that void, searching for reconnection. Likewise, a suicide creates a tear in the Family Energy Field that is hard to overcome. That sense of sudden death through violence or accident is never far from our heart and mind.

Until we participate in a Constellation exploring death, we may have little idea of death's far-reaching effects. The impact of death in our Family Lineage must be integrated into our consciousness; otherwise, it will linger as unresolved feelings. Fear, anxiety, and even mistrust can all be healed through Constellations with Representatives for those who have died. We enter the Family Energy Field and enact a ritual of remembering that becomes a pathway to healing our relations. Death is especially hard on those closest to the one who has passed. In this kind of Constellation, we're able to compassionately witness death's effect on our grandparents, parents, siblings, or our own children and grandchildren.

Our loved ones pass, some peacefully, some elderly, many before their time and more than a few through disease or accident. When we place Representatives in a Constellation for our relatives who have died, we bring them back into our consciousness. The Veil of Forgetting lifts for a brief time and we can receive information from them and from the Family Energy Field. By including them in our consciousness, they can teach us about the cycle of life, sharing invaluable knowledge for our Soul. Although we cannot change fate, we can change the way our consciousness holds it.

Our love for those who have passed is reaffirmed, deepened, and strengthened when we honor them in Constellations. We reestablish and maintain our connection to them. Simply observing a Representative for death can open a pathway of understanding that cannot be fully understood through mental reflection or talking. The Family Energy Field itself informs us how death has steered the direction of the system as well as individual members. We can also observe those still focusing on the deceased, providing a broader picture over several generations of how death has shaped the course of our family's consciousness.

Today is a good day to die for all the things of my life are present.

—Crazy Horse (Lakota: Tašúŋke Witkó)

In TCA, we use Words of Empowerment to free us from the forces that hold us back from a peaceful connection with those who have passed. These words engender the qualities of acceptance and compassion, while helping to open a pathway to the realm of Spirit where our ancestors dwell.

Representing Death and the Dead

As explained in the introduction, there are three ways we learn about ourselves in TCA—through being a Client, a Representative, and a Meta-representative. In a Constellation Involving Death, there is both a Representative for the person who died and a Meta-representative for the phenomenon of death itself. Acting both as a Representative for the dead and a Meta-representative for death in a live Constellation have the potential to forever change our perception of life and death. Although practicing a

Constellation exercise alone makes it difficult to immerse ourselves fully in the role of someone who has died or as a Meta-representative, it is possible to receive profound insight from observing these Representatives and being open to receiving what they have to share about death. The field will inform us if are open to it.

Representing a deceased family member in a live Constellation can offer a unique perspective on life and our own eventual passing from this plane of existence. At first, a Representative may feel discomfort or sadness. As the Constellation unfolds, the Representative often experiences a tremendous appreciation for the life they lived, and even the timing and circumstances of their death. Time and time again, Representatives report feelings of completeness, absence of physical or emotional pain, and a sensation of drifting away. The dead appear to hold no grudges. They accept their fate, are at peace, and wish for us the same.

We are just drops of water
Making up the sacred jug of life
Praying to be poured onto the hollow ground
Being part of the nurturing of life
Evaporating when our work is done
Returning to the sacred jug of life

—Peter

A Meta-representative standing in for the phenomenon of death can offer distinctive insights into death as it affects all of humanity. Representing this phenomenal influence in a Constellation allows for a non-personal understanding of this realm of consciousness. The phenomenon of death is of service to life, called upon when needed, retreating when its work is done. It appears to be neutral and indifferent in the form it takes, even in suicide. It is we, the living, who judge. In contrast, Meta-representatives tell of feelings of non-attachment and yet tremendous compassion for the dead as well as the living.

Act of Reconciliation with Death

The Act of Reconciliation is a practice of finding peace with what is, what has occurred, and what is inevitable and close at hand. Performing the **Act of Reconciliation** is a powerful tool for feeling our connection with a loved one. It also allows us to face a Meta-representative for death. The Act of Reconciliation with Death is similar to the full prostration of bowing. It is a complete, circular movement of healing that incorporates eye contact, touch, and body movement. A physical connection such as holding a hand or gently touching the body of the Representative who has died is an essential component in the resolution process. It creates an interchange and balancing of energies between the Client and Representative. In your Constellation experience, we encourage you to touch the figurine with a finger or two to make the physical connection with the Representative.

The Act of Reconciliation with Death guides you to

> >> **Acknowledge** death by looking at the Representative;
> >> **Accept** through touching the physical body of the Representative; and
> >> **Agree** by making eye-contact with the Meta-representative for death, and then orienting your body to face in the direction of life.

Looking into the eyes of death helps to release your attachment to the loved one. To progress on life's path requires turning your back on the past, not forgetting but also not dwelling. You must be willing to look to the future to move on with your life. Through the Act of Reconciliation, those loved ones who have died can become your spiritual allies and guides.

Time, patience, and silence are the cornerstone of Constellations that revolve around death of a loved one. When the timing feels right, the Representative of the dead lays on the floor, face up. The physical movement of lying down is a powerful representation of life transitioning to death. Once death is presented in this way, the Client is encouraged to look at the Representative lying on the floor. At this stage, the Client is usually in the Mental Level of Consciousness: Acknowledging What Is.

Approaching the Representative helps the Client shift into the Emotional Level of Consciousness and the process of accepting.

Next, a Meta-representative for the phenomenon of death enters the Constellation and positions him/herself within the Client's line of sight. This accentuates the finality of death and the limitation we have as human beings to change the course of fate.

Entering the Vesica Pisces, the Client kneels beside the Representative thus beginning the Act of Reconciliation. As acceptance deepens, emotions continue to flow and then clear. The Facilitator offers Words of Empowerment to help underscore and reinforce the relationship. The Client touches the arm, holds the hand, or rests his or her head on the belly or chest of the Representative until he or she becomes calm. Touching helps the healing and the finding peace process. Next, the Client removes her or his hands, another gesture of letting go.

The final stage—agreement—begins when the Client, standing again, makes eye contact with the other Representatives in the Constellation. Finally, he or she faces the Meta-representative for death. This may be very difficult as it's an act of total surrender to a force greater than one's self. It may also re-stimulate emotions of loss or regret. But it's necessary to fully release the dead to experience the Spiritual Level of Consciousness.

Words of Empowerment such as, "I entrust my mother to you now" or simply "I agree" can support this process. A simple head bow, chin to the chest, finishes the interaction with the Meta-representative. As the Client turns, putting death behind and looking towards life and the future, the Act of Reconciliation with Death is complete.

These processes of accepting and agreeing transport us to the broader understanding that Soul-level Consciousness can provide. When we connect with our ancestors' Souls, we connect to their essence—pure energy unencumbered by personality. This connection will support our life until it's our time to pass.

Coming to Peace with Miscarriages and Stillbirths

To die without being forgotten is to be eternal.

—Lao Tzu, Taoist philosopher

According to the American College of Obstetricians and Gynecologists, anywhere from ten to twenty-five percent of all clinically recognized pregnancies end in miscarriage and most miscarriages occur in the first twenty weeks of pregnancy. Stillbirth, which occurs in about one in 160 pregnancies, is defined by the National Stillbirth Society of America, as "the intrauterine death and subsequent delivery of a developing infant that occurs beyond twenty completed weeks of gestation."

To a mother or father, a miscarriage or stillbirth will likely feel like a great loss. Many families tell a story of a child or sibling that did not come to life. Mothers, particularly, carry the weight of regret, of what could have been, in their hearts. TCA creates a space for acknowledging the Soul of the child and of accepting and agreeing to the situation as it transpired. In cases where there were a number of miscarriages between live births or a child was stillborn, there is usually a felt sense of an empty space between siblings. Creating a Family of Origin Constellation with a Representative for the unborn is a way to help bridge the perceived distance between siblings. This act of making a place for a miscarriage or stillborn child can be enormously healing.

The phenomenological influence of death—on us, our relationships, and our family—comes in many forms. None should be dismissed or undervalued. Instead, each death needs to be explored with an open heart and mind. Like disease and illness, death has many lessons to share if we're willing to pause and listen. Some deaths will pass like a gentle wind; others will leave deep and lasting imprints on our Soul. For many, loss of pregnancy is one of those imprints.

Role of Parent, Role of Child

There is one simple thing wrong with you —
You think you have plenty of time ...

—Don Juan Matus, Yaqui shaman

By agreeing to our parents, just as they are or have been, we free each other and help them enter the next phase of their eternal journey. In their own way, all Constellations prepare us for our own death by assisting in the release of Entanglements. Lighter, we can transition with more ease and grace. One of the Soul Agreements between parent and child is how we enter and exit life. Our parents come first and establish the necessary conditions. They are responsible for creating and nourishing our life, particularly in the early stages when we are unable to survive on our own. In return, we may have the honor of balancing the scale of responsibility by assisting our parents in closing their affairs and helping them exit life. This is the Order of Balance, of giving and receiving.

Just as it is difficult for us as infants to adjust to life, it is often hard to leave our bodies and the material realm when our time comes. It is much easier if children, siblings, partners, and/or other loved ones are there to assist the process of letting go. In the Egyptian Book of the Dead,[18] it is written that in order to reach the *Duat*, or Afterlife, one must die with his or her heart "as light as an ostrich feather." This teaching inspires us to die with no hard feelings towards another and to be at peace with those who are about to die.

Our Soul feels great joy when we assist another in making the transition from one realm of reality to another. For example, finding peace with our parents prior to their death can create a blessed experience of death for them—and us. Without that peace, a parent's death can feel incomplete. Unresolved feelings may continue to linger and weigh on us. Regardless

---

18   Reginald Muata Ashby, *The Egyptian Book of the Dead: The Book of Coming Forth by Day—Pert M Hru* (Miami: Cruzian Mystic Books, 2005)

of our role—parent or child—death affords an unparalleled opportunity to come to a sense of completion and peace. Entering life and leaving life bookend our Soul agreements as parent and child. Death's arrival is an opportunity to help our parent's birth into the next phase of their existence. If we're fortunate enough to be present with our parents(s) during the dying process, we may discover an unexpected new portal into the next phase of our life.

A Constellation Journeyer
Alma — Seeking Truth

I was compelled to do a Constellation on an event that occurred in my father's life, prior to my birth, when my father was a young man in the military. One night, while driving under the influence of alcohol, he accidentally hit and killed a man who was walking along the side of the road. He served a period of time in a military prison. During his incarceration he chose to stop speaking, even to his family. This incident was held as a secret in our family and never spoken about. When I was around ten years old, my mother told me about what had happened and then forbid me to ever speak of it to him or anyone else. I remember at that young age feeling fear, sadness, and confusion.

I believe my father carried a lot of guilt, anger, and shame throughout his life. Being his child, I also carried some of those same feelings for him into adulthood. In an effort to deal with my own pain and confusion around this event I believe I repressed what I had been told. I didn't remember this story about my father's life before starting Constellation work.

As I began my journey with the Constellation Approach, I started to have dreams about my father and his life. As these dreams persisted I contacted my aunt and asked her to share with me what she knew about my father and this part of his life. As the story slowly emerged, I was able to piece together what had happened. I began to see how this secret had an impact on everyone in my family. It hindered our ability to speak our truth and effectively communicate with one another.

In my Constellation I witnessed my father standing across from the man whose life he had taken. I initially felt fear and the judgments I had projected onto my father throughout my life. Then, I felt deep shame and grief over the fact that he had taken another person's life. I watched the Representative for the man who had died fall to the ground, to the position of death. I also watched my father's Representative fall to the ground, choosing to lie beside his victim. I realized in that moment that a part of my father had given up and was choosing not to fully live because of what he had done. It was as if my father was stuck somewhere between life and death. I lay my head on my father's chest, surrendering to the waves of grief passing through me. I felt the deep love I have for him, and my heart opening to forgiveness for all that had passed.

After some time, I felt peace emerge in the field and I understood the Soul agreement my father shared with this man whose life he had taken. I also understood a piece of the Soul agreement between my father and me. Through his secret and bearing witness to the truth of his life, he was teaching me about love and forgiveness.

My experience in the Constellation around this secret death allowed me to acknowledge, accept, and ultimately agree to all that had happened in my father's life. I also realized that this event was no longer mine to carry. I was able to energetically release the guilt and shame I had been carrying, and open my heart to forgiveness, and to the deep love and compassion I feel for my father.

Words of Empowerment Practices

Here are some **Words of Empowerment** to practice reflecting reality, reinforcing, or reconciling with Death and your Family Lineage.

Words that reflect reality:

There is a place in my heart for you.

You left too early for me.

I miss you.

I acknowledge that it was your time.

Said to a Meta-representative:

You are greater than me.

Yes.

Words that reinforce:

I accept that it was your time.

I accept that your time is coming soon.

I'll stay a little longer.

*You are still my father/mother/sister/brother/
wife/husband/friend.*

Said to a Meta-representative:

Please.

I'll leave him/her with you.

I entrust him/her with you now.

Words of reconciliation:

In honor of you, I'll do something good with my life.

I respect your fate.

When it is my time, we will meet again.

Peace, peace, peace between us.

Said to a Meta-representative:

I agree to all of it.

Thank you.

Notice how you feel when you find the 'right' words for the phenomenological influence of Death for yourself and on your Family Lineage.

Reflections on Death

Complete the following journal reflections concerning Death and your Family Lineage:

Father's Lineage:

>> In my Father's Lineage the death that had the most influence was—who, when, and how did they die?

_____

_____

_____

>> This death affected my father in the following ways:

_____

_____

_____

Mother's Lineage:

>> In my Mother's Lineage the death that had the most influence was—who, when, and how did they die?

_____

_____

_____

>> This affected my mother in the following ways:

_____

_____

_____

Family of Origin:

>> The death(s) that had the most effect on my Family of Origin was/were:

_____

_____

_____

>> This death affected my family in the following ways:

_____

_____

_____

>> And me specifically in the following ways:

_____

_____

_____

Current Family: (self, partner, children, adoptive, stepchildren, grandchildren, great grandchildren)

>> In my current family, death is present in the form of

_____

_____

_____

>> In my partner's life, the death that had the most influence was—who, when, and how did they die?

_____

_____

_____

>> This death affected my partner in the following ways:

_____

_____

_____

>> My children are affected by death in the following ways:

_____

_____

_____

Myself:

» The influence of death that currently has the most effect on me is

_____

_____

_____

» This influence affects me in the following ways:

_____

_____

_____

» The deaths that I perceive on the horizon are—who, and when do you feel they may pass?

_____

_____

_____

» I feel that I have, how much time before my own death:

_____

_____

_____

>> Those that will be most affected by my death are

_____

_____

_____

Complete your reflections with the words:

"These are some of the facts regarding Death and my Family
Lineage, as I know them to be."

Chapter 10

War and Conflict

Since wars begin in the minds of men,
It is in the minds of men that peace must be constructed.

—Ananada Guruge, Buddhist scholar

Countless families have been affected by the tragic repercussions of war and violence on a massive scale. A century and a half ago, slavery and the Civil War tore America apart. To this day, immigrants flee zones of conflict to the United States and other countries in search of freedom. Greater Europe has not experienced peace lasting more than fifty years. Africa, the Middle East, and Asia have lived in varying states of perpetual conflict for most of this century. What we as nations experience through war and conflict translates, at a microcosmic level, into our Family Lineages. Our ancestors and family members, and we ourselves, continue to pass on deep grudges, resentments, prejudices. These attitudes are the conflicts that we carry into the world to reenact or to be resolved. The Family Lineage represents our first allegiance: we feel a sense of belonging, obligation, and responsibility to our people.

Out of Love and Loyalty, human beings will fight to the death for their family, nation, and religion, waging war with those they believe threaten their existence. A quest for domination and power drives humanity to the most ruthless ends. Violence, in whatever form, occurs because of an inherent belief in our right to harm others. A sense of superiority in all its manifestations has always been the leading cause of death. Whether carried out either to protect or reinforce our belonging to a tribe, country, nationality, or race, hundreds of millions of people have died or been killed for their beliefs.

In conflict, each side believes itself to be right and the other to be wrong. Conflict starts as thoughts that translate to feelings that escalate finally into action towards another human being. The Thread of Consciousness of Conflict is handed to each generation to deal with as it will. Some carry it forward, vowing never to forgive or forget. Others choose a path of reconciliation. TCA is one path towards reconciliation.

Victims and Perpetrators

An eye for an eye will only make the whole world blind.

—Mahatma Gandhi

Wars, conflicts, violence, and invasion of any type create **Victims** and **Perpetrators**. These twin energies are carried within the consciousness of the Individual and Family Energy Fields. The more traumatic the incident(s), the more far-reaching the consequences are to the self and one's Family Lineage. Spiritual understanding, particularly when personal violence has occurred, happens when a victim can move past her or his desire to punish, and when the perpetrator no longer desires to turn away from their actions. In order for victims to find peace, they need to acknowledge and accept the perpetrator(s) and agree to leave the event in the past. Perpetrators must acknowledge their actions, accept, and agree to take responsibility for any harm done.

The reconciliation between a victim and a perpetrator is the reuniting of two opposing energies. It's a rebalancing of giving and receiving that had occurred in a harsh or harmful manner. Reconciliation only happens when each side finally sees the other as a human being and as a Soul of equal value, one no better or worse than the other. In the realm of the dead, there is no separation; all individuals and groups are alike, balanced over generations and lifetimes, and switch between the roles of victim and perpetrator.

If parents don't come to peace with their conflicts, their children carry the energies of victim or perpetrator into their lives and relationships. Often, children of victims become the next generation of perpetrators. They feel the right of aggression because of what may have happened to their ancestors. Similarly, children of perpetrators may become the next generation of victims. Embodying parental and societal guilt, they may have difficulty feeling the right to be successful and happy.

Each generation has the opportunity to heal or continue the victim-perpetrator energies within their Family Consciousness. When each of us does the necessary work of balancing the victim-perpetrator energies we carry within, we stand a far better chance of living in peace and happiness. The next generation will benefit from the reconciliation work that we do.

Contemplation

>> Do you feel more like a victim or perpetrator?
>> Is your Family of Origin's consciousness more like that of a of victim or perpetrator?
>> Which lineage carries which energy?

The Bonds of Creating Life and Taking Life

Peace is not a relationship of nations. It is a condition of mind brought about by a serenity of soul. Peace is not merely the absence of war. It is also a state of mind. Lasting peace can come only to peaceful people.

—Jawaharlal Nehru, former Indian P.M.

It's inevitable that violence and murder will rend a Family Lineage. This tearing of the family fabric occurs because acts of violence shatter the life-affirming bonds that are meant to hold family members together.

The strongest bonds among individuals, families, and groups are those involving the bonds of life and death. Through the birth of a child, a **Soul Bond** is created between the parents regardless of the circumstances of conception. They will always be the only biological parents the child has. She will always be the mother of his child; and he will always be the father of her child. Because bloodlines extend through the parents into the two branches of the Family Lineage, birth also connects the extended families. In this way, every human being bonds four family lines together—the father's and the mother's paternal and maternal lineages, respectively. Creating life through birth is a **Bond of Joy** that connects us.

According to the same systemic order, taking the life of another person also creates a Soul Bond between individuals and their families. Life is sacred. When life is destroyed through violence, the Order of Balance (giving and receiving) is tipped and requires rebalance. Sometimes this process can take generations.

The person who takes another's life is responsible for that loss. Their Family Lineage, driven by love and loyalty, will find a way to help repay it. Each of us feels partially responsible, even if unconsciously, for violent acts committed by members of our Family Lineage and the Soul Groups with whom we are entwined.

The Rings of Influence (Chapter 5) that shape and steer our lives include nationality, religion, political affiliations, and—in the case of war and conflict—the armies that we support and their acts. None of us are innocent. An act of killing creates a **Bond of Sorrow** that connects us as individuals, families, and sometimes as extended groups, nationalities, and nations.

TCA creates a container for all parties to find meaning and come to peace with what is—through acknowledging, accepting, and agreeing to the truth as it is. No matter how horrific an act is, the perpetrator remains part of the Family Energy Field. That individual needs to be included as "one of us" or inevitably he or she will be represented by a member of a future generation.

A person who has killed another human being is still a son or daughter, father or mother, brother or sister, uncle or aunt, and remains so regardless of his or her deeds. For the victim's family too, Constellations are an opportunity to heal the wounds of violence that quickly become internalized. Facing a Representative for the perpetrator allows the family member to gradually acknowledge the person as human, accept his/ her actions, and agree to their collective fate. Eventually, the Client moves towards the perpetrator—both standing together in the Vesica Pisces. In silence, a return to balance and a transformation may occur. By consciously releasing the past, we are freer to move on with life.

Peace finally arrives when we stop demanding retribution for actions we cannot accept. Leaving the responsibility for their actions to the perpetrators themselves and agreeing to fate as it has appeared between all parties—without further claim—is the best chance to break the cycle of violence between families. But such a degree of acceptance usually requires a brave and attentively facilitated journey at the Soul level. We cannot rationalize our way to acceptance when extreme violence has occurred in our life or the lives of the people we love.

In certain deeply traumatic and painful situations, numerous Constellations may be necessary to achieve resolution. Even then, some feelings may never completely resolve. War, conflict, murder, sexual abuse, assault, and rape are all too common in human experience. We can only wonder if one ever fully recovers from such horrific ordeals. Nonetheless, each Constellation allows for a slow healing of our wounds, showing us how to meet the energies of our most trying circumstances and reclaim the lost parts of ourselves.

Veterans of War and Conflict

War is the father of all things.

—Heraclitus, philosopher

As Constellation Facilitators we have frequently witnessed the effects that war and conflict have had on both men and women. Women in the U.S. military now account for roughly 15% of all active duty service members, and there are close to two million female veterans in the United States. TCA specifically helps veterans with trauma from combat and/ or experiencing the effects of conflict, occupation, and other hostilities. Some veterans carry a heavy burden of guilt and shame for events that they witnessed or participated in while serving in the military. Feelings of helplessness and responsibility for actions beyond their control are recurring themes in our work with veterans.

The Act of Reconciliation with Death introduced in the previous chapter is one healing tool that can help veterans address the loss of comrades and friends. Their losses are not limited to combat, however, according to the Veterans Administration; twenty-two veterans a day commit suicide.[19] Constellations also help veterans come to peace with the enemy they encountered during their time of duty. Long after their military service ends, many veterans still find it difficult to come to peace with the other side in the conflict. When a veteran finally sees the enemy as someone who also acted through love and loyalty to country and beliefs, he or she restores balance, inclusion, and peace for the Soul.

Women often carry the burdens of conflict in other ways too. Soldiers leave their mothers, sisters, wives, and partners only to return to those same women for acceptance and healing of their wounds. After the external conflict has ended, the women at home (and their children) try to recreate a peaceful family life. TCA offers strong support for veterans, spouses, and children of veterans, but it's important to remember that all of us are responsible for creating a peaceful existence together. As we explore the wars and conflicts of our Family Lineage, we may become more willing to actively support a path of peace.

---

19   Justin Worland, "The Bill Could Help Veterans with Mental Health," *Time Magazine* (February, 2013)

War, Conflict and the Heart Chakra

All war is a symptom of man's failure as a thinking animal.

—John Steinbeck, author

The Meta-influences of War and Conflict create both separation and connection. As explained earlier, one function of the chakra system is to constantly respond to the energies of separation and connection affecting all the levels of our consciousness.

The Meta-influences of War and Conflict are associated energetically with the Heart chakra, the 'I-thou' connection, or love. To live life from the consciousness of loving our self, family, and humanity is a central purpose of our existence and one of the highest human achievements. Yet it is a continual practice to keep our hearts open and to care for all our fellow human beings, particularly after conflict. Inevitably, when we are at war or conflict with others, we detach and separate from them. Hurting others shuts off the heart's emotional energy of acceptance, and we lose connection to our humanity.

It's easy for the compassion and care that we naturally possess to become buried in our heart region. A shell of protection forms, and we live in isolation. Purposely harming others or being harmed halts the positive progression of our human and Soul nature and ultimately leads to feelings of despair.

Of the three phenomenological influences, war and conflict are the most detrimental to our being; they have the most dramatic repercussions on who we are. TCA War and Conflict Constellation can help open and activate the Heart chakra in a powerful way, bringing us closer to peace with ourselves and our Family Lineage.

Constellations Involving War and Conflict

To effectively participate in Constellations involving War and Conflict, we must first Suspend Moral Judgment, let go of our beliefs about right and wrong, good and bad, and remember the guiding principles of TCA:

>> Everything is done out of Love and Loyalty to our family, nationality or nation.

>> Everyone has the right to belong.

>> Everyone is entitled to her or his own fate.

>> There is a balance that occurs over time and generations.

Without these principles it would be easy for everyone involved in the Constellation, including the Facilitator, to stand in judgment of the perpetrators.

A War and Conflict Constellation includes the Client, Representatives for members of the Family Lineage involved, and Meta-representatives for the war or conflict. These three components reflect the levels of evolving consciousness: personal, familial, and societal. In turn, the Constellation becomes a mirror for the polar energies of victim and perpetrator as well as the tension held within the Client's Individual Energy Field.

When you no longer perceive the world as hostile, there is no more fear, and when there is no more fear, you think, speak and act differently.

—Eckhart Tolle

Once the Constellation is set, the Client observes the reactions of the Representatives and then enters the field. The Client uses these TCA practices—Words of Empowerment (Ch. 4), Three Words that Heal (Ch. 6), The Bow (Ch. 6), and the Act of Reconciliation with the Dead (Ch. 9)—to progress through the Emotional Level of consciousness. To come to peace with lasting spiritual understanding requires surrendering to Soul Level consciousness that exists beyond the identities of victim or perpetrator. Participating in a live Constellation as a Representative and Meta-representative provides the opportunity to learn how these phenomenological influences shape the evolution of consciousness of families, societies, and nations.

Conflicts Held in the Body

Conflicts begin in the mind and end in the body. When a person is physically assaulted, the bruises and scars may eventually disappear, but the physical body holds a memory of the incident. Whatever is not resolved is stored as cellular memory waiting to be processed at a later date. The place where we were wounded is often where the memory is buried in the form of energetic or molecular compression. Sexual interactions that cause negative feelings are usually stored in the second chakra located around the genital area (creation); emotional wounds of relationship in the fourth around the heart area (love); the pain of verbal abuse in the fifth around the throat area (communication); and mental cruelty in the sixth chakra around the "third eye" area between the eyebrows (vision).

In all likelihood, unresolved ill feelings held towards another will eventually make us sick. They tend to fester and to accumulate, trickling from the mental level into our emotions, eventually to be digested by the only means left—the physical body. The ill or dis-eased body seems to demand an opportunity to heal the underlying thoughts and feelings that contributed to the illness or disease.

Most people are in some kind of conflict with their own body. These conflicts stem from judgments internalized towards our body as well as from judgments we may have of our parents' bodies, since we are an extension of their physical forms. How many of us can truly say, *I am at peace with my body?* In our love and loyalty to our parents and ancestors, we work consciously or unconsciously with these "body conflicts" throughout our lives. Each of us attempts in our own way to find peace with the body we inherited.

Contemplation

>> Where in my body am I holding old physical wounds, traumas, or assaults?
>> Am I holding ill feelings towards another person?
>> Where in my body am I holding these feelings?
>> What are my feelings and judgments regarding my parents' bodies?
>> Which of my body parts am I in conflict with?

A Constellation Journeyer
Joe — War Inside and Out

I am a United States Marine and combat veteran of the Vietnam War. I have completed a series of Constellations revolving around the war and my conflicted feelings about being a part of it. *Semper Fidelis—Always Faithful* is the motto of the United States Marine Corps, a vow amongst Marines confirming brotherhood and to never leave anyone behind. That vow was the centerpiece of my survivor's guilt.

In my first Constellation, there were Representatives for my brother Marines, those who were killed, the few survivors, the enemy (Viet Cong and the North Vietnamese Army, the Vietnamese people), and the war protesters at home. I needed to acknowledge what had happened in that war. I was in a leadership position, responsible for the men under my command. I felt responsible for their deaths. Near the end of the Constellation the Facilitator told me to turn away from my dead comrades. I refused, stating that I could never turn my back on a brother Marine, *Semper Fidelis—Always Faithful*. The Constellation ended and I felt unresolved.

Some months later, while reflecting on the choices I had made in life, the realization came that each of those men in my platoon who died had made their own choice to be there. They made their own life decisions, just as I had, choosing to go to war. It was not my place to take responsibility for the choices they made, and by extension I was not responsible for their deaths. They chose their own destinies, and there were no rewards or punishments, only the consequences of their choices. For some, it was their final choice. I had held myself captive by being always faithful, in life and in death. That was a profound revelation for me. Their deaths were not mine to carry any longer. This realization changed my whole life.

During my second Constellation, looking at Representatives for the dead Vietnamese soldiers, I realized they were no longer my enemy. They too made their choices. We were equals, men protecting their country. It was clear they felt the same towards me. There was no ill will left between us. My third Constellation was about saying "farewell." There were five other survivors besides myself from our platoon, men I had not seen or spoken to in over forty years. We never thought to say good-bye. We had survived, we were immortal, and this would never end. I needed to acknowledge that these men served with me and I with them. I needed to accept all that had happened between us, with honor and respect. This Constellation was a completion for me with those with whom I had served and survived. By the end I no longer felt alone.

Each of these Constellations was a necessary precursor to what would ensue over the final two. The last formal Constellation was essentially a re-enactment of the first, with representatives of *all* the parties involved in the war—myself, my parents, and all the dead, Marines and Vietnamese alike. This time I was able to pay homage to each, acknowledging, accepting, and agreeing that these things had happened between us. Unlike the first Constellation, the outcome was different, proving how the right words, spoken at the right moment, have a power beyond belief. Instead of being told to turn away, in essence, to turn my back, the Facilitator said, "It's time to face a new direction," and gently turned me as I willingly followed. The new direction was the first step on a new path.

There was still one more step to go, unguided and unplanned. On Father's Day 2012, I visited the Vietnam War Memorial, commonly called, "The Wall." I went with my wife, Nancy, who has been with me at every Constellation, and my youngest son, Pat. I had avoided this trip for nearly thirty years, telling myself that I feared the ghosts that I would find there. The life I had been living, this place I had existed in, was not heaven.

It was a Constellation unto itself: The Wall held the energy of that conflict, the names etched on it, the visitors, veterans, families, and tourists, unknowing Representatives. It was a Constellation of healing and reconciliation. My tears bathed the wounds of my Soul as my hands touched the names of those that I had known. I felt my heart being freed of a grief-filled burden, finally knowing that these men whom I had honored for so long reflected that honor back unto me.

Words of Empowerment Practices

Here are some Words of Empowerment to practice reflecting reality, reinforcing, or reconciling with War and Conflict and your Family Lineage.

Words that reflect reality:

I see now the effect war has had on you.

You paid a high price to survive.

War/conflict is a part of our family.

This conflict has separated us for too long.

Said to a Meta-Representative:

You are greater than I.

Yes.

I acknowledge your place in our Family Lineage.

Words that reinforce:

I accept that this was your fate.

This conflict does not need to keep us apart any longer.

You are stronger because of this.

I, too, carry this conflict.

Said to a Meta-representative:

Please.

I accept the gifts you have brought.

Because of you, I/we am/are here.

Words of reconciliation:

In honor of you, I will live differently.

Thank you for carrying this so I did not have to.

I agree.

Let's find another way together.

Said to a Meta-representative:

I agree to all of it.

Thank you.

Notice how you feel when you find the 'right' words for the phenomenological influence of War and Conflict for yourself and on your Family Lineage.

Here are some Words of Empowerment to practice reflecting reality, reinforcing, or reconciling if you were a victim or perpetrator of harm.

Words that reflect reality:

Victim to perpetrator:

I acknowledge that this happened between us.

I can see you now.

You are the one responsible.

Perpetrator to victim:

I am the one.

You are innocent and I am guilty.

Yes.

Words that reinforce:

Victim to perpetrator:

I have carried this for a long time.

You have been with me since that time.

Your actions have had a great effect upon me.

I accept all that has happened between us.

Perpetrator to victim:

I have never forgotten.

You suffered because of my actions.

Please.

Words of reconciliation:

Victim to perpetrator:

I take responsibility for my part in what happened.

I leave your responsibility with you.

You are free to go.

Thank you.

Perpetrator to victim:

I take full responsibility for my actions and any harm I have caused you or your family.

I am willing to do whatever is necessary to bring balance.

May we both find peace.

Notice how you feel when you find the 'right' words that heal the energies of victim and perpetrator that you may carry.

Reflections on War & Conflict

Complete the following journal reflections concerning War and Conflict in your Family Lineage.

Father's Lineage:

>> In my Father's Lineage, the war(s), conflict, or situation causing victimization that influenced him were the following:

_____

_____

_____

>> Family member(s) who served or were directly involved in war, conflict, or victimized include the following:

_____

_____

_____

>> These experiences affected my father in the following ways:

_____

_____

_____

Mother's Lineage:

≫ In my Mother's Lineage, the war(s), conflict, or situation causing victimization that influenced her were the following:

_____

_____

_____

≫ The family member(s) who served or were directly involved in war, conflict, or victimized include the following:

_____

_____

_____

≫ These experiences affected my mother in the following ways:

_____

_____

_____

Family of Origin:

≫ The war(s), conflict, or situation causing victimization that had the most effect on my Family of Origin include the following:

_____

_____

_____

>> These experiences affected my family in the following ways:

_____

_____

_____

>> These experiences affected me specifically in these ways:

_____

_____

_____

Current Family: (self, partner, children, adoptive children, stepchildren, grandchildren, great-grandchildren)

>> In my Current Family, the member(s) that are presently serving, or have served and were directly involved in war, conflict, or victimized are/were the following:

_____

_____

_____

>> These experiences affect my family in the following ways:

_____

_____

_____

>> These experiences affect me specifically in these ways:

_____

_____

_____

Myself:

>> I have experienced the energies of being a victim in the following situation(s) and with this person/ these people

_____

_____

_____

>> I have experienced the energies of being a perpetrator in the following situation(s) and with this person/ these people

_____

_____

_____

Close your journal reflections with these words:

"These are some of the facts regarding War and Conflict
in my Family Lineage as I know them to be."

Chapter 11

Immigration and Migration

Just as love survives the death of a loved one,
the love for one's country lives on long after a change of citizenship.

—Lisa Iversen, constellation facilitator

In 2013 over seven million American households moved from one state to another. There are millions more who moved within a state, leaving parents, siblings or other close relations. All of these people had to leave something in order to get something. Each move we make disconnects us from one place and attaches us to another. For centuries, immigration has offered the promise of a new beginning, the possibility of a better future for self, family, and the next generation. Members of every nationality, race, ethnicity, and religion have immigrated to other shores—e.g., the United States—to seek a better life for themselves and their families. We are all seekers and searchers, constantly on the quest for a better way of life.

Yet, the cost of migrating sometimes means forgetting our geographical roots. In these migratory times, we can easily forget those roots and the price that's been paid for our (or our ancestors') fresh start. If we are living in any country other than the one where our distant family members lived, then someone in our Family Lineage sacrificed for us to be here. Or, perhaps it is *you* who paid the price of separating from your family, homeland, and first language.

These universal patterns of immigration and migration add multi-layered complexities to our Family Lineage. Often our maternal and paternal lineages come from completely different places, languages, and customs. In the previous chapter we saw how war and conflict can drive us in pursuit of safety and security. Through this next series of Constellations we will come to understand how those routes that our ancestors followed have influenced where we are today.

Constellations involving Immigration and Migration allow us to honor our ancestors and their homelands by acknowledging the physical, emotional, and spiritual journey our Family Lineage took over the generations. When we honor our ancestors, we connect to the life force that ultimately supports our Soul's journey. Immersing in our Family Energy Field and connecting to the phenomenological influences of our **Country of Origin** or our **Family Lineage Countries of Origin** links us to the energies of those homelands. Every Country of Origin has its own distinct qualities and attributes that are transmitted through the Meta-representatives to the Client. They are unique to each Client and Constellation. Sometimes they manifest as feelings of love, appreciation, or peace. Some clients have reported hearing words, phrases or even songs spoken in an unfamiliar language as they face the Meta-representative.

Along the path one must turn back in order to seek oneself.

—MengZi, philosopher

Ultimately, as we stand in the Vesica Pisces with our ancestors and Countries of Origin, feelings of pride and dignity for our ancestors and their homelands begin to filter into our awareness. We have a visceral sense of where we came from, how we arrived, and the price paid for a better life as well as an expanded understanding of what it means to own the Countries of Origin of our Family Lineage. As we experience gratitude and appreciation for our lineage and the geographical roots of our heritage, we become filled with a new sense of pride, strength and self-confidence.

Immigration, Migration and the Root Chakra

Issues involving Immigration and Migration are connected primarily to the Root or Earth chakra. Located at the base of our perineum, this chakra opens downward towards the earth. It connects with—and gathers—the energies of the ground upon which we stand. These earth energies that are harnessed through our Root chakra help us to withstand and weather the challenges of life. When our Root chakra becomes energized, it also connects us to our ancestral homelands and our present home.

Being rooted in one place for long periods of time or over several generations, deepens natural connections to the earth. Immigration and Migration, on the other hand, separates us from our ancestors and more importantly, from the earth. The longer we remain in one geographical location, the more appreciation we usually acquire for our natural surroundings. Over time we naturally want to protect and preserve the land in which we live. When we separate from our homeland and disengage the Root chakra, we lose a fundamental connection to nature and the land of our familial forbearers.

Reconnecting to our ancestral Country (or Countries) of Origin gives us a new appreciation not just of our ancestors but also of their love and attachment to the land. When we embody that same love, we will cherish it wherever we settle. In this way, we can begin practicing peace with the land—living with it—not against it.

Constellations Involving Immigration

Immigrants often feel a pull between their Country of Origin and the country in which they now reside. We often hear Constellation participants describe this state of limbo as 'no man's land,' a place in between worlds, "not there but not fully here."

In Constellations involving Immigration, two Meta-representatives stand in for the Client's homeland and for their current country of residence. These two Meta-Representatives hold the creative tension within the Family Energy Field. One releases; the other receives. For instance, a Client who left Mexico to live in the United States would place Meta-representatives for these two countries allowing them to feel the pull each exerts upon them.

There's another predicament that's common among first-generation Americans. First-generation children often find themselves trying to find a way to balance the values of the old country and the new. In this Constellation the Client places a Meta-representative for the Country of Origin of the parent(s), a Representative for his/her parent(s), themselves, and a Meta-representative for the United States. The Order of Balance—giving and receiving, loss and gain—occurs over three generations: the first generation are those left in the old country, the second generation are those who immigrate, and the third are the children born in the new country.

Multi-generational Immigration Constellations can focus on one side of the Family Lineage or both. A parent, grandparent, great-grandparent, and distant ancestor are each placed until the one who remained behind is represented. If a person is not sure of his or her ancestry, he or she can place a Representative for a distant relative and a Meta-representative for a County of Origin he/she feels may be part of the lineage. Simply using the name "Great-great-grandfather" or "Great-great-grandmother" will rekindle the energetic connection. The Client can then individually acknowledge his or her ancestors and the sacrifices they made, thanking each for their contribution to the evolution of the Family Lineage.

> *I had always hoped that this land might become a safe and agreeable asylum to the virtuous and persecuted part of mankind, to whatever nation they might belong.*
>
> —George Washington

Next, the Client moves along the trans-generational line to approach the County of Origin. In a live Constellation, a Meta-representative who stands in for a country or homeland generally remains stationary. Like the homeland itself, he/she cannot move. Clients and Representatives eventually enter into the Vesica Pisces of this Meta-representative, where the connection is strengthened and becomes rooted in the Individual Energy Field. There, the Client can receive the blessing and transmission of consciousness from the Meta-representative.

A Constellation Journeyer
Anne — Gratitude

As I looked into my father's eyes and connected especially with my grandfather and great-grandfather through the representatives, my dormant roots awakened. Along with grief for what had been long lost, I felt a strong, beaming love. Gratitude arose for the hard lives they lived, for the great changes and loss they endured, and all that happened that in turn gave me my own adventurous life.

At the end of my father's line stood a Meta-representative for Ireland awaiting my attention. As I looked back through this lineage, something stirred in my mind and to my surprise, I remembered our soul agreements extending from Ireland through one generation to the next to me. I could see what each of the men evolved: a deep love for family, the land, and animals, and prospering through their life service. Ireland held its own soul agreement to evolve poverty to a new truth of abundance.

This constellation initiated a deep connection and conscious dialog with my soul and a comfort in knowing it is here now to direct me as I move forward into my new endeavors.

———— ◆◆◆ ◄————

Being a Meta-representative in a live Constellation is a unique opportunity to experience how consciousness is expressed at a societal level. It enhances our appreciation for the immense diversity and equality passed on to us through our Countries of Origin, nationalities, and homelands. Similar to how we feel pride for our family's Countries of Origin, being a Meta-representative for other nations offers us insight into their unique offerings. Representing Countries of Origin broadens our perspective on life, makes us more respectful of all nations and nationalities. The unconscious judgments and prejudices we often project on "the others" becomes transformed into understanding, compassion, respect. We naturally begin to see them with a more conscious and peaceful Soul.

Constellations Involving Migration

In a Constellation involving Migration, the Client chooses Meta-representatives for the important places he or she has lived, including his/her current home, as well as Representatives for the significant relationships associated with each place. For instance, placing Representatives for the important teachers and mentors in our lives helps us appreciate how we have been supported—and also the synchronicity of places, events, and influential people on our life journey. Migration Constellations can serve as a kind of timeline of our life, allowing us to see and feel what we have gained and lost through our Soul's journey from one place to another. The Client begins with her or his birthplace, then progresses through each new setting and person.

By using Words of Empowerment and physical practices like bowing with each Representative for our loved ones, we can honor the effects migration has had on our closest relationships. For example, there may have been a significant relationship that did not work out, or a certain place is where we met our current partner. Some friendships have survived, others have not. But as we reflect on these movements through Migration Constellations, we can honor them all. We can Acknowledge

What Is, accept both the good and the difficult, and agree to all the routes we have traveled to arrive where we are today.

We can also think of Immigration and Migration as a process of uprooting and replanting. Seeds of ritual, tradition and ceremony are carried within the hearts of those who leave, eventually to be planted in a new land. There, they take root while blending with the local living energies, thus creating a third way. Like migrating birds distributing seeds from faraway places, migrating people bring and share their collective wisdom wherever they settle.

A Constellation Journeyer
Sabine — Healing the Split of Generations

I was born and raised in Germany. Both my parents were involved in World War II: My mother as an adolescent worked in a German labor camp (BDM— Bund Deutscher Maedchen), and my father as a prisoner of war in the United States. With the end of the war, they lost their homes and all possessions. They were forced to leave because that part of Germany was occupied and annexed by Poland. In World War I, my father's parents also lost everything and were forced from their homes by the Russians. My great grandparents, grandparents, parents, and children were all separated from their homes and homeland by war and ultimately Polish occupation. At twenty-six, I chose to leave my country to marry an American. My mother had died five years earlier, and my father had remarried. I did not feel like I belonged there anymore. I wanted to know what the impact of all this was on my life.

My Constellation included Representatives for each World War, my mother and father, his mother and grandmother, Germany, and the United States. As I set up the Constellation I was flooded with the recognition that this was big, the power of the wars huge, way beyond any control I had over anything. I wanted to connect to the wars, surrender to their power and the effect they had on my family. I bowed to them and was surprised when I felt a feeling of love arise. I began to feel a deep longing for my father, a longing I had never allowed myself to feel.

Unlike previous Constellations, I had no hesitation moving close to my father. I surrendered to him and was able to let my love for him affect me. I melted into his field and the fields of my ancestors, the grandmother and great grandmother who surrounded me. I could feel the split between us all healing. I felt a deep appreciation for my father and my fatherland, Germany. I saw how I was carrying the split, being like them; split off from my homeland and native language, my mother tongue.

After resolving with the wars, my father and grandparents and I turned towards the Meta-representative for Germany. Sadness and grief overcame me immediately. I began sobbing, my body shaking. It felt like I was re-experiencing the death of my mother once again, but this time even deeper. This was accompanied by an enormous feeling of betrayal and guilt. I was the one who had left this time. As I kept looking at Germany, my feelings turned into love, and I spoke the words, "thank you," followed by deep bowing to both my mother and my homeland. I realized this is where it all began: my mother who gave me life and Germany. I turned towards the Meta-representative for the United States and immediately felt a certain kind of freedom and a sense of peace and gratitude. As I slowly approached the USA, the word "please" came up, and I began to bow. Standing in front of the USA, looking back at Germany, I felt great peace and pride. I also felt the strength of being German and all that comes with that.

The split I carried was from the women in my family lineage. By leaving Germany, my homeland, my mother tongue, I left my mother and the gifts she gave me, including a more full life. I lived this split by becoming like the men in my family—doing, achieving, thinking, fighting, rebelling—continuing to fight wars on the inside. I carried that for the men and thus kept being split off from women.

Since the Constellation, I am aware of a sweet connection with my mother and the women in my family as well as my father. I feel connected to both of them, not one or the other. I am in touch with a deeper sense of gratitude for life, Germany, and the United States, feminine and masculine, life and death.

Words of Empowerment Practices

Here are some Words of Empowerment to practice reflecting reality, reinforcing, or reconciling with Immigration and/or Migration and your Family Lineage.

Words that reflect reality:

I acknowledge the sacrifice you made.

You paid a high price to leave/stay.

Because of you, I am here.

You stayed and I left.

Our fate was different.

I am better because of you.

It is only distance.

Because of you I have a different life.

Please.

Words that reinforce:

I accept that this was your fate.

I accept the gift you have given me.

We are stronger because of you.

You belong to all of us.

I had to leave.

You helped me at that time.

Yes.

Your blood is my blood.

There will always be a place in my heart for you.

Words of reconciliation:

I will remember you in ritual.

You are free to choose.

You helped the next generation.

You left for us, too.

I agree to all of it.

I will take the best of both.

We are together again.

I will not forget.

Thank you.

Said to a Meta-Representative:

Please.

Yes.

Thank you.

I take you as you are.

I take you back now.

Please bless me.

We began with you.

Our family lives on.

Your roots run deep in me.

Your land was good for me.

I acknowledge your place in our Family Lineage.

Notice how you feel when you find the 'right' words for the phenomenological influence of Immigration and Migration for yourself and your Family Lineage.

Reflections on Immigration and Migration

Complete the following journal reflections concerning Immigration and Migration in your Family Lineage.

Father's Lineage:

>> In my Father's Lineage, his ancestors immigrated from and/or migrated within (country) to

_____

_____

_____

>> His ancestors that immigrated and/or migrated are (parent, grand parent, aunt, uncle, etc. and their names if known)

_____

_____

_____

>> The reasons for my father's ancestor's immigration and/or migration are

_____

_____

_____

>> These immigrations and migrations affected my father in the following ways:

_____

_____

_____

Mother's Lineage:

>> In my Mother's Lineage, her ancestors immigrated from and/or migrated within (country) to

_____

_____

_____

>> Her ancestors that immigrated and/or migrated are (parent, grand parent, aunt, uncle etc. and their names if known)

_____

_____

_____

>> The reasons for my mother's ancestor's immigration and/or migration are:

_____

_____

_____

≫ These immigrations and migrations affected my mother in the following ways:

_____

_____

_____

Family of Origin:

≫ Within my Family of Origin, my father, mother, and sibling(s) immigrated from (country) to country (countries):

_____

_____

_____

≫ Within my Family of Origin, my father, mother, siblings migrated within the country from (where) to (where):

_____

_____

_____

≫ The reasons for their immigration and/or migration are

_____

_____

_____

>> These immigrations and migrations affected my family in the following ways:

_____

_____

_____

>> These immigrations and migrations affected me specifically in the following ways:

_____

_____

_____

Current Family: (self, partner, children, adoptive children, stepchildren, grandchildren, great-grandchildren)

>> In my Current Family, the member(s) who has immigrated/migrated or is in the process of immigrating/migrating is/are

_____

_____

_____

>> The reasons for his/her immigration and/or migration are

_____

_____

_____

>> These immigrations and migrations affect my family in the following ways:

_____

_____

_____

>> These immigrations and migrations affect me specifically in the following ways:

_____

_____

_____

Myself:

>> I have immigrated from (country) to

_____

_____

_____

>> I have migrated within country from (where) to (where):

_____

_____

_____

>> The reasons for my immigration and/or migration are

_____

_____

_____

>> My immigration and migrations affects my family in the following ways:

_____

_____

_____

>> My immigration and migrations affect me specifically in the following ways:

_____

_____

_____

Close your journal reflections with these words:

> *"These are some of the facts regarding Immigration and Migration in my Family Lineage as I know them to be."*

Chapter 12

Religion

God has no religion.

—Mahatma Gandhi

Religion is an ever-present force in our lives and has influenced nearly every aspect of civilization. We don't have to look far to see how religion has also contributed to the conflicts plaguing our world. To come to peace with our hidden or unconscious attitudes towards other religious traditions we must first come to peace with the religion(s) we ourselves were born to.

Religion or a code of shared beliefs in God—in its many different forms, traditions, practices—bonds many families together, but differences in religious beliefs can also divide family members, both living and dead. Our mission in TCA is to help heal the wounds of separation from our ancestors' traditions and to strengthen our connections to the original source of spiritual strength passed on through the generations. Just as we chose our family, we also chose all that came with them, including the family religion(s). It doesn't matter whether we have rebelled or devoutly followed our ancestors beliefs. The only requisite is our willingness to explore religion as it existed in our Family Lineage.

The religious traditions of our family, even if there appeared to be none, offer a way for us to connect to the fourth Level of Consciousness, Spirit. This level of consciousness transcends the rational mind, offering us an opening to the mysteries of our existence. Spirit is the divine synchronicity that occurs in our lives, the all-permeating force that guides us. It is also the realm of our deceased ancestors and the source from which all originates and all returns. Through TCA we can enter into conscious relationship with Spirit through familial Representatives and Meta-representatives for Religion.

One pathway to Spirit is through acknowledging, accepting, and agreeing to how our Family Lineage practiced their religious traditions, so that we can be truly free to practice our connection to Spirit as we wish. The approach helps us to release any conflicts we have with the religion(s) of our ancestors and opens another avenue of spiritual connection to strengthen and support our journey of finding peace.

Religion and the Crown Chakra

Religion is associated with energy of the Crown chakra. Our uppermost chakra, it extends from the top of our head and signifies a direct spiritual awareness. As we approach issues surrounding religion, we activate the energies of the Crown chakra to help us resolve our conflicts and find peace with the gods of our ancestors.

Just as the Root chakra connects us to the earth, the Crown chakra links us to Spirit. Traditionally, religion has been a great force connecting us to Spirit—but it has also served to separate us from Spirit as well. When we are not at peace with the religious beliefs of our Family Lineage, our Crown chakra remains partially closed, limiting our potential for full spiritual connection and empowerment.

The basis for our human nature, our humanity, is the balance in our hearts between the Above and the Below, Spirit and Earth. When our Root chakra is open to the healing energies of our ancestral homelands and our Heart chakra is receptive through releasing conflicts, our Crown chakra can begin to fill us with the presence of Spirit. Each of the preceding Constellations in this book has the potential to activate a different stream of energy and strength. So, it is now possible to imagine our entire chakra system awakened, activated, and pulsating from our previous Constellation practices. Opening the Crown chakra through a Religion Constellation will strengthen our Individual Energy Field, but in addition, it offers us the possibility of a truly different future by healing separations of the past and opening us to peace and enrichment in all areas of our lives.

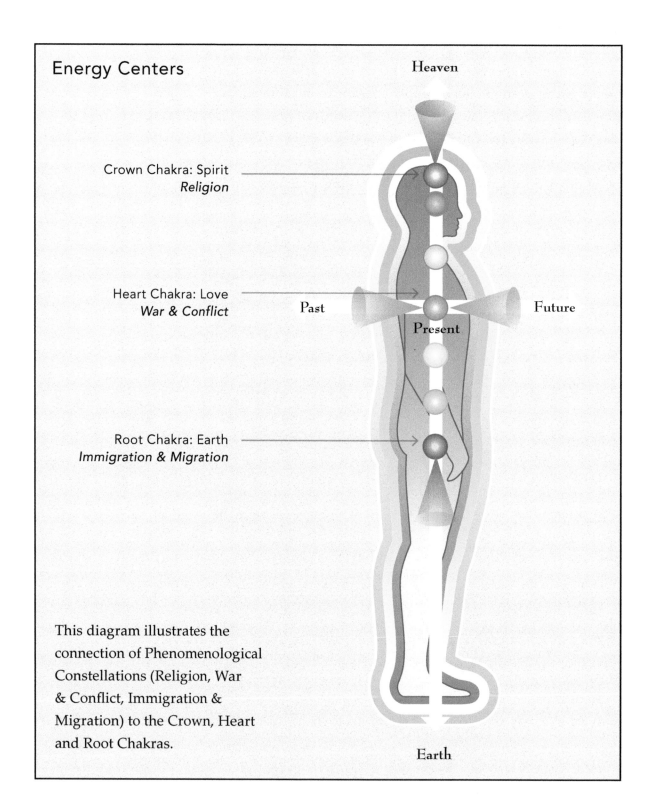

Energy Centers

Heaven

Crown Chakra: Spirit
Religion

Heart Chakra: Love
War & Conflict

Past

Future

Present

Root Chakra: Earth
Immigration & Migration

This diagram illustrates the connection of Phenomenological Constellations (Religion, War & Conflict, Immigration & Migration) to the Crown, Heart and Root Chakras.

Earth

Constellations Involving Religion

Compassion can be put into practice if one recognizes the fact that
every human being is a member of humanity regardless of differences in
religion. Deep down there is no difference.

—Tenzin Gyatso, 14th Dalai Lama

The phenomenological influence of Religion is best represented by a Meta-representative for either the Father's or Mother's Lineage. If the influence of religion is particularly strong, extending back several generations, grandparents and great-grandparents may also be represented. Or, when two different religious traditions are present in a family (a common occurrence) e.g., Christianity and Judaism—both parents should be represented as well as both religions. In a case where the parents' religions are reflected by different Countries of Origin, Meta-representatives may also be placed for each country.

Once the Constellation is set, we observe the placement of the Representatives and Meta-representatives. Sometimes, powerful insights emerge concerning the effect religion has had on different family members, the system as a whole, or the Client. Using Words of Empowerment, the Client begins to acknowledge, accept, and agree to the spiritual choices of his/her relatives. Once again, it is important for the Client to enter the Vesica Pisces with the Meta-representative, to allow for resolution and peace to occur. During this process, the Crown chakra widens, creating a deeper connection to Spirit at the Soul level of consciousness. A bow by the Client further enhances the Crown chakra to open and receive the transmission of spiritual consciousness into his/her Individual Energy Field.

Just as there may be a family member who carries the burden of physical disease or mental illness for a family, we have frequently observed in Constellations that there may be a family member who is more spiritually predisposed than the rest. The form it takes can vary from a devoted religious practice to following a path of atheism. Whatever the specifics, he or she seems to have made a Soul Agreement to keep the flame of Spirit alive for the family—even if it manifests as denying the existence of a higher power. A Representative for this family member may be placed in the Constellation from the beginning—or whenever it feels appropriate. In TCA we've found this inclusion to create a long-lasting feeling of gratefulness for a spiritual element that is too often dismissed in our materialistic worldview.

The last phase of the Constellation begins when the Client moves into position at the front of the generational line following the Order of Precedence. The Father's Lineage stands behind his/her right shoulder, the Mother's Lineage behind the left shoulder. The Meta-representatives for Religion stand behind the ancestors. In a live Constellation, Representative gently places a hand on the shoulder of the person in front of them until the Client is touched by his/her parents. Then, the Representatives allow the consciousness of Spirit to be transmitted forward through the generations of the Family Lineage to the Client. In a figurine constellation, we recommend touching each Representative with the index finger, beginning with the Meta-representative for Religion and ending with the figurine for our self.

This constellation for Religion is the last Constellation directly related to our Family Lineage. Bowing to the spiritual choices of our ancestors' is the last gesture of respect before proceeding to face non-family members. In the Relationship Constellations, that will be introduced next.

As you've undoubtedly come to see, TCA helps us move from separation to connection. Over and over, we are able to uncover our Soul connections with loved ones and the powerful Meta-influences that have shaped parts of our life. But to connect deeply, we have to surrender the patterns that separate. We call this phase of the process **Conscious Closure**. It means saying good-bye, accepting, and agreeing to *everything* that occurred, so that negative Threads of Consciousness don't linger and continue to entangle us with the past. When a relationship or life situation comes to its natural conclusion, Conscious Closure allows the goodness and blessings to remain while releasing us from that which no longer serves us. The learning that arose from our connection is weaved into the tapestry of our life's wisdom. We have the choice in all of our relationships to move into genuine communion with the other as well as truthfully acknowledging her/his Soul and the effect she or he has had on our life. Then, through the practice of Conscious Closure, each of us is free to follow our Soul's path, wherever it may lead.

Not Christian or Jew or Muslim
Not Hindu, Buddhist, Sufi or Zen,
Not any religion or cultural system.

I am not from the east or from the west,
Not out of the ocean or up from the ground,
Not natural or ethereal,
Not composed of elements at all.

I do not exist,
Am not an eternity in this world or the next,
Did not descend from Adam and Eve or any origin story.

My place is the placeless, a trace of the traceless.
Neither body nor Soul.

I belong to the Beloved,
Have seen the two worlds as one and that one call to and know.

First, last, outer, inner,
Only that breath breathing Human Being.

—Jelaluddin Rumi,
(trans. by Coleman Barks)

A Constellation Journeyer
Susan — Religion as a Bridge to Love and Acceptance

When I was growing up, my family was moderately religious in the Judaic tradition. I lived near many of my mother's family, attended *yeshiva* with my cousins, kept kosher, and went to an Orthodox temple. Although logistically close with them, I judged them all harshly and spent years wishing I had the nerve to run away.

My father's family all lived about an hour away and we visited them on weekends. None were religious or kosher. I felt more connected to them than to my mother's family. My father died when I was thirteen years old. He'd been the glue that held his family together and without him there didn't seem to be a reason to connect with us. They gradually disowned my immediate family, and I longed for many years to reconnect with them.

As an adult I chose to not practice my religious traditions. I told myself for decades I didn't need to be religious, that I was "better than them" because I found the spiritual path. But the more I embraced spirituality and distanced from religious traditions, the more pain I felt, and the deeper the split became with my family. I was stuck between two worlds: religion versus spirituality. I needed to find a way to bridge both, to connect more meaningfully with my family.

For my Constellation I chose representatives for my parents, grandparents, and a meta-representative for Judaism. As I stood looking at them I was flooded with emotions. I felt judgments around the lack of education and simpleness of my mother's family and then shame for judging them. I felt longing for my father's family along with the sadness of being rejected. I was critical yet vulnerable, wishing things were different.

The Constellation revealed that my actions played a role in being stuck and the story I'd been telling myself had another side. My own hardness perpetuated hurt and disconnection from both sides of my family. To move forward I needed to accept my mother's family into my heart to heal the part that rejected and judged them so harshly. I also realized I needed to let go of the longing for inclusion from my father's family that I craved so intensely and accept things as they were.

Until I could accept them for who they are, I wasn't allowing others to accept me. My judgments of them and of myself got in the way, but through the Constellation's resolution process those barriers could now begin to dissolve. I could feel my heart softening and opening to a new way of being. I could see that there was love and acceptance within my family. As the judgments melted, I could allow love to flow among us.

By the end of the Constellation I could embrace Judaism, passed down from my mother's family out of love and tradition. The Meta-representative stood behind me, and I gradually felt supported by its presence. I no longer felt the obligation that I'd pushed back at for decades. I could feel genuine appreciation and connection to my spiritual foundation through the support of Judaic traditions from my mother's family. I was also able to reconnect to my father's lineage through that same spiritual foundation at the Soul level. I could hold and accept both the spiritual and religious parts of me, the traditions from both lineages, and know that there is love on both sides of my family.

I have a new appreciation for the love and closeness of my mother's family and their traditions without the guilt of not following those traditions. I have a special place in my heart for the loving memories from my father's family without the intense longing I felt. I acknowledge, accept, and agree to all that has been passed down to me. I can carry my foundational values of love and acceptance—grounded in my religious and spiritual belief—into my life, my work, and all my relationships.

Words of Empowerment Practices

Here are some Words of Empowerment to practice reflecting reality, reinforcing, or reconciling with Religion and your Family Lineage.

Words that reflect reality:

I acknowledge your religion.

Because of you, I have faith.

You gave me what you believed.

I follow in your steps, in my way.

I am better because of your beliefs.

It has been hard for me at times.

Please.

Words that reinforce:

I accept your religion.

I accept the gift you have given me.

I am stronger because of you.

You did what was best for you, and for me.

I had to find my way.

You gave me my foundation.

Yes.

Words of reconciliation:

You are free to choose.

I understand now.

I agree to your choices.

I agree to all of it.

I will take the best of both.

Your faith was good.

I will not forget.

I will continue in my way and you can continue in yours.

Thank you.

Said to a Meta-Representative:

Please, yes, or thank you.

I take you as you are.

I take you back now.

Please, bless me.

You were the right religion for me.

We are a part of you and you are part of us.

Our family is better because of you.

Your truth runs deep in me.

I see now you have always been here.

I agree to your place in our Family Lineage.

Notice how you feel when you find the 'right' words for the phenomenological influence of Religion for yourself and on your Family Lineage.

Reflections on Religion

Complete the following journal reflections concerning Religion in your Family Lineage:

Father's Lineage:

>> In my Father's Lineage, the religion(s) was/were

_____

_____

_____

>> Who practiced the religious traditions? In what form?

_____

_____

_____

>> This religion(s) affected my father in the following ways:

_____

_____

_____

Mother's Lineage:

>> In my Mother's Lineage, the religion(s) was/were

_____

_____

_____

>> Who practiced the religious traditions? In what form?

_____

_____

_____

>> This religion(s) affected my mother in the following ways:

_____

_____

_____

Family of Origin:

>> The religion(s) that had the largest impact on my Family of Origin was/were

_____

_____

_____

>> Who practiced the religious traditions? In what form?

_____

_____

_____

>> This religion(s) affected my Family of Origin in the following ways:

_____

_____

_____

>> And this religion affect me specifically in these ways:

_____

_____

_____

Current Family: (self, partner, children, adoptive, stepchildren, grandchildren, great-grandchildren)

>> In my Current Family, the religion(s) is/are

_____

_____

_____

>> My partner's religion is/are

_____

_____

_____

>> Who practices the religious traditions? In what form?

_____

_____

_____

>> What religious traditions do your children, grandchildren, great-grandchildren currently practice? In what form?

_____

_____

_____

Myself:

>> My religion is/are

_____

_____

_____

>> The form that I practice religious tradition is/are

_____

_____

_____

>> Currently, I practice no religious tradition, but based on my awareness of the Family Energy Field, I am connected to

_____

_____

_____

Close your journal reflections with the words:

These are some of the facts regarding Religion in my Family Lineage, as I know them to be.

Chapter 13

Relationships

We are all a little weird and life's a little weird,
and when we find someone whose weirdness is compatible with ours,
we join up with them and fall into mutual weirdness and call it love.

—Dr. Seuss, cartoonist

Every intimate connection we have presents us with a unique opportunity to learn and grow, to deepen and expand our consciousness. In relationship, we are each other's teachers. Intimacy naturally creates friction that exposes our vulnerabilities and opens us to emotional and spiritual growth. Whether a relationship is brief or enduring, involves physical intimacy or not, those relationships when the heart and Soul connect deeply are never forgotten. They remain with us long after proximity has faded.

One of the many mysteries we explore regularly in the Constellation Approach surrounds our Soul's choice of partners and spouses. We try to include *all* the elements and energies we carry with us—our Family of Origin, Father's and Mother's Lineages, Siblings, the effects of Physical Disease, Mental Illness, Death, War and Conflict, Immigration, Migration and the Religion of our ancestors. Our commitment is to free ourselves from

the past and activate the true healing powers of our Ancestral Lineage—
so that we can be fully present for a loving encounter with the other. An
encounter grounded in peace.

For most of us, our first experience of relationship is what we see in our
parents and sometimes grandparents. Regardless of how their relationships
evolved, they fundamentally affect the core of how we experience the
world of "you" and "I." Our beliefs regarding commitment, intimacy, trust,
and care for another person are created from our parents' relationship. We
borrow from them what is good and successful, and try to leave behind
what does not seem to serve our personal needs or evolution. Here are
three facets of relationship that we encourage you to reflect on:

Contemplation

>> How did love "look" in my family?
>> How did the family conscience shape my
understanding of relationship?
>> How can I support the flourishing of love in my
current relationship?

The Constellation Approach enables us to look closely at our parents'
relationship as well as our current and previous significant relationships.
Some think of this part of the process as disentanglement. But TCA also
allows us to recognize the Soul of those others, the gifts we have received,
and the agreements made. One consequence of Relationship Constellations
is that they help create greater healthier, more fulfilling relationships.

In the previous chapters we've been exploring ways to find peace
with family members, with whom we are connected through bloodlines.
A relationship with a partner is more mysterious however; marriage
or a similar long-term commitment is often a kind of spiritual peace
treaty. Each of us explores our willingness to find ways of living in peace
through a mutual pact of caring and concern for the other's wellbeing. But
first, let's look at our past relationships for an understanding of what we
carry forward into the present. This, too, is a crucial part of the process of
finding peace.

What We Bring into Relationship

Living together is an art.

—Thich Nhat Hanh, Zen Buddhist monk

All of us bring our family's value system, attitudes, and secret codes of behavior into our relationships as couples. Through bonds of love and loyalty to our family we secretly hold beliefs such as "My family is better" or "My way of handling situations is 'the right way.'" Inevitably, feelings of guilt and innocence play out whenever there is a conflict of values between two family systems. Such conflicts often arise during holiday seasons when different family traditions and values come into play. If we give in to our partner's traditions, we may well have a guilty conscience; but if we remain loyal to the traditions of our own Family of Origin, insisting our way is best' our conscience reassures us that we are "innocent."

Of course, there are numerous other arenas in which two family systems will meet. All of these crossing points are opportunities for learning, sharing and evolving:

- Sex
- Food
- Money
- Religion and ritual (holidays, prayer, gift giving, celebrations)
- Love (expressing and withholding)
- Health and illness
- Conflict (fighting and resolving)
- Time (vacation, relaxation, time apart)
- Caring for other family members

At any of these crossing points, a third way is always possible—merging the best of both partners but also creating something new.

The Orders of Love in Relationships

One way to begin moving towards peace in relationships is to understand how the fundamental Orders of Love also apply in family systems—*Precedence, Inclusion and Balance*—also applies in relationships. There are two additional Orders that apply: *Everything is done out of love and loyalty* and *Everyone is entitled to their own fate.* When one or more of these basic orders is out of alignment—through inequality, devaluing or disrespecting the other or his/her family—disharmony will result.

The Order of Precedence is central to the love between couples. The relationship takes priority over all things, constantly needing to be nourished and maintained. It is the root from which everything that flourishes in and from the relationship depends. A couple's love is the foundation on which all things in a family are built. It is of foremost importance and needs to come first.

The Order of Inclusion encompasses everything from each person's Family of Origin and all that has occurred between the couple. Nothing can be ignored; otherwise, it will manifest in the relationship in unconscious ways. An attitude of inclusion means *acceptance of what is* without prejudice or moral judgment. This order is not an absence of boundaries, but rather a receptive consciousness that includes both the good and the difficult.

From the moment that two people are united by their Karma, they should spend every moment in search of harmony.

—Dilgo Khyentse Rinpoche,
Vajrayana master

Each parent needs to be acknowledged and respected for their place in our lives, regardless of their behavior. If a child takes the side of one parent, he or she gradually loses the other. Later, he or she will unconsciously continue the chosen parent's battle in relationship, or choose a partner to represent the lost parent. Parents or family members who are displaced, forgotten, or disregarded will be included—albeit unconsciously—through the partnering choices we make.

Giving to and receiving from one another are the hallmarks of balance in a healthy, loving relationship.

The Order of Balance is maintained over time, throughout the course of the relationship, from one generation to the next and by way of all that emerges from this love. Couples receive first from their parents' relationship, and then create together, passing on something new to the next generation. Children are the most evident example of a couple's creative expression, but becoming parents is not the only way partners contribute to the evolution of life. The possibilities for creating balance in relationship and contributing to life over time and from one generation to the next are limitless.

Love, Loyalty and Fate

"Everything is done out of love and loyalty to the Family Lineage" means that we repeat family patterns in relationship either to be similar to, to do it for, or to do it better than a member of our lineage. This is our *blind* attempt to contribute to the evolution of our family conscience and to improve the collective experience of relationship in our family system. To shift out of Blind Love, TCA traces the origins of our actions. Once discovered, we shine a light upon our behavior. In this way our love becomes *enlightened.* We're able to honor the positive patterns that have come to us through our Family Lineage—consciously taking what is good—and leaving what no longer serves.

"Everyone is entitled to their own fate" conveys a universal truth: our parents' relationship and all that happened between them is their fate as a couple. By respecting and agreeing to our parents' relationship and choices (their Soul Agreement), we can truthfully examine our own relationship(s). If we skip this step, we remain in a state of judgment, partially focused on our parents and limit the possibility of a mature awareness—not to mention finding peace in our own lives.

Similarly, if we as parents are in judgment of, or competition with, our children's partner (e.g., "This woman will never love him as much as I do" or "This man will not protect and provide for her as much as I can."), we hinder our capacity to let go of our children. Since letting go requires a great deal of trust in the partner our child chooses, we sometimes have difficulty allowing them their own fate. But consciously releasing them can support their union and allow it to thrive. By rooting us in our own Soul consciousness, TCA helps us to accept everyone's fate and to trust in the mystery of life itself.

Treatment of Each Other

Like father like son; like mother like daughter.

—Thomas Draxe, theologian

We learn how to treat each other by observing our parents and the relationships of those around us as we mature. Daughters learn how to behave towards and value men primarily from watching their mothers, but also from observing older sisters and other female family members. Sons learn how to treat and respect women mostly from witnessing their fathers, but also from watching the way brothers, uncles, and other male relatives act towards female family members. If parents have love and respect for each other, then sons and daughters will naturally emulate them in their own relationships. The Constellation Approach uncovers the negative attitudes we may have inherited and strengthens our positive perceptions to help create healthier, more loving relationships.

Balance in Relationship

Sometimes we experience pain or get hurt in relationships. Maintaining the Order of Balance requires retribution or redress in some form. If our partner hurts us and we do not hold him/her accountable, resentment builds, causing us to adopt a victim-like superiority. Over time, this victim consciousness weighs on us and can potentially destroy our relationship.

Happiness is forgetful. Unhappiness remembers everything and keeps bringing it up.

—Bert Hellinger

When we feel hurt and express our disappointment, we are really saying, "You hurt my love for you," or "You hurt the love in our relationship." Bringing to awareness the victim and perpetrator energies that often exist in intimate relationships is an essential component of the Constellation Approach. Interestingly, the one who causes hurt instinctively desires to be held accountable. Hence, causing harm to a person we care about can be a direct path to awakening our consciousness—only if we take responsibility and feel true remorse. Transforming our interactions in this way enables us to maintain a state of balance in our relationship.

Bonds

Another issue that arises in Relationship Constellations involves bonds. Love between partners is limited by the degree to which each partner is bonded to the parent of the opposite sex. The intensity of the bond is usually determined by resentment or deep love. Both bonds have a strong magnetic pull.

Resentment involves a strong negative attachment that keeps us in a state of conflict. Our resentment for a parent of the opposite sex will naturally emerge in our intimate relationships. On the other hand, deep love and loyalty can keep us overly attached to our parents and prevent us from being fully available. For example, a son must leave the energetic sphere of his first love, his mother, to move into manhood. If he does not transform the bond of boyhood attachment, no woman will ever live up to his image of the feminine. Similarly, a daughter must leave the sphere of her first true love—her father's energy of provision and protection—to fully become a woman and be available for another. If a woman remains overly bonded with her father, her partner may come to feel inferior, unable to live up to an idealized image of the masculine.

In a Relationship Constellation we not only feel the powerful effects of being open to intimate relationship, but also the energetic support and encouragement moving through us from the Family Energy Field. To achieve real and lasting success in relationship, we need to figuratively 'turn our back' to our parents. This helps opens our front body chakras to be available for connection with the other and allows the support of the

Family Lineage to enter through our back-body chakras. Reorienting our Individual Energy Field through a Relationship Constellation channels the strength of the male lineage in support of the son—so he can face the feminine in all her power. Similarly, it allows the female to be supported by her female lineage in standing up to the potency of the masculine. This Constellation enables us to maintain a powerful energetic connection with our parents while also being open and available for relationship to flourish. A clear, unimpeded stream of consciousness can then flow from our Family Lineage into us, through us, and into our relationship as well.

Consider your parent of the opposite sex and ask yourself:

>> Is my bond with him/her one of resentment or of love?
>> Am I at peace or in conflict?
>> How far have I moved away from his/ her energetic pull?
>> How close am I to the energetic pull of my parent of the same sex?

Ways of Being in Relationship

A relationship is like trying to build a boat
as it is floating down the river.

—Peter

Observer, Caretaker, and **Equal Exchanger** are three kinds of roles that show up frequently in relationship. The first two invariably lead to problems for couples. The third offers the most opportunity (and best chance) for giving and receiving over time. Balance and equality need longevity and spaciousness to find their equilibrium. Stability does not happen overnight.

The **Observer** has a tendency to withhold in various ways, is less involved, and may even seem removed, as if watching from a safe distance. He or she feels innocent and superior to his/her partner while internally experiencing emptiness and dissatisfaction in the relationship. The behavior stems from rejecting or judging his or her parents and their relationship. He or she will bring these qualities into any relationship they are in.

The **Caretaker** is constantly giving, caring for the other person, and helping the family. She/he feels innocent, appears to have few needs, and avoids being indebted to her/his partner. But the Caretaker feels a deep inner loneliness. Her or his behavior comes from taking on responsibility for one or both parents when young. She/he is secretly angry at the parent of the opposite sex for not doing his/ her job in taking care of the spouse, and over time has become bitter, identifying as a victim in relationship.

The **Equal Exchanger** feels a sense of equality and thrives on a continual shift between giving and receiving. He/she feels an appropriate balance of innocence and guilt within the relationship. An Equal Exchanger compliments, praises, willingly supports, and appreciates the other's personal growth—feeling joy and pleasure for the most part. These actions come from accepting his/her parents' relationship as it is (or was) rather than staying stuck in 'the middle' between mother and father.

We cannot reach love without immense gratitude in our hearts.

—Arnaud Desjardins, spirtual teacher

It's important to learn ways to balance what we give our partner and what we receive from her or him. No two people can give equally in all things, at all times, in a relationship. In a general sense the one who has more should give more, yet also allow and accept that what the other can give in return is enough. When the Order of Balance is achieved, both partners will feel at peace with one another.

As noted above, the way we function in relationship is based on learned and inherited traits from our family. Try to identify how your parents related to each other, and then how *you* act in relationship based on the three roles just described—Observer, Caretaker, and Equal Exchanger. This will aid your movement towards peace—all the more so if you're facing challenging circumstances such as being without children, a terminated pregnancy, dealing with infidelity, etc.

Without Children

According to the 2013 U.S. Census Bureau report, roughly twenty percent of all adults in America are childless. Similar to not having a sibling, not having a child also has an observable impact on our consciousness. TCA can help us explore the reasons for our Soul's choices and also assist couples without children in their desire to contribute to the evolution of consciousness through their partnership. For couples experiencing infertility, a Constellation can help clear Entanglements and strengthen their connection to each other and to their Family Lineage.

Terminated Pregnancy

"My dear child …
I am now giving you a place in my heart, and you shall have a part of
the good that
I shall bring about in memory of you and consideration of you."

—Bert Hellinger[20]

For some individuals who experience a terminated pregnancy there are feelings of being unresolved, either within themselves or with their partner. The Constellation Approach practice of Suspending Moral Judgment creates an environment in which a woman, a man or both can come to resolution and find peace.

---

20   Bert Hellinger, trans. by Ralph Metzner, *On Life and Other Paradoxes; Aphorisms and Little Stories from Bert Hellinger* (Phoenix: Zeig, Tucker & Theisen, Inc., 2002)

We believe there is a three-way Soul Agreement and energetic bond between the biological parents and the Soul of the unborn. A triangular Constellation that includes the Client, a Representative for his/her partner, and a Representative for the unborn can bring unresolved feelings of guilt and responsibility to full consciousness. Approached with the utmost respect, these Constellations have the potential to heal the deepest feelings of doubt or regret.

The specific circumstances in the Client's life at the time of the decision to terminate are represented in the Constellation, so that they may be integrated and held in the core of his/her being truthfully. This process of healing the past allows both partners to move forward in life with more acceptance and compassion.

Infidelity

There are certain patterns that tend to surface around issues of infidelity. One is love and loyalty to a family member. We may fail at fidelity because one or both of our parents did. By acting in a similar way we try to balance feelings of guilt and innocence—*I'll be like you.*

Sometimes we are drawn to an unfaithful partner to feel what our parent or grandparent experienced. In that case, our loyalty to victimhood is as much an act of Blind Love as it is a perpetration—*I understand you a little better now.*

Infidelity may also be a means of punishing our partner for what she or he has not done. We feel hurt, wronged, or neglected in some way, but are unable to come to a conscious resolution with our partner. Instead, we make an unconscious attempt to return balance to our relationship.

There is another pattern of infidelity that does not involve sexuality at all, although it can feel as if there is a force drawing one of the partners away from the relationship. This third entity creates a wedge between the couple, causing strife and feelings of abandonment or "less than." The pattern can take the form of an addiction to alcohol or drugs, gambling, excessive work or other kinds of harmful self-absorption.

In this case, we are unknowingly trying to resolve an entanglement from our Family Lineage and may be unaware of its effects on our relationship. Yet, infidelity is a Thread of Consciousness that rarely goes unrecognized by our partner or children. In Relationship Constellations, it is best represented and understood as a Meta-influence—which will affect everyone until it is acknowledged.

Relationship Constellations

Ah, this lonely road of love
Not for the faint of heart

Together-alone
We travel along
Always wanting more

Holes and boulders
Block our way

This is not an easy highway
Smooth to ride

More a steep, dangerous trail
Many twists and turns
Drop-offs and falls

Easily lost with
No one to guide you
Many have gone before
Surely more to come

For those who choose to
Walk this road

Know there is no other way to reach
The land of love.

—Peter & Jamy

A marriage or committed relationship brings together two Family Lineages and each person's history of intimate relations, including the effects of phenomenological influences. Because entanglements or disconnection with our Family Lineage are at the root of many relationship issues, Relationship Constellations may include any aspect of the nine preceding Universal Themes or Strands of Awareness. These Constellations are a culmination of the themes, issues, ideas, and points of guidance that we've been exploring until now.

Some of the other major influences from our previous intimate relationships include: first marriages, other partners with whom we have had children, terminated pregnancies, and any individuals with whom we have unresolved issues from the past. All of these relationships and ties need to be acknowledged, accepted, and agreed to in order to move on freely, unencumbered. For many of us, we find it difficult to fully accept the previous relationships of our partners. If there is reason to believe that the Entanglement resides with a previous relationship, she or he will be represented in the Constellation.

There are four phases in a Relationship Constellation:

>> **Phase One** begins with a brief interview process during which the Client identifies an issue. Next, the Facilitator and Client determine who should be represented, including possible Meta-representatives.

>> **Phase Two**, Representatives are chosen and placed by the Client or Facilitator, or a participant of the Constellation group may voluntarily select himself/herself A Systemic Approach Constellation can uncover the Entanglements in the Client's Family Lineage. The Phenomenological Approach uses Representatives for the Client, his or her partner, and the Meta-influences of the partner's Family Lineage. This process allows the Client to observe what the partner is bringing into their relationship. In both approaches, the field will reveal the Orders of Love that are involved as well as the pathway to resolution. Throughout the process the Client notes the placement of Representatives and their reactions.

>> When the Client enters the field, **Phase Three**, the disentanglement process, begins. Based on what actually emerges within the Constellation, additional Representatives may be added to one or both Family Lineages until the disentanglement process is complete. A Representative for the current partner is the last Representative with whom the Client will interact.

>> After complete resolution with Family members and Meta-representatives, **Phase Four** begins. The Client now turns to face the partner's Representative and moves towards him or her, making a transition through the four Levels of Consciousness to enter the Vesica Pisces. As the Client's chakras align with the partner's

Representative, it becomes possible for her or him to experience spiritual healing in the form of acceptance, understanding, peace, and appreciation.

If the Client's partner is physically present, the Constellation may culminate with the Client facing his or her partner. Time is allowed for genuine eye contact—looking through the windows of the Soul—to recognize each anew. Their interaction may end here, or the Client's partner may enter the Constellation and together the couple moves into the Vesica Pisces. Eventually, they turn slowly and offer their backs to all in the Constellation—so that they can receive the blessings and support of their parents and ancestors.

A Constellation Journeyer
Michael — "I Don't Need to Heal a Woman to Receive her Love"

I was separated from my first wife and had been waiting six months for her to complete the legal process of the divorce, when I did my first Constellation. Even though I had great doubts before I married her, I believed that my love was strong enough to make the marriage work. But it hadn't worked. I felt dejected about my prospects for relationship and wanted to learn more about my unconscious patterns.

I knew my relationship with my mother, whose father died suddenly when she was fifteen, influenced all my connections with women. She was the youngest child and bore the impact of his death most intensely. As I grew up, her pain and rage came out in ways that were confusing to me. I tried to heal my mother so she could give me the love I needed. I repeated this pattern with my relationships; I attracted women who were wounded.

When I began the Constellation I placed Representatives for my mother, her father, and myself. After placing the Representatives, I wept deeply. I grieved for my mother's love and felt her unexpressed grief for her father. The depth of feeling surprised me. Seeing my mother look at her father and embrace him, I felt how much she missed him. I felt my grandfather for the first time, as a real person who had lived as one of my ancestors, not just an abstract figure in my mother's life. I swam in clouds of mystery as great movements happened inside me. I was in unknown territory.

Then, I took my place in the Constellation. When I looked at my grandfather he said, "Thank you for being there when I could not." I began to understand the reality of what had existed invisibly between my mother and me. I had attempted the impossible—tried to heal the pain of the loss of her father. It became clear to me that these were agreements to which we had deeply and silently colluded that would always result in failure.

When my mother moved closer to her father, I saw her relax in his presence. I felt relief knowing it was not my obligation to resolve this traumatic experience for her. The Facilitator invited me to turn with my back to them, to feel their strength and support behind me. It felt unsafe because of memories of my mother's anger and cruelty to me. I turned to face them feeling more secure and relief. This was a good place to end. There would be more opportunities in the future to resolve the limiting images I carry from my mother of women.

The Constellation created profound shifts inside of me. My relationship with my mother has changed dramatically. I see her in new ways and don't take personally what happened between us. I feel freer to create my own life in ways that are right for me. I understand that my mother chose, for deeper reasons, life experiences for the growth of her soul. It's not my responsibility to intervene in her fate. I have compassion for her life's journey. I am deeply grateful for all she did for me as my mother.

Two significant events occurred within the week after the Constellation. My first wife signed the legal documents and began finalizing our divorce. With time I have come to better understand my part in creating the marriage, and take responsibility for all I did in the relationship. The second was I had breakfast with an acquaintance. Although feeling raw and vulnerable from the Constellation, I trusted she would be open to my state of being. We eventually began dating, and are now happily married.

A Constellation Journeyer
Kelly — Finding Acceptance

Despite how much I respected Chuck and loved being with him, I found myself caught in an internal conflict. On one side I was judging him for everything, from his choice in socks to the way he was making decisions in our business. On the other hand, I knew he was a knowledgeable and intelligent man whom I respected.

I could also be very sensitive to any real or perceived judgment I felt from Chuck. I knew I needed to try something different to break my pattern of judging him and my hypersensitivity to any judgment I felt from him. It was hurting us both.

As I placed the Representatives for my mother and father, I was very aware of the judgments they had towards each other in their twenty-two years of marriage and in the twenty-five years since they divorced. I became even more connected to it when I placed a Meta-representative for Judgment. I felt the pain of disapproval in my parents' marriage: my father's beliefs that my mother was manipulative and too emotional, and my mother's beliefs that my father was emotionally disconnected and unforgiving.

I felt they should have been more accepting as parents. I had been judging them in the same way they had judged me. I turned to each of them and said, "I feel I am better than you." Then, after a few minutes, "I accept you fully as my mother and father." I felt lighter for having acknowledged my part of the judgments in our relationships.

As my gaze shifted from the eyes of my parents to Judgment, I felt how heavy judgment was in my own marriage. I wanted desperately to leave

Judgment with my parents. I became aware that in some ways Chuck had taken the place of my parents.

The Meta-representative for Judgment began moving slowly from behind my parents to stand face to face with me. I felt trapped by my inability to figure out a way to deny Judgment, unable to move beyond them. I was feeling unbearably stuck before the Facilitator said, "Kelly, it's important to acknowledge your judgments."

I breathed deeply, looked into Judgment's eyes and began to accept my judgments and all they came with. I started to see the Soul Agreements I had with my parents. By helping me become aware of how painful it is to give and receive judgment, they had encouraged me to find a new way, a path to acceptance. With this new knowledge I was able to say "Yes" to Judgment and to my parents. I felt my agreement to all that happened between us in our family deepen with each repetition of the word.

I turned to face the Representative for Chuck. As I looked at him, I felt both the pain from the judgments I had held for him and hope for a different way of being together. Tears flowed down my cheeks as I said, "I have judged you. I want to find a new way of being with you now." I bowed to him, touching my forehead to his, so grateful for his strength to remain true to himself in the times I had acted as if I were better than him.

As I've stepped into my life with Chuck, I realize how beautifully counter-intuitive TCA can be. By trying to deny my judgments I had been harshly judging myself too, only adding to my tension and frustration. I came to see that the only way I could end this fight was to acknowledge and accept having judgments. I no longer feel a burning desire to tell him what he should wear or the constant need to second-guess his business decisions. I breathe easier in these moments rather than wanting to get him to change. In accepting my judgments they have softened and some have even faded. This allows me to see Chuck more clearly and to connect with him more deeply.

Words of Empowerment Practices

Here are some Words of Empowerment to practice reflecting reality, reinforcing, or reconciling with Relationships.

Words that reflect reality:

Your relationship is your business.

I see you both a little differently now.

I will always be your daughter/son.

I am leaving soon.

I am becoming his wife/her husband soon.

He/she will come first then.

I acknowledge your relationship as it is.

I acknowledge all you bring.

It is the right relationship for you.

We are both responsible.

Words that reinforce:

My children come first.

Your children come first.

You are the right one for me.

I belong to you and you belong to me.

Please bless me as I leave.

I accept your relationship as it is.

I accept all that has happened between us.

You are right for each other.

We carry this together.

I honor all that the two of you have been through.

Please take me as I am.

Yes.

Words of reconciliation:

You have my blessing.

I wish you well.

I'll stay as long as I can.

I agree to all of it.

I'll take you fully and all that comes with you.

I agree to all that has happened between us.

Let us find another way, together.

You are free to go.

Thank you.

Notice how you feel when you find the 'right' words for your Relationships.

Reflections on Relationships

Complete the following journal reflections concerning the Relationships in your Family Lineage. Base your answers in this section on the previous Universal Themes — Family of Origin, Father, Mother, Siblings, Disease/Illness, Death, War/Conflict, Immigration/Migration, and Religion. As you complete the reflection questions, it may be helpful to refer back to previous chapters.

Father's Lineage:

>> The major influence(s) that my father brought from his Family Lineage into the relationship with my mother, including significant previous relationships and children, are the following:

_____

_____

_____

_____

>> These major influences affected my parents' relationship in the following ways:

_____

_____

_____

_____

Mother's Lineage:

>> The major influence(s) that my mother brought from her Family Lineage into the relationship with my father, including significant previous relationships and children, are the following:

_____

_____

_____

_____

>> These major influences affected my parent's relationship in the following ways:

_____

_____

_____

_____

Myself:

>> The major influence(s) that I bring from my Family Lineage, including significant previous relationships and children, into my current or a future relationship, are the following:

_____

_____

_____

_____

>> These major influences affect my relationship in the following ways:

_____

_____

_____

_____

Current Family:

Partner/Spouse:

>> The major influence(s) that my partner/spouse brings from his or her Family Lineage, including significant previous relationships and children, into our relationship, are the following:

_____

_____

_____

_____

>> These major influences affect our relationship in the following ways:

_____

_____

_____

_____

Children, adopted children, grandchildren, stepchildren or great grandchildren:

>> The major influence(s) that my children, adopted children, grandchildren, stepchildren, or great-grandchildren bring from his or her Family Lineage, including significant previous relationships and children, into their relationships, are the following:

_____

_____

_____

_____

>> These major influences affect or may affect his or her relationships in the following ways:

_____

_____

_____

_____

Partner/Spouse:

>> The major influence(s) that my children's, adopted children's, grandchildren's, stepchildren's or great-grandchildren's partner /spouse bring from his or her Family Lineage, including significant previous relationships and children, into their relationships are the following:

_____

_____

_____

_____

>> These major influences affect or may affect his or her relationships in the following ways:

_____

_____

_____

_____

Close your journal reflections with the words:

These are some of the facts of the Relationships in my Family
Lineage as I know them to be.

PART IV

Agreeing
To
Our Soul Nature

Chapter 14

The Last Barrier to Peace

I am the captain of my Soul.

—Nelson Mandela

Our quest thus far has been a multi-layered exploration of the first two perennial questions—"How did I get here?" and "Why am I here?" Now, with our ancestors standing at our backs, we can attempt to cross the last barrier of agreeing to our Soul nature, finding peace with ourselves so that we may embrace our lives fully. Being at peace with all that is and was frees us, but it also invites us to confront—and live—a different reality.

We cannot turn back, blame others, or live in regret. Instead, we are being challenged to take full responsibility for our life journey, to release our attachments to the past. We bow to all that has transpired and focus on moving towards our future. Like a vessel, we're ready to catch the strength of our ancestors' wind in our sails. Well prepared, we can chart our course with the wisdom and guidance of our Soul nature—the real captain of our ship.

In another way, our path has brought us full circle, back to the core of ourselves and the prospect of exploring the third perennial question— "How shall I live my life?" Or, as the Zen Buddhist teacher asks the student through a *koan* (question), "What was the shape of your original face before you were born?" In other words, what are you bringing forward into life? What was your original Soul's vision before you incarnated?[21]

Journey of the Soul

The Soul is the truth of who you are.

—Marianne Williamson, spiritual teacher, author

Our life is really our Soul's journey disguised in human form. Each of us has the capacity to align with our Soul nature if we choose to. Once we become awake and aware, our lives are never the same. We see that each human Soul is on their own path, living his or her life—an almost endless variety of forms across the planet. The CEO and the trash collector are equal in the pursuit of their Soul nature. They learn, grow, and evolve as their Soul chooses—the same as everyone else.

But our destiny is determined by our awakened actions in relation to our unique fate. Agreeing to our Soul nature requires *knowing who we are,* not from an egocentric point of view, but from the center of our being, with open-mindedness and peace. When we understand who we are, we can develop insight into *how to live*—how to move forward, how to act, and how to contribute meaningfully—to personal, familial, and societal consciousness—for the benefit of all.

Take care of your thoughts, for they will become words.
Take care of your words, for they will become actions.
Take care of your actions, for they will become habits.
Take care of your habits, for they will become your character.
Take care of your character, for that will shape your destiny.

—attributed to the Talmud, Mahatma Gandhi,
the Dalai Lama and other sources[22]

---

21 Ralph Metzner, *The Six Pathways of Destiny* (Berkeley: Regent Press, 2012)
22 Ralph Metzner, *Eye of the Seeress - Voice of the Poet* (Berkeley: Regent Press, 2011), pg. 83.

The Constellation Approach

To be in deeper, more creative relationship with Soul consciousness, each of us must look in the mirror and examine who we have become. The way forward charted by the Constellation Approach encourages 'becoming' through reflection and contemplation—so that we may merge our human nature with our Soul nature. Joining these seemingly dual states of being can be abetted by three distinct yet mutually dependent and interconnected facets of who we are—our **Familial Archetypes, World Work,** and our **Inner Feminine and Inner Masculine.**

Familial Archetypes

We are now ready to experience our family within the context of our present lives and world. Let's consider the four fundamental Familial Archetypes that we inhabit during our lifetime. For men, they manifest as son, brother, partner/spouse, and father. For women, they appear as daughter, sister, partner/spouse, and mother. We can think of other possible relational roles as extensions of these basic four. For a woman, a niece or aunt is a daughter and sister first. Becoming a mother precedes being a grandmother. Men are the same, only manifesting in their masculine roles. A nephew stems from being a son, an uncle from being a brother, and a grandfather from being a father.

A male may become

> Son, brother, partner/spouse, father, nephew,
> uncle, step-, adoptive-father,
> grandfather, great grandfather

A female may become

> Daughter, sister, partner/spouse, mother, niece,
> aunt, step-, adoptive-mother, grandmother,
> great grandmother

Familial Archetypes

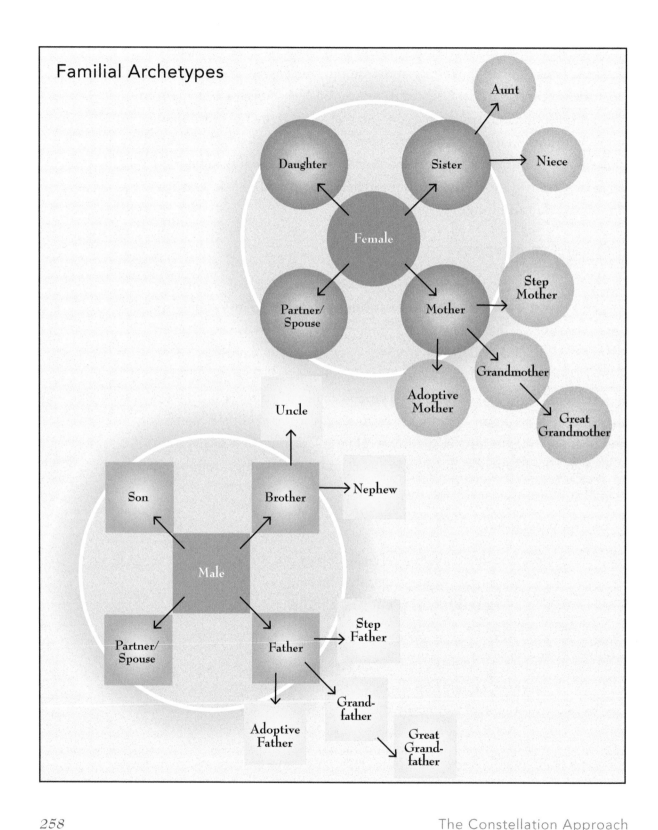

These Familial Archetypes continue to manifest as we mature along the timeline of our lives. They shift and change as our families grow and decline. We are son or daughter as long as our parents are alive. We will always be their child; however, when they die, our role as daughter or son ceases. We become each archetype by way of our own distinctive Family Energy Field.

We have agreed to these Familial Archetypes. How could it be any other way? If we have consented to our family and all the circumstances of our Family Lineage, then our Soul has agreed to these archetypal roles. Through the practice of the Constellation Approach, Familial Archetypal Constellations provide insight into these four main archetypal relationships, allowing our next evolutionary steps to appear.

A Constellation Journeyer
Jane—Wife, Mother, Daughter

I chose three figurines to represent the Familial Archetypes of wife, mother and daughter. As I looked at these figurines representing who I had become at sixty-one-years old, I was immediately drawn to the figurine for being a mother. This was where I felt most committed. I realized a lifelong commitment to my sons on the Soul Level.

When I looked at the figurine for myself as wife, I immediately felt the self-destructive nature that my husband and I both carry. We don't take care of ourselves, particularly physically. I saw how easily I follow his patterns of unhealthiness. I recognized how interconnected we are. I felt how we had both given up in certain ways, though we were still drawn together. We balance each other. I knew he needed me, and I, him.

Looking at the figurine of myself as daughter I became aware that my self—destructive tendencies originated as a sister and daughter. My mother and several of my sisters drink excessively and do not care for their physical well-being. I knew I needed to shift my consciousness from daughter to wife.

As I moved the three figurines close together, I could feel the front of my body opening, my heart softened. I felt a rebalancing of energies occurring within me. I began to understand my life, my purpose. I felt as if I were stepping into my life. I understood the importance of my Soul connections with my husband and sons whom I care for. Suddenly the potential of my life opened up to me. I wanted to step into my life in a different way. It was as if my Soul was showing me the direction I needed to go. My heart felt like it just kept opening more and more.

TCA practice of pausing, reflecting, and contemplating reveals an awakened way of being in these archetypal roles. Consider the Familial Archetypes as reference points for the Soul aspects of your current family relationships.

Choose figurines for your main Familial Archetypes and one for yourself. Then move your figurine before each one to gain insight into the current roles you inhabit at this time in your life.

Contemplation

>> How have I done up to this point?

>> How am I doing now?

>> How would I like to move forward?

World Work

Quiet the mind and the soul will speak.

—Ma Jaya Sati Bhagavati, spiritual teacher

The next archetypal consideration as we move forward to take our rightful place in the world is our societal archetype, or how we express our vocation in the world—our World Work. Within the "perennial wisdoms found among the indigenous peoples' of each continent" (or shamanic traditions), there were four original ways of being present in the world—the warrior, teacher, healer, and visionary. [23]

As our world has developed and grown, two other vocational archetypes have emerged—the explorer and the builder. With regard to the Soul's incarnational intention for this life, our teacher Ralph Metzner has written that "The Soul chooses one or more of these six great archetypal pathways."[24] His hypothesis helps us understand the ways in which

---

23   Angeles Arrien, *The Fourfold Way: Walking the Paths of the Warrior, Teacher, Healer and Visionary* (San Francisco: Harper, 1993).

24   Ralph Metzner, *The Six Pathways of Destiny* (Berkeley: Regent Press, 2012)

our Soul may have chosen to manifest—beyond Familial Archetypes. A Constellation involving our World Work can give us an expanded view of our Soul nature. Metzner adds, "We may have glimpses in dreams, messages from Spirit, as well as contacts with teachers and role models that inspire us on finding our way, our unique destiny."[25]

The Six World Work Paths[26]:

>> *Warrior/Guardian/Reformer/Activist:* One who seeks to protect and defend natural and social systems against invasion or corruption or toxicity.

>> *Teacher/Historian/Social Scientist/Journalist:* One who seeks to communicate and inform others concerning history, society, policies, economics, and current affairs.

>> *Healer/Shaman/Therapist/Peacemaker:* One who seeks to repair, regenerate, rebalance, and resolve conflicts in natural and social systems.

>> *Artist/Musician/Storyteller/Poet/(Visionary):* One who seeks to inspire others by revealing and expressing beauty and harmony in the world.

>> *Explorer/Scientist/Seeker/Pioneer:* One who seeks to expand and deepen knowledge of nature, life, cosmos and psyche.

>> *Builder/Organizer/Producer/Engineer:* One who seeks to build systems, both material and social-that support and further life in all its aspects.

According to Metzner, "Each of the pathways is not only a career or profession, our work in the world; each is also, at a deeper level, a pathway of spiritual development that the Soul has chosen."

---

25   Ibid.
26   Ibid.

Which of the Six World Work Paths are you currently pursuing? Although most people identify with some percentage of each one, try to choose the three that best describe your World Work. Placing a figurine for yourself and one for each of these three pathways will help you receive insight and guidance.

Contemplation

>> Why would my Soul choose these pathways?

>> How are they related to my family lineage?

>> What do I want to contribute to society?

A Constellation Journeyer
Ofelia—Embodying the Healer

I placed different archetypal aspects of myself: "daughter, sister, wife, mother, and healer. I could see that sister was suffering. She and I began to cry.

Looking into the eyes of my sister representative, I felt so much love for her. I wanted to hold her and make her feel better; but I knew that this would ultimately not help either one of us. So I said to her, "I honor your fate"" and stepped away from her. I turned towards daughter and healer. My intuition told me that daughter held the key to my healer. I just didn't know how.

I placed daughter in front of wife and mother, and placed healer in front of them all. I then stood to the left of healer and took her hand, but it wasn't quite right. I then moved in front of healer and leaned my back into her (the representative). The energy around and inside of me began to vibrate. My heart raced! This was it. It was as if I had just gotten behind the wheel of a very fast race car. The energy got stronger. I kept hearing "I embody the healer." I was no longer the driver of this race car; I became the race car!

I saw and felt myself fully wrapped in the wings of my mother's and father's lineages. I understood that my soul's purpose in this lifetime is to embody the healer more fully as my World Work.

Since my constellation I have a lot more energy and drive. I am clearer and more focused on what I want in my life. It has been easier to let go of the people and things that do not feed my soul. I had never allowed myself to experience the "healer" inside of me. Now my healer and I are one for the first time. I know and feel that part of my soul's true essence.

Inner Feminine and Inner Masculine

God turns you from one feeling to another and teaches you by means of opposites, so that you will have two wings to fly, not one.

—Jelaluddin Rumi

We facilitate Constellations with the Familial Archetypes and the Six World Work Paths to create a physical representation of where our Soul journey has led us. These two sets of Representatives echo how our Soul is revealing itself at this time in our life. With these insights, we can now turn to face the two inner aspects of our being, the Inner Feminine and Inner Masculine.

Throughout our lifetime, we attempt to achieve harmony between the two opposing yet interdependent forces of feminine and masculine. We begin our attempts at harmony through our parents, siblings, and other relationships—each of them external representations of feminine and masculine. But now that journey leads us back to our innermost self.

Consciously or not, we either work towards peace and accord between these two life forces, or we find ourselves in disharmony. We were born into physical form either as feminine or masculine. Many, who believe we chose our parents, also believe that we chose our gender. Regardless, we are expected to act and respond in particular ways because of our gender—and also follow the behavioral patterns of the collective we were born into. In reality, however, we carry a part of each gender within us.

The struggle between the feminine and masculine is an unrelenting battle that continues to rage on our planet, as it has for millennia. For world peace to occur, we begin by accepting the feminine and masculine as they present themselves in our Family Lineage. Once we accept those fully, we are free to explore the ongoing conflicts between our own Inner Feminine and Inner Masculine. The Constellation Approach prepares us to sign an essential peace treaty so that both energies can live in balance within us.

According to the tradition of Alchemical Mysticism, each of us possesses an inner nature that is both masculine and feminine. Our Inner Masculine is vital, generative, and expressive. Reflected on our right, solar side, its nature is linked to the energies of the sun. It is considered to be vibrant and electric—both protector and provider. The Inner Masculine has attributes of investigating, probing, searching, penetrating. The Inner Feminine or lunar side is receptive and magnetic. Its nature, reflected on our left side, is like the moon's energetic influence on the tides, reaching out yet drawing inward. Our Inner Feminine is emotional, sensory, perceptual, nurturing, and caregiving.

In Taoism, our masculine nature is described as *yang*, bright, the external principle. Our feminine nature or *yin* is internal, dark, deep and mysterious like the sea. Depicted as white (*yang*) or black (*yin*) in the Taijitu symbol, one can't exist without the other. Within *yang* is *yin* and within *yin* is *yang*.

In yogic traditions the energetic pathway or *nadi* that runs up and down the right side of our body called the pingala—is considered masculine. This pathway is dynamic, active, and associated with extroversion, corresponding to the left side of the brain. The feminine *nadi* on the left side of our body is called *ida*. Associated with introversion and being magnetic, it is linked to the right side of the brain, our intuitive nature. Both pathways are extrasensory in function, playing a part in our empathic and instinctive responses to life.

The *ida* and *pingala* intersect with each chakra and interconnect with a third perpendicular energetic pathway in the center of our body. Called the *sushumna*, it is the vertical axis that allows us to express our Soul nature through our masculine and feminine sides; it is also said to connect heaven and earth.

Through the alchemical process of the Constellation Approach, we can transform our prejudices and misperceptions about the opposite—by opening to what is inside us. We can enter into communion with our own dual nature, joining our Inner Feminine and Inner Masculine to unite the polarities and create an inner marriage. The king and queen, solar and lunar, dynamic and receptive, logical and intuitive become one within the

Vesica Pisces of our open human hearts. With empathy for all that we have experienced in this lifetime and an awakened awareness, we can come to peace with our Inner Feminine and Inner Masculine gaining unprecedented access to the fullness of our innermost self.

As philosopher Ken Wilbur observed, "The point is … to unify and to harmonize the opposites, both positive and negative, by discovering a ground which transcends and encompasses them both."

A Constellation Journeyer
Mary — Welcome Back

Standing across from the Representatives for my Inner Masculine and Inner Feminine I felt confusion, anger, and then awareness. My masculine side looked down upon my feminine side. I was judging a part of myself so harshly, a part I hardly even knew. Did I have the courage in this moment to walk toward my feminine? Would she accept me? Could I surrender to what she had to offer? I felt like the prodigal daughter, full of doubt and shame, wondering if my past actions and loyalties would be understood, and if I would be permitted into the feminine consciousness.

As I approached, I could feel the divine feminine love and still wondered if I would be accepted. As I entered the Vesica Pisces all I heard was, "Welcome back." Those two words sank into me. I cried tears of relief and felt myself surrender. I understood the next steps I needed to take in relation to my own feminine nature.

I needed to own her by being more present in my relationships and profession. It was important to step into owning who I am as a woman and share with the world what I had learned. I had to begin my workshops and continue to write. I knew that I needed to embrace my Inner feminine more fully in my roles as wife, mother, daughter, sister, healer, and teacher.

Place three figurines—one for yourself and one each to represent your Inner Masculine and Inner Feminine. Notice which way each is facing, how far apart each is from the other, and pay special attention to the inner aspect of yourself you are least comfortable with. Allow yourself to readjust the figurines as you feel drawn to, and notice any insights you may receive. Slowly move your figurine into the Vesica Pisces of each, allowing more time to reflect.

Contemplation

>> What arises as I face my Inner Feminine?

>> What arises as I face my Inner Masculine?

>> What perceptions do I need to release to come to peace with both facets of myself?

Soul Nature

The Soul is a lamp, whose light is steady,
For it burns in a shelter where no winds come.

—Bhagavad Gita (6.19)

The Soul acts through the Familial Archetypes, the pathways of our World Work, and our Inner Feminine and Inner Masculine. Connecting with our Soul consciousness points us in a direction that allows us to focus our intention and take the next steps to fulfill our destiny. The Soul has a greater vision of the interconnectedness of life itself and provides us with a guiding voice, if we are willing to listen.

As "the light within life" described by the alchemists, the Soul informs our choices, offering wise counsel that helps shape our character. These two aspects of our being are conjoined since birth. Many names express our Soul nature—divine spark, basic goodness, core essence. *Anam* in Gaelic, *atman* in Hindu, *yechidah* in Hebrew, and Holy Wind *(nichi'i)* for the Navajo. It is our Higher Self, Christ Consciousness, Buddha-nature and God's throb.

Standing before our Soul nature is the culmination of the Constellation Approach process—an opportunity to integrate fully all that has come before. This is the final Constellation in our Immersion Program. It requires a desire and willingness to go beyond our rational mind, to release attachment to psychological and religious interpretation, and to move into divine communion with the other—our Soul that has lived within us, always. This transcendent Soul communion expands us and allows 'direct knowing' to happen. Information in the form of images, feelings and sensations intensifies; there is often a sense of linear time suspending itself. Apparent differences in our human personality seem to recede as our Soul nature is recognized more fully.

Once in alignment, our human nature becomes the servant of our Soul. Our Soul, in turn, becomes the guardian of our character. Both can walk together as one. Through the sacred ceremony of a Constellation, there can be a profound, life-transforming experience of this unity. Finally, the light within us has the luminosity and spaciousness to emanate through all areas of our life.

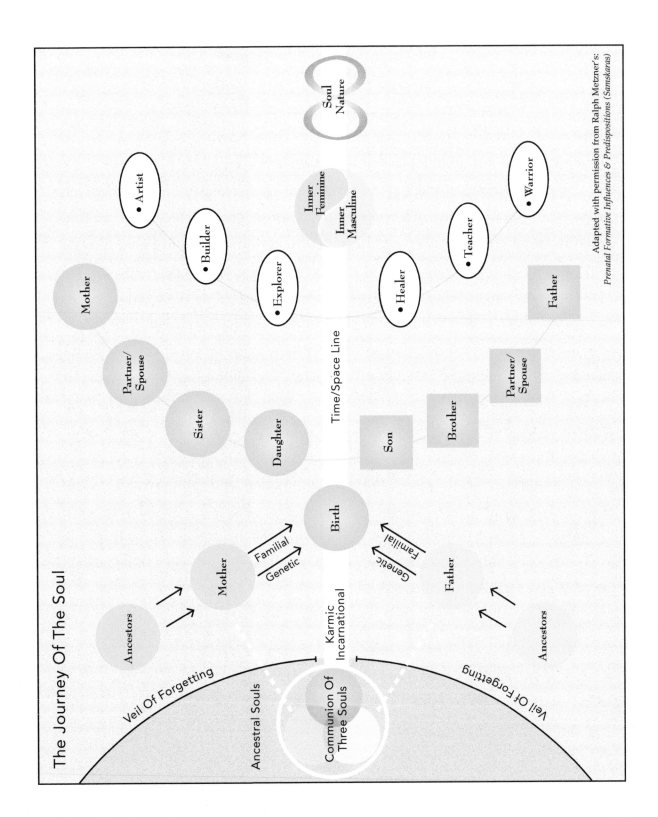

The Journey Of The Soul

Soul Nature

Artist
Builder
Explorer

Inner Feminine
Inner Masculine

Healer
Teacher
Warrior

Mother
Partner/ Spouse
Sister
Daughter

Father
Partner/ Spouse
Brother
Son

Time/Space Line

Birth

Ancestors
Mother
Familial
Genetic

Karmic Incarnational

Genetic
Familial
Father
Ancestors

Veil Of Forgetting
Ancestral Souls
Communion Of Three Souls
Veil Of Forgetting

Adapted with permission from Ralph Metzner's:
Prenatal Formative Influences & Predispositions (Samskaras)

A Constellation Journeyer
Patricia—Facing my Soul

I turned to stand in front of the representative for my soul. I stated my full name and agreed to what was, what is and what will be.

As I closed my eyes and stepped towards my Soul's nature I passed through eons of time and many lifetimes—just flashing like a very rapid motion picture. With my eyes still closed I saw before me a magnificent figure of light with giant wings. Suddenly I was at a much higher vibration. As I stood beside my Soul my beliefs regarding myself seemed so small. All the experiences of daughter, sister, mother, wife, entrepreneur in this lifetime faded—no longer having importance. The wholeness I felt with my twin soul next to me brought the masculine/feminine balance within. I felt deep self-love. In some sort of ethereal manner I gained insights from the lessons learned in my archetypal roles and in that moment I recognized I am the Divine. I am so much more than I ever knew.

Afterward, I sat in silence for almost an hour, as multiple waves of feeling and insights came over me one after another. Often it seemed they were coming from many directions all at once and yet inside my being. It was as if I was accessing wisdom from other aspects of myself. It was a holographic experience. I was "stunned" for days.

Chapter 15

Myths of the Soul

*The images of myth are reflections of the spiritual potentialities of
every one of us. Through contemplating these, we invoke their powers
in our own life.*

—Joseph Campbell

Ancient mythologies of indigenous peoples, gods and goddesses, devas
and deities have inspired and guided our vision as facilitators and teachers
of the Constellation Approach. Myths are "clues" that assist us, as Joseph
Campbell notes, in "finding a way of experiencing the world that will
open us to the transcendent that informs it, and at the same time forms
ourselves within it... That is what the soul asks for."[27]

The two of us have been especially captivated by those myths that
lend deeper meaning to our Soul's origin as well as a healing vision for
our lives. Several of the myths continue to have a powerful impact on
our work facilitating Constellations. We offer two of these timeless myths

---

27   Joseph Campbell, *The Power of the Myth* (New York: MJF Books, 1988)

here in the hope that they will continue to awaken you to the quintessence of your Soul's true nature, to the "rapture of being alive."[28]

The Myth of Er

The Myth of Er, the tenth and last chapter of Plato's *Republic* (fifth century B.C.) tells the story of the soldier Er's near-death experience on the battlefield. Throughout the night while hovering between life and death, Er arrives in the astral realm where he is shown the Soul's incarnational pathway onto the road of life. He watches as three primeval goddesses called *Moirai*, the Fates, craft each Soul's life from a single thread. *Clothos*, the youngest spins; *Lachesis* measures; and *Atropos*, the elder, cuts the thread when our time on earth is done. The Fates then hand the Soul a token that will determine details of its destiny.

Ushered beneath the grand throne of the creator Goddess *Ananke* (Necessity) as she turns her life-giving spindle, the Soul is born. Each life is indispensable, its purpose unalterable. Consider for a moment how the spindle of Necessity and the Fates' token are reflected in our experience of the Ten Strands of Awareness and Threads of Consciousness along the Rope of Time. We have been coming to understand our Soul's unique purpose: that "what we live *is* necessary to be lived"[29]; everything that has happened has already happened, for "whatever we are, could not have been otherwise."[30]

The Myth of Er continues. Before each Soul is born into human life, it crosses the Plain of Oblivion and drinks from the River Lethe (forgetfulness). The incarnational 'lot' of family, relationships, world work, etc., is all eradicated, erased and emptied from the mind. At daybreak, Er opens his eyes to find himself lying on a funeral pyre surrounded by his family. Since Er himself was not allowed to drink the

---

28   Ibid.
29   James Hillman, *The Soul's Code: In Search of Character and Calling* (New York: Grand Central Publishing, 1996)
30   Ibid.

waters of forgetting, he was able to recount his experience of the Soul's journey to others.[31]

Much like this life-nourishing myth, the Constellation Approach encourages us to awaken to our Soul's place and purpose on earth, including those mysteries our Soul chose before we arrived.[32] The second myth, which we share below, is called the Hymn of the Pearl. This too, takes us on a Soul expedition that can enlighten us in ways both intimate and epic.

Hymn of the Pearl

From tattered parchment found in Central Asia to the Egyptian discovery of earthenware jars containing the Nag Hammadi scrolls, many influential scriptures about the life of the Soul have been uncovered in the last century. The "fabulous narrative poem"[33] known as the Hymn of the Pearl is found in the *Acts of Thomas* of the *New Testament Apocrypha*. It has been preserved, treasured, and translated from several ancient languages, and is considered "one of the most attractive documents in Gnostic literature."[34]

The tale begins in the east, at the "House of the Highest Ones" in heaven with three main figures—the "Father of Truth," the "Mother of Wisdom," and a brilliant, young, Prince.[35]/[36] The Prince is sent out on an arduous journey to re-claim the One Pearl from a fierce and terrible serpent. But before he left his beloved home, his parents did one important thing:

---

31   Chrysovalantis Petridis, *Plato's Mythologizing of the Myth of Er* (Portland: Inkwater Press, 2009)

32   James Hillman, *The Soul's Code: In Search of Character and Calling* (New York: Grand Central Publishing, 1996)

33   Willis Barnstone, *The Other Bible* (New York: Harper & Row, 1984)

34   Ibid.

35   Ibid.

36   Ralph Metzner, *The Life Cycle of the Human Soul: Incarnation, Conception, Birth, Death, Hereafter, Reincarnation* (Berkeley: Regent Press, 2011)

They made a covenant with me
and wrote it in my heart so that I would not forget:
'When you go down into the material world
and bring back the One Pearl
which lies in the center of the sea
and is guarded by the fierce dragon,
you will have your robe of glory
and the royal cloak and with your Twin
you will inherit the Kingdom.' 37/38

The young Prince, plunged fully into the trance of the earthly plane—just as we often do. Eating and drinking, he is lulled into the unconscious realms; he forgets his bejeweled robes, his royal parents, his mission, and especially the covenant of finding the One Pearl. We, too, may become similarly distracted in our lives and sometimes addicted to our illusions. Feeling blameful, victimized and unsatisfied with our family and the circumstances of our life, we suffer, believing ourselves to be separate and alone.

There is a turn of events in the story, arriving by way of a mystical, shape-shifting eagle, carrying a 'voice memo' from the Prince's parents: "From your father, the King of Kings, and your mother, Mistress of the East … Awake and arise from sleep … Remember you are the son of Kings...."[39]

Slowly, the Prince shakes off his delusion, recalls the covenant written inside his heart, and charms the dragon into sleep by repeating the names of his Father and Mother over and over again. He seizes the Pearl from the "snorting serpent"[40] and heads homeward towards the east. On his way, the Prince meets the noble ambassadors from his parents' house who've come to escort him home. He gazes upon the garment that the noble ones hold out for him:

---

37   Ralph Metzner, *Diving for Treasures: Poems & Epilogs* (Berkeley: Regent Press, 2015)

38   Willis Barnstone, *The Other Bible* (New York: Harper & Row, 1984)

39   Ibid.

40   Ibid.

As I gazed on it
suddenly the garment became a mirror
of myself. I saw in it my whole self,
and in it I saw myself apart,
for we were two entities
yet in one form…
with one kingly seal.[41]

This "robe of many colors, embroidered with gold and silver threads, with rubies and sapphires and emeralds and seams fastened with diamonds"[42] is said to hold all knowledge (*gnosis*). It mirrors our Soul's true nature with its luminosity and divine light.

In the sacred work of the Constellation Approach we remember the names of our parents and Ancestors and honor all that they experienced and endured before our arrival. We, too, can merge our human nature with our Soul nature and retrieve our rightful inheritance—the One Pearl. In the words of the Prince, "I put on the beautiful robe of many colors all around me … I bowed … and adored the majesty of the Mother-Father. They received me, rejoiced in me and with them in the Kingdom"[43] they bestowed their Ancestral Blessing upon me.

---

41 Willis Barnstone, *The Other Bible* (New York: Harper & Row, 1984)

42 Ralph Metzner, *Diving for Treasures: Poems & Epilogs* (Berkeley: Regent Press, 2015)

43 Ibid.

Chapter 16

Agreeing to All of It

Oh, may this be the one
Who will bring forward
The good, true and beautiful in
Our family lineage;
Oh, may this be the one who will
Break the harmful
Family patterns …

—Old European ancestral song [44]

Together, we reached inside our pocket for the key of desire and unlocked the Doorway of Existence. As our ancestral tree was revealed to us, the ground beneath our feet began to rumble, unearthing our long-held familial misperceptions. Approaching closer, we noticed a pathway leading to our patrilineal and matrilineal roots. We acknowledged and accepted our origins. Slowly connecting with our ancestors, we transformed discomfort, becoming less afraid.

---

44   Angeles Arrien, *The Fourfold Way: Walking the Paths of the Warrior, Teacher, Healer and Visionary* (San Francisco: Harper, 1993)

Steadying ourselves, we drew nearer to the tree. Upon it were posted a myriad of questions, inviting us to reclaim the names of our tribe and the hidden stories of our clan. As we discovered answers and spoke Words of Empowerment, new openings occurred throughout our mind-body. We continued on our way, meeting the Souls and circumstances of our lineages that molded us into who we have become. But then, we stepped into the Vesica Pisces with them and our inner images began to change.

Next, we took our position in the Order of Precedence, feeling for the first time perhaps, our rightful place in our Family of Origin. With pride, we could now stand stronger in our self, feeling more at peace with all that was and all that is.

Agreeing to our mothers and fathers, sisters and brothers forever changes how we think, feel and speak about them. The tenor of our speech carries a positive energetic frequency that touches the listener's heart. Indeed, when negativity is released towards the people we love, we become like beacons of light. Our light and lightness of being attracts and affects those nearest to us, family members, friends, and associates. Inner peace is palpable.

> *I agree to all that was,*
> *All that is and all that*
> *I am becoming.*

> —Joan LoMonaco, TCA graduate

Agreeing to the path of our ancestors allows us to choose whether we follow in their footsteps—or take a completely different route. It lessens the guilt we may feel for being different or seeking an alternative way to live our life. We can come to peace with our choices, recognizing they have been steered by our Soul for reasons larger than our own personal gain.

'Agreeing to all of it' is direct access to compassion, the natural state of the Soul. It creates a state of deep appreciation and gratitude within, and is vital to the transformation of consciousness. Without this agreement, there can be no understanding; without understanding, there can be no compassion; and without compassion we cannot attain the peace our Soul yearns for.

The practice of 'agreeing to all of it' means we are willing to be inclusive, welcoming, non-rejecting, and truly tolerant to others' views. 'Agreeing to all of it' is also the portal that allows us to enter an awakened state, releasing projection and attachment. Everyone and everything reveals its importance and purpose on the spiritual plane. No one, no-thing is better or worse; hierarchy dissolves and we find ourselves on an even playing field. We rest in the tranquil sea of transcendent insight comprehending the interconnectedness of all things.

I do not at all understand the mystery of grace — only that it meets us where we are but does not leave us where it found us.

— Anne Lamott, novelist

Each of us has contributions to make towards peace on our planet by bringing the vibration of peace into every area of our lives. 'Agreeing to all of it' gives us the strength to stand in the present moment, face our future, and activate our Soul's destiny as peacemakers. This is the potential and promise of the Constellation Approach.

In closing, we invite you once again to feel the powerful energetic connection to your Family Lineage by naming and claiming your birthright:

"I am_____

the son/ daughter of

_____."

Let all the other Words of Empowerment that you have embodied during this process flow freely from within you. And finally

"I Agree to All of It."

PART V

Constellation Experiences

Dear Constellation Journeyer—

Part V is designed to help you experience Constellations. The "Constellation Experiences" in this section correlate to the Ten Universal Themes associated with each chapter in Parts II and III. These experiences are opportunities to practice what you have learned. (Remember that the process of connecting with your Family Lineage begins with the answers to your Reflections and the specific Words of Empowerment you choose).

We encourage you to keep a journal to record the insights you may receive as each Constellation builds upon the preceeding one. By the time you complete the Constellation Experiences you will have created your own path to **Finding Peace Through Your Family Lineage**.

The initial steps for Setting Up your Constellation Experience are the same for each Constellation. We list them here so you can familiarize yourself with the process. We recommend that you enter this experience with the same agreements we described in Part I—with desire, an open heart and a willingness to explore your Soul nature.

>> Gather numerous small figurines that will act as Represenatives for family members and phenomonological influences. (e.g., chess pieces, crystals, shells, rocks, small spice bottles, nail polish). Be sure to have one figurine for yourself.

>> On a sturdy surface, like a table, desk, or countertop, create your Constellation using the figurines as Representatives. Allow yourself to be the *observer* looking into your Constellation.

>> As you place each member, call the respective name aloud or silently — either way, the Soul will hear. If you don't know the specific names, say the name *Grandfather* or *Grandmother* for example, followed by the surname, if you know it.

>> Take your time. Allow the Constellation to arise from your own inner image. Place the pieces however you are intuitively drawn to do so. You

cannot do this incorrectly. Simply breathe and allow your Constellation to unfold.

We wish you well on your journey of finding peace, making peace and keeping peace with your Family Lineage.

—*Jamy & Peter*

Constellation Experience #1

Your Family of Origin

1. Open your journal to a new entry. Title it "Reflections on my Family of Origin."

2. Gather numerous small figurines including one for yourself. e Create your Family of Origin Constellation using the figurines as Representatives. Allow yourself to be the *observer* looking into your Family of Origin. Represent three generations, grandparents, parents, and yours.

4. As you place each member, call the respective name aloud or silently—either way, the Soul will hear. If you don't know the specific names, say the name *Grandfather* or *Grandmother* for example, followed by the surname, if you know it.

5. Take your time. Allow the Constellation to arise from your own inner image. Place the pieces however you are intuitively drawn to do so. You cannot do this incorrectly. Simply breathe and allow your Constellation to unfold.

6. Place the figurines in relation to each other. Begin by placing your father and mother, then your siblings in birth order, including yourself. Add your paternal and maternal grandparents even if you did not know them.

7. Notice directions Representatives face, patterns, and groupings. Observe and become aware of your feelings. Rearrange the figurines as you are drawn. Observe your reactions; notice your feelings and any insights you may receive. Pause. Continue this process until you feel a sense of completion.

8. Create the final arrangement by placing everyone in the Order of Precedence and Inclusion. Place your grandparents next to each other, from left to right; paternal grandfather, grandmother, maternal grandfather, grandmother. Place your father in front of his parents and your mother next to him in front of her parents. Place your siblings in birth order next to your mother. Leave your birth order space open.

9. Pause, observe your reactions; notice your feelings and any insights you may receive. Place your figurine in your rightful place. Let yourself feel what it's like to be in your family. (See diagram)

10. Select one or more of the **Words of Empowerment to Your Family of Origin** (from page 80) and say aloud or silently. Experiment with different Words of Empowerment. Observe and become aware of your feelings and any insights you may receive.

11. Journal about your experience with your Family of Origin Constellation.

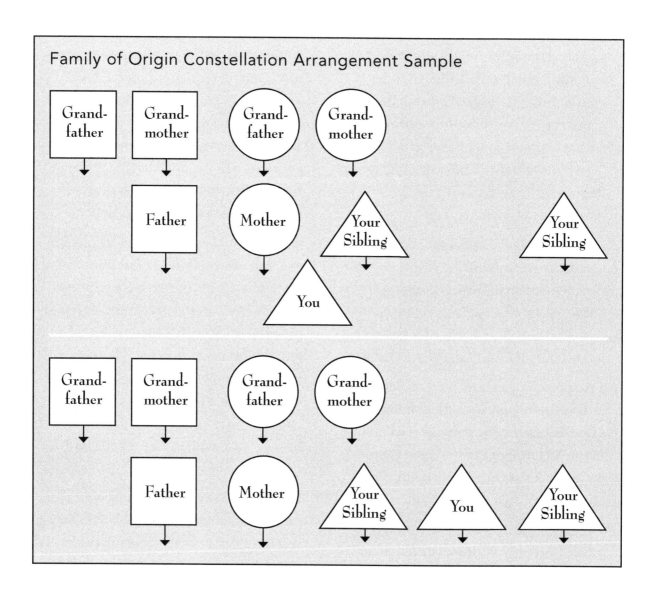

Family of Origin Constellation Arrangement Sample

Constellation Experience #2

Your Father's Lineage

1. ʿOpen your journal to a new entry. Title it "Reflections on my Father's Lineage."

2. ʿGather numerous small figurines including one for yourself

3. Allow yourself to be the *observer* looking into your Constellation.

4. As you place each member, call their name aloud or silently—either way, the Soul will hear. If you don't know the specific names, say the name *Grandfather*, for example, followed by the surname, if you know it.

5. Take your time. Allow the Constellation to arise from your own inner image. Place the pieces however you are intuitively drawn to do so. You cannot do this incorrectly. Simply breathe and allow your Constellation to unfold.

6. Place the figurines in relation to each other. Begin with your father, his parents, and his siblings. Include representatives for significant relationships, wives, and children prior to or after your mother. Eventually add his grandparents (your paternal great grandparents).

7. Notice directions Representatives face, patterns, and groupings. Observe and become aware of your feelings. Rearrange the figurines as you are drawn. Observe your reactions; notice your feelings and any insights you may receive. Pause. Continue this process until you feel a sense of completion.

8. Place everyone in the Order of Precedence and Inclusion. Looking at the Constellation from back to front, place your great grandparents and grandparents. Align your father in birth order with his siblings in front of his father and mother. Representatives for significant relationships, wives or children prior to or after your mother are placed to the side.

9. Place the figurine for yourself in front of your father. Imagine your father standing before you. Choose one of the **Three Healing Words:** "please," "thank you," or "yes." Repeat three times slowly to him.

10. Select one or more of the **Words of Empowerment for Your Father** (from page 92) and say aloud or silently.

Experiment with different Words of Empowerment.

11. Create the final arrangement by turning your figurine to face forward, with your Father and his Lineage standing behind you in the position of support and strength. Observe and become aware of your feelings and any insights you may receive. (See diagram)

12. Journal about your experience with the Father's Lineage Constellation.

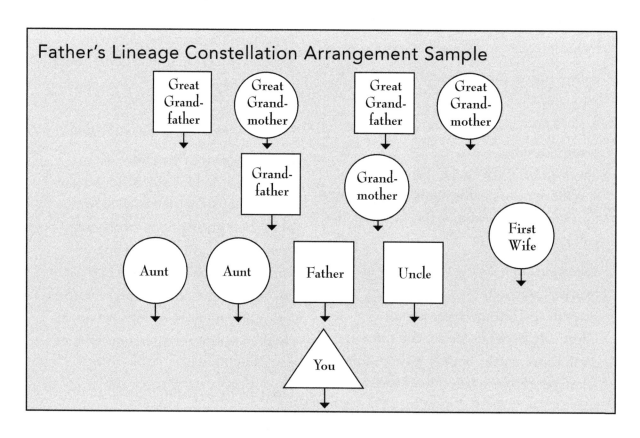

Father's Lineage Constellation Arrangement Sample

Constellation Experience #3

Your Mother's Lineage

1. Open your journal to a new entry. Title it "Reflections on my Mother's Lineage."

2. Gather numerous small figurines including one for yourself.

3. Allow yourself to be the *observer* looking into your Constellation.

4. As you place each member, call their respective name aloud or silently—either way, the Soul will hear. If you don't know the specific names, say the name *Grandfather*, for example, followed by the surname, if you know it.

5. Take your time. Allow the Constellation to arise from your own inner image. Place the pieces however you are intuitively drawn to do so. You cannot do this incorrectly. Simply breathe and allow your Constellation to unfold.

6. Place the figurines in relation to each other. Begin with your mother, her parents, and her siblings. Include representatives for significant relationships, husbands, and children prior to or after your father. Eventually add her grandparents (your maternal great grandparents).

7. Notice directions Representatives face, patterns, and groupings. Observe and become aware of your feelings. Rearrange the figurines as you are drawn. Observe your reactions; notice your feelings and any insights you may receive. Pause. Continue this process until you feel a sense of completion.

8. Place everyone in the Order of Precedence and Inclusion. Looking at the Constellation from back to front, place your great grandparents and grandparents. Align your mother in birth order with her siblings in front of her father and mother. Representatives for significant relationships, husbands or children prior to or after your mother are placed to the side.

9. Place the figurine for yourself in front of your mother. Decide how you would like to incorporate **The Act of Bowing** to your mother (the head bow, the waist bow, or a full prostration).

10. Imagine your mother standing before you. Choose one of the **Three Healing Words:** "please," "thank you," or "yes." Repeat three times slowly to her.

11. Select one or more of the **Words of Empowerment to Your Mother** (from page 110) and say aloud or silently. Experiment with different Words of Empowerment.

12. Create the final arrangement by turning your figurine to face forward, with your Mother and her Lineage standing behind you in the position of support and strength. Observe and become aware of your feelings and any insights you may receive. (See diagram)

13. Journal about your experience with the Mother's Lineage Constellation.

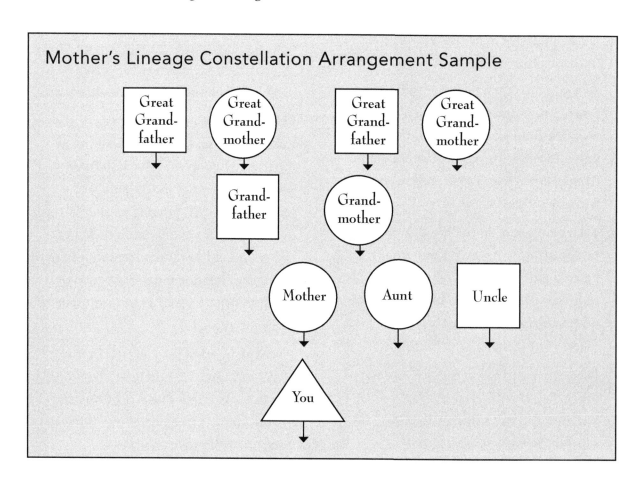

Mother's Lineage Constellation Arrangement Sample

Constellation Experience #4

Your Sibling Relationships

1. Open your journal to a new entry. Title it "Reflections on my Sibling Relationships."

2. Gather numerous small figurines including one for yourself.

3. Allow yourself to be the *observer* looking into your Constellation.

4. As you place each member, call his or her name aloud or silently—either way, their Soul will hear. If you don't know the names, say the name "Brother/Sister" or "Aunt/Uncle" for example, followed by the surname.

5. To best understand your Sibling relationships, it is helpful to first observe your parents' relationships with their own siblings. On the left side of the working area, begin by placing in birth order your father and his siblings. Then place your mother and her siblings in birth order on the right side of the working area. Start with biological siblings from the same set of parents (your grandparents).

6. Take your time. Allow the Constellation to arise from your own inner image.

Place them however you are intuitively drawn. You cannot do this step incorrectly. Simply breathe and allow your Constellation to unfold.

7. Notice patterns and groupings in the way representatives are facing. Based on the answers in your Reflections, become aware of your feelings in relation to your aunts and uncles. For example, you might notice an uncle who may have been excluded, an aunt who was particularly important to you, or a parent's sibling who remained unresolved with the family.

8. In front of these two groups of figurines, place your biological siblings in birth order and a figurine for yourself. Notice your feelings and any insights you may be receiving.

9. Rearrange the figurines as you are drawn. Observe your reactions. Notice your feelings and any insights you may be receiving. Rearrange the figurines again. Pause, observe, and notice your feelings and insights. Like a slow-

moving chess game, play until you feel a sense of completion.

10. Create the final arrangement by moving your father and mother to the center. Place them side-by-side, facing forward, your father on the left, and your mother on the right. Arrange your father's siblings along the left and your mother's siblings along the right, forming a loose arc. Place your siblings in birth order, also facing forward.

11. One by one, place the figurine for yourself in front of each of your siblings. Select one or more of the **Words of Empowerment to your Siblings** (from page 126) and say them aloud or silently three times. Experiment with different Words of Empowerment with different siblings. You may also incorporate a Bow of respect or gratitude if you wish. (See diagram)

12. Finish your Sibling Relationship Constellation by placing yourself in birth order among your siblings. *(The Order of Precedence)*

13. For Blended Families: You may place your half/ step-siblings into the Constellation as they came into your family. Note your feelings and reactions. Choose Words of Empowerment and say them aloud or silently.

14. Journal about your experience with the Sibling Relationship Constellation.

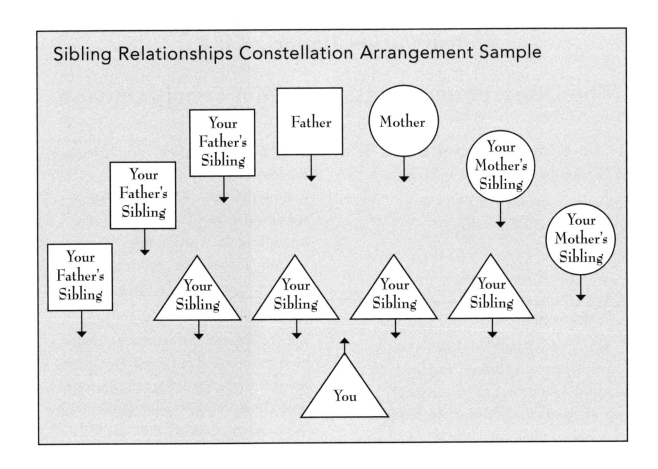

Sibling Relationships Constellation Arrangement Sample

Constellation Experience #5

The Diseases and Illnesses of Your Family Lineage

1. Open your journal to a new entry. Title it "Reflections on Disease and Illness.

2. Gather numerous small figurines including one for yourself.

3. Allow yourself to be the *observer* looking into your Constellation.

A. Systemic Approach:

4. Set up your Family of Origin using the **Systemic Approach**. Include both sets of grandparents. As you place each member, call their name aloud or silently. Either way, their Soul will hear. Then, place a Meta-representative for the primary disease/illness that is part of your paternal lineage, naming it aloud. Place the Meta-representative however you are intuitively drawn. Repeat for your maternal lineage.

5. Take your time. Allow the Constellation to arise from your own inner image. You cannot do this step incorrectly. Simply breathe and allow your Constellation to unfold.

6. Based on the answers in your Reflections, become aware of your feelings in relation to these diseases/illnesses. Beginning with the disease/illness of your Father's Lineage, notice who has been affected and how. Repeat for your Mother's Lineage. Allow your awareness to broaden.

7. Rearrange the figurines as you are drawn. Observe your reactions; notice your feelings and any insights you may receive. Pause. Rearrange the figurines again; observe your feelings and insights. Continue this process until you feel a sense of completion.

8. Create the final arrangement by placing everyone in the Order of Precedence and Inclusion. Looking at the Constellation from left to right, place your father, mother, and siblings in birth order. Grandparents stand behind their children, grandfather on the left and grandmother on the right. Place the two Meta-representatives beside or behind the family member you feel they are most connected to at this time. (See diagram)

9. One at a time, place the figurine for yourself in front of the Meta-representative and the family member most connected to it.

10. Select one or more of the **Words of Empowerment for the Representative and Meta-representative** (from page 148) and say it aloud or silently three times. Experiment with different Words of Empowerment. You may also incorporate a bow of respect or gratitude if you wish. (See diagram)

11. Finish your disease and illness Constellation by placing yourself in the Order of Precedence, birth order, among your siblings.

12. Observe your Family Lineage and the Meta-representative for the Strand of Awareness of disease and illness. Become aware of the Threads of Consciousness and the gifts that these phenomenological influences have had on yourself and your Family Lineage.

13. You can repeat this Constellation for other illnesses and diseases or add additional Meta-representatives to the Constellation at this time.

14. This Constellation may be performed for your Current Family, Partner, and Children.

B. Phenomenological Approach:

1. If you are carrying a particular disease or illness that has not occurred previously in your Family Lineage (non-Systemic), set up a Constellation using the **Phenomenological Approach:** Choose a figurine to represent yourself and a Meta-representative for the disease or illness.

2. Select one or more of the **Words of Empowerment for the Meta-representative** and say aloud or silently three times. Experiment with different Words of Empowerment. You may also incorporate a bow of respect or gratitude if you wish.

3. Place the Meta-representative beside or behind your figurine. Simply observe, become aware of your feelings and any insights that arise.

4. Journal about your experience with your Disease/Illness Constellation.

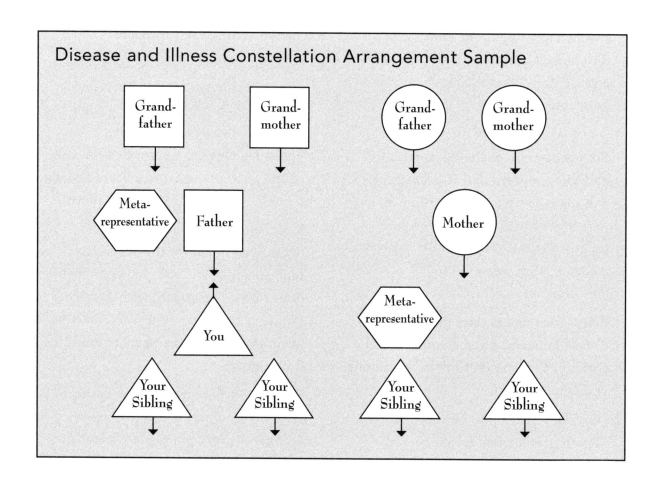

Disease and Illness Constellation Arrangement Sample

Constellation Experience #6

The Deaths that Affected Your Family Lineage

1. Open your journal to a new entry. Title it "Reflections on Death."

2. Gather numerous small figurines including one for yourself.

3. Allow yourself to be the *observer* looking into your Constellation.

4. Based on the answers in your Reflections decide who should be represented in your Constellation. Whose death do you want to look at? Which lineage— Father's, Mother's, or Family of Origin? Who else was affected? As you place each member, call their name aloud or silently—either way, their Soul will hear. Begin the Constellation set-up with the Representative who has died, standing up.

5. Take your time. Allow the Constellation to arise from your own inner image. You cannot do this step incorrectly. Simply breathe and allow your Constellation to unfold.

6. Become aware of your feelings in relation to this loved one's death. Notice who has been affected and how. Allow your awareness to expand.

7. Take the figurine for the loved one who has died and, in the same location, place it flat on the table, as if lying on their back. Observe your reactions and notice your feelings and any insights you may be receiving. Rearrange your figurine to stand next to this Representative. Pause and notice your feelings and insights.

8. Touch the Representative who is lying down with one finger. Select one or more of the **Words of Empowerment** (from page 166) and say them aloud or silently three times. Experiment with different Words of Empowerment.

9. Place a Meta-representative for death near the Representative and opposite the figurine for yourself. Observe your reactions and notice your feelings and any insights you may be receiving.

10. Select one or more of the **Words of Empowerment for the Meta-representative** and say aloud or silently three times. Experiment with different Words of Empowerment. Complete the interaction with a slight bow.

11. Create the final arrangement by leaving the Representative who has died and the Meta-representative for death where they are. Turn everyone else to face forward. Take your figurine and move it to the front of the Constellation. This symbolizes moving into life and leaving death behind. (See diagram)

12. Observe your Constellation and the Meta-representative for the Strand of Awareness of Death. Become aware of the Threads of Consciousness and the gifts that this phenomenological influence has had on yourself and your Family Lineage.

13. You can repeat this Constellation for other deaths that have affected yourself, your Family Lineage, or your Current family.

14. Journal about your experience with your Constellation involving Death.

Phenomenological Approach (if you are facing a potentially terminal situation):

1. Set up a Phenomenological Constellation using a figurine Representative for yourself, your loved one, and a Meta-representative for death.

2. Select one or more of the **Words of Empowerment for the Representative and the Meta-representative** and say aloud or silently three times. Experiment with different Words of Empowerment. You may also incorporate a bow of respect or gratitude if you wish.

3. Place the Meta-representative beside or behind your loved one's figurine. Simply observe, become aware of your feelings and any insights that arise.

4. Journal about your experience with the Strand of Awareness of Death.

Reflections on Death Constellation Arrangement Sample

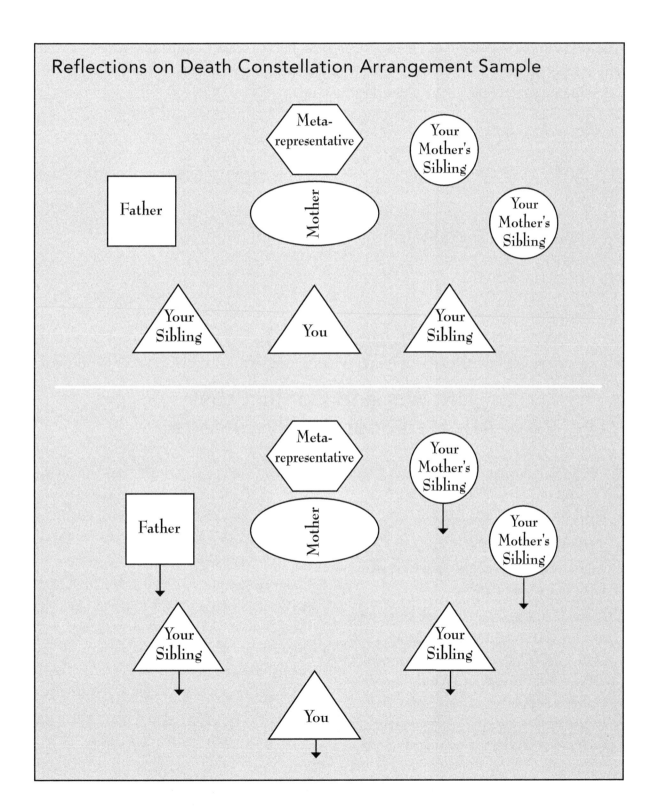

In addition to the Constellations below focused on the War and Conflict that Affected Your Family Lineage, there are four other Constellation Experiences related to reconciling victim and perpetrators. We encourage you to set them up, if

>> A family member was a victim of harm

>> A family member was a perpetrator of harm

>> You were a victim of harm

>> You were a perpetrator of harm

Constellation Experience #7

The War and Conflict that Affected Your Family Lineage

1. Open your journal to a new entry. Title it "Reflections on War and Conflict."

2. Gather numerous small figurines including one for yourself.

3. Allow yourself to be the *observer* looking into your Constellation.

4. Based on the answers in your Reflections; decide who should be represented in your Constellation. Which war or conflict do you want to look at? Which lineage— Father's, Mother's, or Family of Origin? Who else was affected? As you place each member, call their name aloud or silently—either way, their Soul will hear. Place upright any Representative(s) who has died as a result of the war or conflict. Finally, place a Meta-representative for the war or conflict.

5. Take your time. Allow the Constellation to arise from your own inner image. You cannot do this step incorrectly. Simply breathe and allow your Constellation to unfold.

6. Become aware of your feelings. Notice who has been affected and how. Allow your awareness to broaden. Allow

yourself time to really look at the Meta-representative.

7. Take the figurine(s) for the loved one(s) who has died as the result of war or conflict and, in the same location, lay it flat on the table as if lying on their back. Observe your reactions and feelings, and notice any insights you may receive.

8. Rearrange the standing figurines as you are drawn.

9. Place the figurine that represents you near the Representative(s) who has died. Touch the prostrated Representative(s) with one finger. Use **Words of Empowerment** to honor their life and their passing (see Chapter 9 on Death).

10. Rearrange the standing figurines again as you are drawn: Beginning with the eldest generation, place your figurine in front of each Representative. Select one or more of the **Words of Empowerment** (from page 186) and say them aloud or silently three times. Experiment with different Words of Empowerment. Complete with each Representative.

11. Place your figurine in front of the Meta-representative. Select one or more of the **Words of Empowerment for the Meta-representative** and say aloud or silently three times. Experiment with different Words of Empowerment. Complete the interaction with a slight bow.

12. Create the final arrangement by leaving the Representative(s) who has died where he/ she is. Place the Meta-representative for war or conflict where you are drawn. Turn everyone else to face forward. Move your figurine to the front of the Constellation, also facing forward. This placement symbolizes moving into life and leaving the war or conflict with the past. (See diagram)

13. Observe your Constellation and the Meta-representative for the Strand of Awareness of War and Conflict. Become aware of the Threads of Consciousness and the gifts that this phenomenological influence has had on yourself and your Family Lineage.

14. Repeat this Constellation for other wars and conflicts that have affected you, your Family Lineage, or your Current Family.

15. Journal about your experience with your Constellation involving War and Conflict.

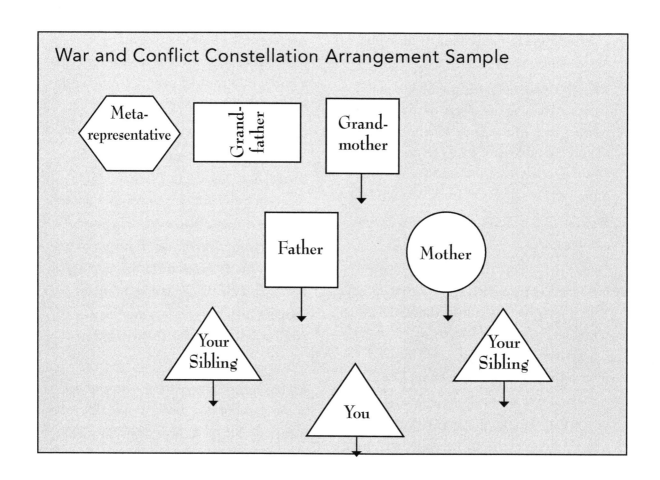

War and Conflict Constellation Arrangement Sample

Constellation Experience #8

If a family member(s) was a victim of harm

1. Place figurines to represent the victim(s) in your Family Lineage, the perpetrator(s), and a figurine for yourself.

2. Place a Meta-representative for the conflict/event/situation that occurred (e.g., robbery, physical assault, sexual boundary violation).

3. Become aware of your feelings. Notice who has been affected and how. Broaden your awareness. Allow time to fully observe each Representative and the Meta-representative.

4. Placing your figurine in front of or near the victim(s), select **Words of Empowerment** to acknowledge them, accept them, and agree to their fate. Complete the interaction with a slight bow.

5. Placing your figurine in front of the perpetrator, select one or more of the **Words of Empowerment** and say aloud or silently three times to acknowledge them, accept what has happened, and agree to all of it. Complete the interaction with a slight bow.

6. Leave the responsibility for their actions with them.

7. Place your figurine in front of the Meta-representative. Select one or more of the **Words of Empowerment to the Meta-representative** and say aloud or silently three times. Experiment with different Words of Empowerment. Complete the interaction with a slight bow.

8. Rearrange the figurines by placing the victim(s) and perpetrator(s) standing next to each other. Place the Meta-representative beside the perpetrator.

9. Place your figurine several inches in front of the victim(s), perpetrator(s), and Meta-representative, facing forward. This symbolizes moving into life, leaving the conflict and energies of victim—perpetrator in the past and with them.

10. Journal about your experience with your Constellation involving Victim—Perpetrator.

Constellation Experience #9

If a family member(s) was a perpetrator of harm

1. Place figurines to represent the perpetrator(s) in your Family Lineage, the victim(s), and a figurine for yourself.

2. Place a Meta-representative for the conflict/event/situation that occurred (e.g., robbery, physical assault, sexual boundary violation).

3. Become aware of your feelings. Notice who has been affected and how. Broaden your awareness. Allow time to fully observe each Representative and the Meta-representative.

4. Placing your figurine in front of, or near the victim(s), select **Words of Empowerment** to acknowledge them, accept them and agree to their and your family member's fate. Complete the interaction with a slight bow.

5. Placing your figurine in front of the perpetrator(s), select one or more of the **Words of Empowerment** to acknowledge them, accept what has happened, and agree to all of it. Be sure to acknowledge that they are still part of your Family Lineage. Complete the interaction with a slight bow.

6. Leave the responsibility for their actions with them.

7. Place your figurine in front of the Meta-representative. Select one or more of the **Words of Empowerment to the Meta-representative** and say aloud or silently three times. Experiment with different Words of Empowerment. Complete the interaction with a slight bow.

8. Rearrange the figurines by placing the victim(s) and perpetrator(s) standing next to each other. Place the Meta-representative beside the perpetrator.

9. Place your figurine several inches in front of the victim(s), perpetrator(s), and Meta-representative, facing forward. This symbolizes moving into life, leaving the conflict and energies of victim—perpetrator in the past and with them.

10. Journal about your experience with your Constellation involving Perpetrator—Victim.

Constellation Experience #10

If you were a victim of harm

1. Place a figurine to represent yourself and the perpetrator(s).

2. Place a Meta-representative for the conflict/event/situation that occurred (e.g., robbery, physical assault, sexual boundary violation).

3. Become aware of your feelings. Notice how you have been affected. Broaden your awareness. Allow time to fully observe each Representative and the Meta- representative.

4. Placing your figurine in front of the perpetrator(s), select one or more of the **Words of Empowerment** and say aloud or silently three times to acknowledge them, accept what has happened, and agree to all of it. Complete the interaction with a slight bow.

5. Leave the responsibility for their actions with them.

6. Place your figurine in front of the Meta-representative. Select one or more of the **Words of Empowerment to the Meta-representative** and say aloud or silently three times. Experiment with different Words of Empowerment. Complete the interaction with a slight bow.

7. Place your figurine several inches in front of the perpetrator(s), and Meta-representative, facing forward. This symbolizes moving into life, leaving the conflict and energies of victim— perpetrator in the past.

8. Journal about your experience with your Constellation involving Victim— Perpetrator.

Constellation Experience #11

If you were a perpetrator of harm

1. Place a figurine to represent yourself and the victim(s).

2. Place a Meta-representative for the conflict/event/situation that occurred (e.g., robbery, physical assault, sexual boundary violation).

3. Become aware of your feelings. Notice how you have been affected. Broaden your awareness. Allow time to fully observe each Representative and the Meta- representative.

4. Placing your figurine in front of the victim(s), select one or more of the **Words of Empowerment** and say aloud or silently three times to acknowledge them, accept what has happened, and agree to take responsibility for your actions to balance the scales. Complete the interaction with a slight bow.

5. Place your figurine in front of the Meta-representative. Select one or more of the **Words of Empowerment to the Meta-representative** and say aloud or silently three times. Experiment with different Words of Empowerment. Complete the interaction with a slight bow.

6. Move the victim(s) figurine several inches away from your figurine, facing towards their life. Face your figurine in a different direction. Move your figurine several inches away from the Meta-representative. This symbolizes moving into life, leaving the conflict and energies of victim—perpetrator in the past.

7. Journal about your experience with your Constellation involving Perpetrator-Victim.

The next two Constellation Experiences focus on the themes of Immigration that Affected Your Family Lineage and Migration that Affected You or Your Family Lineage.

Constellation Experiences #12

The Immigration that Affected Your Family Lineage

1. Open your journal to a new entry. Title it "Reflections on Immigration and Migration."

2. Gather numerous small figurines including one for yourself.

3. Allow yourself to be the *observer* looking into your Constellation.

4. Based on the answers in your Reflections, decide which lineage—Father's, Mother's, Family of Origin, or Current Family—you want to look at. Have at least three generations represented: those who stayed in the Country of Origin; those who immigrated; and those born, raised, or now living in the new land.

5. In sequential order, place a Meta-representative for the Country of Origin. Then, a figurine(s) for the ancestor(s) who stayed behind, a figurine(s) for who immigrated, a figurine(s) for

who was born in this country, a Meta-representative for the United States, and a figurine for yourself.

6. **If you immigrated**, the Representatives will be the following: Country of Origin, those who stayed, yourself, the United States (or the country you migrated to), and your children, if any.

7. Take your time. Simply breathe and allow your Constellation to unfold one figurine at a time. As you place each member, call the name aloud or silently—either way, their Soul will hear.

8. Become aware of your feelings. Notice the effect Immigration has had on your Family Lineage. Broaden your awareness. Allow yourself time to really look at the Meta-representatives.

9. Rearrange the figurines so they are all facing forward, looking at you.

10. Place your figurine in front the relative(s) who immigrated. Select one or more of the **Words of Empowerment** (from page 202) and say them aloud or silently three times. Experiment with different Words of Empowerment.

11. Place your figurine in front of the relative(s) who stayed behind. Select one or more of the **Words of Empowerment** and say them aloud or silently three times. Complete the interaction with a slight bow.

12. Place your figurine in front of your Country of Origin. Select one or more of the **Words of Empowerment to the Meta-representative** and say aloud or silently three times. Complete the interaction with a slight bow.

13. Place your figurine in front of the relative(s) who was/were born in the United States. Select one or more of the **Words of Empowerment** and say them aloud or silently three times.

14. Place your figurine in front of the United States. Select one or more of the **Words of Empowerment to the Meta-representative** and say aloud or silently three times. Complete the interaction with a slight bow.

15. Create the final arrangement by placing your figurine slightly in front of the United States facing forward. If your children are represented place them next to you. (See diagram)

16. Observe your Constellation and the Meta-representative for the Country of Origin and the United States or destination country. Become aware of the Threads of Consciousness and the gifts that this phenomenological influence of Immigration has had on yourself and your Family Lineage.

17. Repeat this Constellation for the other side of your Family Lineage or Current Family.

18. Journal about your experience with your Constellation involving Immigration.

Immigration Constellation Arrangement Sample

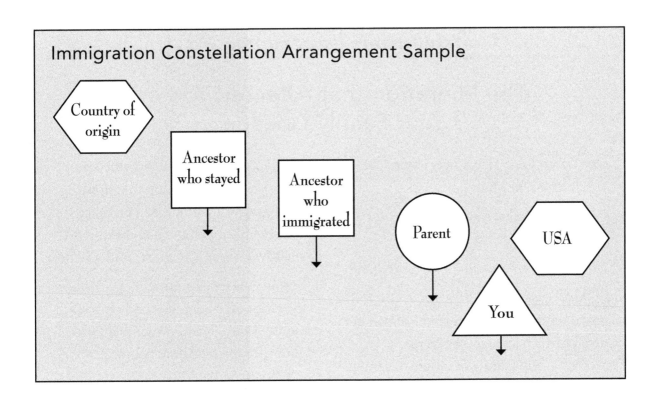

Constellation Experience #13

The Migration that Affected You or Your Family Lineage

1. Open your journal to a new entry. Title it "Reflections on Migration."

2. Gather numerous small figurines including one for yourself.

3. Allow yourself to be the *observer* looking into your Constellation.

4. Based on the answers in your Reflections, decide which lineage—Father's, Mother's, and Family of Origin, Current Family or your own—migration you want to look at.

5. In sequential order, place a Meta-representative for the place of birth. Next to this, place a Meta-representative figurine for relatives associated with the place of birth. Then, place a figurine to represent each significant location lived. Place figurines next to each location to represent important relationships associated with each location. Continue until the current place of living for yourself or the relative you have chosen to work with is placed. Finally, place your figurine.

6. Take your time. Simply breathe and allow your Constellation to unfold one figurine at a time. As you place each member, call the name aloud or silently—either way, their Soul will hear.

7. Become aware of your feelings. Notice the effect Migration has had on your Family Lineage and/or yourself. Broaden your awareness. Allow yourself time to really look at the Meta-representatives.

8. Rearrange the figurines so they are all facing forward, looking at you.

9. Place the figurine for yourself in front of the Meta-representative for the place of birth. Select one or more of the **Words of Empowerment to the Meta-representative** (from page 202) and say them aloud or silently three times. Experiment with different Words of Empowerment.

10. Place your figurine in front of the relative(s) from the place of birth. Select one or more of the **Words of Empowerment** and say them aloud or

silently three times. Experiment with different Words of Empowerment. Complete the interaction with a slight bow.

11. Continue with each location and Representatives until your figurine is in front of your current home. Complete the interaction with a slight bow.

12. Create the final arrangement by placing your figurine slightly in front of your current home facing forward. (See diagram)

13. Journal about your experience with your Constellation involving Migration.

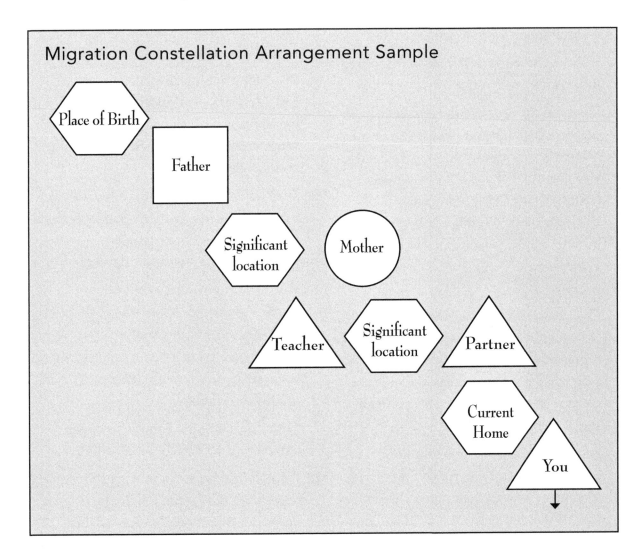

Migration Constellation Arrangement Sample

Place of Birth

Father

Significant location

Mother

Teacher

Significant location

Partner

Current Home

You

Constellation Experience #14

The Religion(s) of Your Family Lineage

1. Open your journal to a new entry. Title it "Reflections on Religion."

2. Gather numerous small figurines including one for yourself.

3. Allow yourself to be the *observer* looking into your Constellation.

4. Based on the answers in your Reflections, decide which lineage—Father's, Mother's, or a combination of both—do you want to look at? If the religious tradition(s) spans several generations, use figurines extending to the great-grandparents. *(parent, grandparent, great-grandparent)*

5. If you have chosen to work with both lineages set up one side then the other. In sequential order, place a Meta-representative for the religious tradition, a figurine(s) for the ancestor(s) of each generation, and a figurine for yourself.

6. Take your time. Simply breathe and allow your Constellation to unfold one figurine at a time. As you place each member, call their name aloud or silently—either way, their Soul will hear.

7. Become aware of your feelings. Notice the effect religion has had on your Family Lineage. Broaden your awareness. Allow yourself time to really look at the Meta-representative(s).

8. Rearrange the figurines until you feel a sense of resolution between the Representatives and Meta-representatives. Reflect on your feelings and insights.

9. Turn all the Representatives to face your figurine, placing them in the generational Order of Precedence (parents, grandparents, great-grandparents).

10. Place your figurine in front of your parents' figurines. Select one or more of the **Words of Empowerment** (from page 221) and say them aloud or silently three times. Experiment with different Words of Empowerment.

11. Continue along the Family Lineage, completing with each Representative.

12. Place your figurine in front of the Meta-representative for the religion(s) of your ancestors. Select one or more of the

Words of Empowerment to the Meta-representative and say aloud or silently three times. Experiment with different Words of Empowerment. Complete the interaction with a slight bow.

13. Create a final arrangement by placing your figurine slightly in front of your parent's figurine, everyone facing forward. Then place your Father's Lineage behind your right side at a slight angle extending backward. Do the same for your Mother's Lineage on your left side. The Meta-representative for Religion will be positioned behind the oldest generation. (See diagram)

14. Observe your Constellation and the Meta-representative(s) for religion(s). Become aware of the Threads of Consciousness and the gifts that this phenomenological influence of Religion has had on yourself and your Family Lineage.

15. Repeat this Constellation for the other side of your Family Lineage or Current Family.

16. Journal about your experience with your Constellation involving Religion.

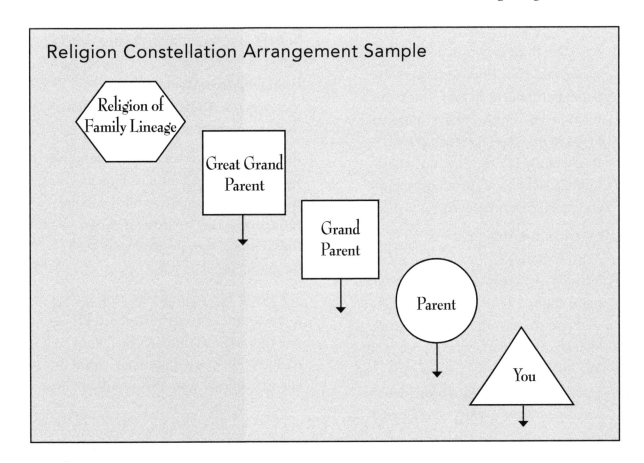

Religion Constellation Arrangement Sample

The three Constellation Experiences that follow focus on Your Parents' Relationship, What You Bring into Relationship, and Your Current Relationship.

Constellation Experience #15

Your Parents' Relationship

1. Open your journal to a new entry. Title it "Reflections on my Parents' Relationship."

2. Gather numerous small figurines including one for yourself.

3. Allow yourself to be the *observer* looking into your Constellation.

4. Based on the answers in your Reflection questions, place Representatives for the major influence(s) on your parents' relationship. These are the things each brought into the relationship from their Family Lineage and the major influence(s) that occurred during the course of their relationship.

5. In sequential order, place a Representative for your father on the left side of your working surface. Then place slightly behind him, figurines to represent the following: any prior significant relationships to your mother, unresolved relationships from his Family Lineage, Meta-representatives for any phenomenological influence that significantly impacted him, such as mental illness, immigration, or death.

6. Repeat for your mother, with her figurine placed on the right side of your working surface. Slightly behind her, situate the major influences she brought into the relationship with your father from her Family Lineage, and life before your father such as previous relationships, child (children) from previous marriage(s), strong religious conviction, or estrangement with a sibling.

7. Be sure to leave enough space in between your mother's and father's figurines to place Representatives for the major influence(s) that occurred during the course of their relationship. (See diagram, Step 1)

8. Take your time. Simply breathe and allow your Constellation to unfold one figurine at a time. As you place each member, call their name aloud or silently—either way, their Soul will hear.

9. Become aware of your feelings. Notice what each parent brought into the relationship. Broaden your awareness. Allow yourself time to really look at each Representative and each Meta-representative.

10. Bring your awareness to your mother and father. Place in between them the major influence(s) that affected their relationship during the course of their time together, such as death of either one or a child, a significant migration or immigration, addiction, severe physical disease, etc. (See diagram, step 2)

11. Become aware of your feelings. Notice all that happened in your parents' relationship. Allow yourself time to really look at each Representative and each Meta-representative.

12. Rearrange the figurines so they are all facing forward, looking at you.

13. Place a figurine for yourself facing the Constellation.

14. If there is anyone or any Meta-influence that you feel an Entanglement with, use the practices that you have learned through TCA to disentangle.

15. Return your figurine to face the entire Constellation.

16. Select one or more of the **Words of Empowerment** (from page 246) and say them aloud or silently three times. Experiment with different Words of Empowerment.

17. Complete the interaction by bowing.

18. You may end here or if you wish to continue with your partner or potential partner turn your figurine to face forward, back open to your Family Lineage.

19. Place a figurine for your current partner or for a potential partner facing your figurine.

20. Say to your partner or potential partner:

This is where I come from.
I bring all of this and more into our relationship.

21. Create the final arrangement by placing the figurine for your partner/potential partner next to you. (See final diagram)

22. Observe your Parents' Relationship Constellation. Become aware of the Threads of Consciousness and the gifts that your parents' relationship has had upon you.

23. Journal about your experience with your Parents' Relationship Constellation.

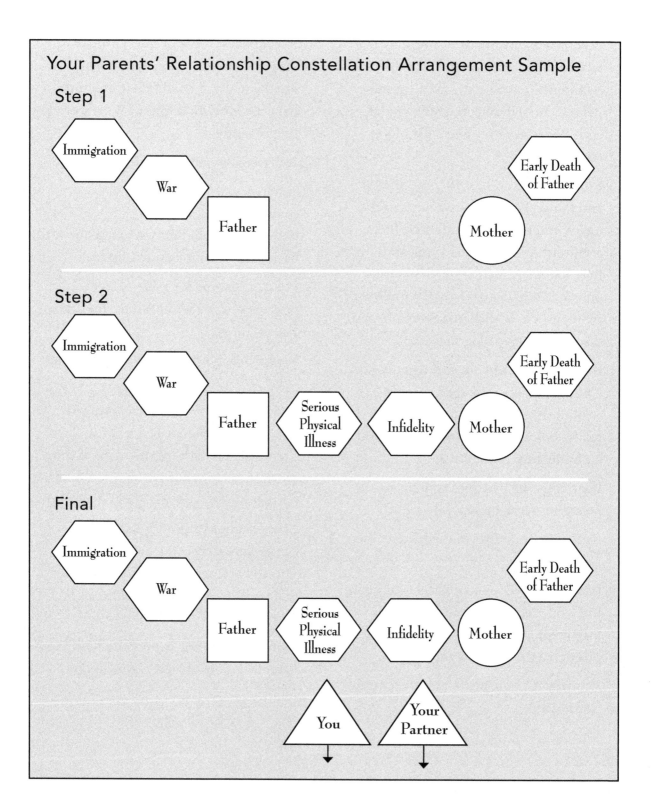

Constellation Experience #16

What You Bring into Relationship

1. Open your journal to a new entry. Title it "Reflections on what I bring into Relationship."

2. Gather numerous small figurines including one for yourself.

3. Allow yourself to be the *observer* looking into your Constellation.

4. Based on the answers in your Reflection questions, place Representatives for the major influence on your life. These are the things that you bring into any intimate relationship from your Family Lineage, and the major influence(s) that occurred during the course of your life.

5. In sequential order place a Representative for yourself, slightly behind your figurine any prior significant relationships, children, terminated pregnancies, unresolved relationships from your Family Lineage, and Meta-representatives for any phenomenological influence(s) such as physical illness, conflict, immigration, religion or deaths that have strongly impacted you.

6. Take your time. Simply breathe and allow your Constellation to unfold one figurine at a time. As you place each member, call her or his name aloud or silently—either way, their Soul will hear.

7. Become aware of your feelings. Allow yourself time to really look at each Representative and each Meta-representative. Broaden your awareness.

8. Turn your figurine to face the Constellation.

9. If there is anyone or any Meta-influence that you feel an Entanglement with, use the practices that you have learned through TCA to disentangle.

10. Return your figurine to the front of the Constellation, facing forward with your back to your Family Lineage and prior relationships. If you have a child (children) from a prior relationship, place him or her next to you.

11. Become aware of your feelings. Notice all that you bring into relationship.

12. Journal about your experience of what you bring into a Relationship Constellation.

Constellation Experience #17

Your Relationship

1. Open your journal to a new entry. Title it "Reflections on My Relationship."

2. Gather numerous small figurines including one for yourself.

3. Allow yourself to be the *observer* looking into your Constellation.

4. Set up and complete your "What I bring into Relationship" Constellation.

5. Based on the answers in your Reflection questions concerning your partner, you will create a Phenomenological Approach Constellation for the major influences on his or her life that you are aware of. These are the things brought into your relationship from his or her Family Lineage and any major influence prior to meeting you.

6. Place a figurine for your partner and slightly behind him or her, major influences brought into your relationship, such as previous relationships, child (children) from previous marriage(s), death of a parent, physical disease, war, strong religious conviction, or estrangement with a sibling.

7. Be sure to leave enough space between your figurine and your partners to place Representatives for the major influence that occurred during the course of your relationship, similar to your Parents Relationship Constellation.

8. Take your time. Simply breathe and allow your Constellation to unfold one figurine at a time. As you place each member, call her or his name aloud or silently—either way, their Soul will hear.

9. Become aware of your feelings. Allow yourself time to really look at each Representative and each Meta-representative associated with your partner.

10. Broaden your awareness as you take in all that your partner has experienced prior to you. Take your time. Let the field show you the Entanglements. Notice if there is anything unresolved for your partner or for yourself in relation to your partner's life. Try to develop a feeling of compassion.

11. Turn your figurine and the figurine for your partner to face each other.

12. Select one or more of the **Words of Empowerment** and say them aloud or silently three times. Experiment with different Words of Empowerment.

13. Complete the interaction with your partner by bowing to him or her.

14. You may end here or if you wish to continue with your partner place Representatives and Meta-representatives in between your figurines for the major influence that have occurred during the course of your relationship such as serious physical disease, death of a sibling, migration, terminated pregnancy, children or infidelity.

15. Observe your Relationship Constellation. Notice if there is anything unresolved between you and your partner. This is where your work lays in finding peace. Become aware of the Threads of Consciousness and the gifts that your relationship has had upon you.

16. Journal about your experience with your Relationship Constellation.

Relationship Disentanglement[45]

Choose a relationship, past or present, where you feel unresolved and may have lingering feelings such as anger, guilt, blame, or resentment. Ask for the assistance of his or her ancestors as well as your own.

Center yourself.

Begin by saying, silently or aloud from your heart, his or her full name:

"Dear_____, I am releasing
all negative emotional reactions, including
guilt, anger, anxiety, resentment, that I have
been holding and projecting towards you. I ask
you to forgive me for any hurts or harm you
believe I have caused you. I take responsibility
for my part of what went wrong in our
relationship, and any harm I may have caused.

I let you take responsibility for your part of
what went wrong in our relationship, and
any harm you may have caused. I am grateful
for the good things, such as _____, _____,
_____, that I received from you.

I wish you well. You will always have a place
in my heart.

---

45   Adapted from a meditation taught to us by Ralph Metzner

Appendix A

Family Constellations — Historical Development

The fundamental idea that the family is an interactive unit affected by past generations and that it operates by a set of unifying principles is at the foundation of Family Therapy. Its evolution can be traced by following the development of influential theories and approaches pioneered by Murray Bowen, Virginia Satir, Salvador Minuchin, the MRI group in Palo Alto, and the Milan Group in Italy.

Beginning in the early 60s, renowned family therapist Virginia Satir recognized that a symptom manifest in one member of the family had a function in balancing the system, and that system had a part in maintaining the symptom. Over time, Satir and others expanded on this concept and established a three-generational model called Family Reconstruction.

Family Therapy grew from practice to theory as Salvador Minuchin began his model of Structural Family Therapy, focusing on family hierarchy and boundaries, and the belief that interventions could aid families in interacting productively. Around the same time, the Milan Group in Italy began to work with families and concluded that many issues involved the family as a whole, not just an individual; they also observed a repetition of patterns from one generation to another.

One of the first therapists to concentrate on the family of origin was Murray Bowen. At the core of Bowen's theory was the concept of differentiation — examining the degree of emotional reactivity to one's family. His focus was helping individuals to avoid becoming "swallowed-up" by predicable family dynamics. Strategic Family Therapy and later Brief Therapy developed as an outgrowth of the work of Gregory Bateson, Paul Watzlawick, Richard Fisch, and the MRI Palo Alto group on patterns of family communication.

Jay Haley, and former wife, Cloé Madanes, emerged as leaders in the field using the teachings and techniques of Milton Erickson, M.D., a distinguished hypnotherapist whose work concentrated on interactive patterns. These are just a few of the major theorists who helped create a body of knowledge and a way of intervening with individuals, couples, and families that went beyond the confines of psychodynamic work. Among their seminal ideas was the notion that the individual symptom should be seen as a function of the whole system—and the therapeutic focus should be expanded to include all members of the family.

In Jacob and Zerka Moreno's Psychodrama methodology, clients assigned family members to act out other roles within the family to help the clients realize unconscious dynamics in the family. Family Sculpting, created by Virginia Satir and advanced by Fred and Bunny Duhl and David Kantor, was considered an effective method of blending the cognitive and the experiential by physically arranging the family members as the client sees them, so that a goal of re-shaping the family could occur. While Family Constellations also use visual representation, the practice is unlike Psychodrama and Family Sculpting in that representatives stand quietly and allow themselves to experience the internal impact of the family dynamics, manifest through the Constellation set up by the client.

Bert Hellinger added significantly to Family Therapy by offering new insights to systemic psychotherapy—what he calls "orders of love." He has shown that love is at work behind all human behavior; that there is a great need for balance in giving and taking, and in gain and loss within any system; and that every member, living or dead, has an equal right to belong. Hellinger's Family Constellations are also distinctive in other aspects, including his focus on the healing power of the Soul.

Appendix B

Key Constellation Approach Concepts

There is no limit to the good you can do in the world, as long as you don't care who gets the credit.

—Fr. Strickland, Jesuit priest

The Essential Steps of a Constellation

The Constellation Approach follows a few essential steps, which can be applied in either a Systemic or Phenomenological Constellation. The first three steps create the Constellation. Steps 3 through 7 takes place within the Constellation Energy Field as the Constellation progresses towards resolution. These seven steps correlate to the Phases of a Constellation in Chapter 4.

1. The Client presents a clear issue to the facilitator. An issue that is related to specific facts and/or persons will achieve the best results. When the Client is direct about his or her need for help with a specific issue, the intention and direction are established for a shift in consciousness to occur.
2. Representatives are selected based on the information presented by the client. They are chosen from the Participant Energy Field, or figurines can be used as described in the Constellation Experiences.
3. The Client or Facilitator sets up the Constellation by placing the Representatives with little or no words spoken. Time is allowed for Representatives to become quiettly attentive and aware of their feelings in relation to the other Representatives. This time also encourages the Client to open up to the Emotional Level of Consciousness.

4. Both the Client and Facilitator observe the Constellation, noticing the directions in which Representatives are facing and any emotional or physical sensations that may manifest. This is the step of Acknowledging What Is.

5. The Client enters the Constellation. Representatives may react by turning their body direction in relation to each other or the Client. Often the Faciliator encourages Representatives to move into relative close proximity depending upon the issue being explored.

6. Words of Empowerment are introduced to facilitate movement through the Levels of Consciousness.

7. The Threads of Consciousness are followed through the Client's Family Lineage, from the eldest generation to the present until resolution occurs for the Client or the Constellation feels complete.

Three Kinds of Constellations

1. **Facilitator-directed Constellations** offer the best learning opportunity because they usually unfold methodically and can be readily understood by beginning participants and students. In this kind of Constellation, the Facilitator guides the process, steering the Client and Representatives towards reconciliation.

2. **Movements of the Soul Constellations** are most affective for participants who are already familiar with the Constellation Approach process and have participated in several Constellations as both Client and Representatives. Representatives in this kind of a Constellaiton have learned to differentiate between emotions or movements that may trigger their own issues, versus staying grounded and fully conscious in their role as a Representative. Representatives move from position to position in the Constelation as guided by Family Soul Consciousness—the "invisible conductor." These un-facilitated movements can give the Client a very different perspective on the issues initially presented. The Client ordinarily does not enter into the

Family Energy Field until several or all of the Representatives have moved from their original placement.

3. **Spirit-Mind Constellations** are reserved for advanced students and participants who have attended numerous seminars. These Constellations involve delicate dance-like movements. Representatives walk slowly, interact wordlessly, and move continually until resolution, as both the Client and Facilitator observe from outside the Family Energy Field. As a participant observing a Spirit-Mind Constellation, it can be difficult to comprehend the meaning of these improvised, spontaneosly choreographed steps. Yet, for the Client, it may reveal hidden personal truths that touch the depths of his or her Soul — another portal of healing. Needless to say, these Constellations require a significant amount of trust on the part of everyone involved. In most cases interpretation is left up to the Client.

The Practice of Rounds

A **Round** is a process in which each person in a Constellation group has an opportunity to speak briefly, one at a time. During seminars as well as the Immersion Program, Rounds strengthen the interconnectedness of the group, clarify purpose, and support the integration process. In the first Round, participants are invited to state the issue they are currently working on or what they would like to receive from a Constellation. When intentions are spoken aloud, they align one's inner compass with the outer world and support movement towards wholeness. This first Round also encourages everyone in the Participant Energy Field to become fully present and invested in their own healing.

The purpose of a second Round (generally, later in the day) is to allow participant to share their experiences of observing and participating in the Constellations. This process is one of integration, giving participants a chance to claim their new awareness, including any emotional catharsis they may have experienced or new insights they have gained. This in turn, grounds the transformation in their body-mind and supports the probability of lasting change.

Being a Representative

The role of a **Representative** in a Constellation is akin to being a musician in an ensemble. Each Representative plays a part in relation to the whole. Like an invisible conductor, the consciousness of the Family Soul directs the flow of energy from one Representative to another, as the Constellation unfolds. Together the Representatives can create a complete composition to heal the Client.

Just as in an ensemble, there are times when a Representative may be more active—like performing a solo. But if the Representative overplays his or her part, the entire composition suffers. A consciously attuned Representative can immerse her/himself in their role and allow the energies to lead them individually, while not losing their connection to the overall progression of the Constellation. The key to being an authentic Representative is to hold an "egoless" state—to to surrender one's personality and any intention of improving or helping the client. It is also important to set aside any personal fear of what the Constellation may reveal.

Before stepping into the role of Representative, consider saying these phrases quietly to yourself:

"I am not (your name)."

"I am the Representative for (the person you are representing—father, mother, sister, grandmother, etc.)."

"I am of service to (the name of the Client) and their Family Soul."

"I am also of service to myself and my Family Soul."

This last statement is a conscious opening to whatever personal healing or learning may occur while one is in the role of a Representative or Meta-represenative.

Natural Movements in The Constellation Approach

There are **Natural Movements** in Constellations that ensure a gentle and harmonious unfolding. For example, the Client or Representative for the Client moves towards the parent, older generation, perpetrator, or Meta-representative, eventually entering the Vesica Pisces. Following these Natural Movements below will help make a strong energetic connection. Once a connection is forged, feelings can be transformed, conflicts dissolved, and powerful shifts in consciousness can occur.

1. **Children move towards their parents.** It is important for the child to enter the Vesica Pisces with the parent. This movement mimics a returning to the source of where we originated.

2. **Younger generations move towards older generations.** If the older generation moves into the Vesica Pisces of the younger generation, it can feel forced, as if going against the natural flow of energy.

3. **Victims move towards Perpetrators.** If the Perpetrator moves towards the Victim, no matter how well intended, the Victim will perceive this movement as a threat and retreat physically or energetically. The Perpetrator must bear the weight of their responsibility and wait for the healing to come to them. Each step the Victim takes toward the Perpetrator is a step in the direction of reconciliation and peace for both.

4. **Immigrants and Migrants move towards their homelands.** Meta-representatives in a Constellation remain mostly stationary in their role as a country or homeland, similar to the land itself. They cannot come to us, either in life or in a Constellation. Clients and Representatives move towards and eventually into the Vesica Pisces of these Meta-representatives, wherein the connection ensues and becomes rooted in our Individual Energy Field.

The Role of Physical Contact

Although most healing in Constellations is accomplished through our Individual Energy Fields, there are times when physical contact can help facilitate the transmission of energy. For example, once we're inside the Vesica Pisces, a tender touch can carry us deeper into our emotions or even elevate us into Soul Consciousness. Never forced or coerced, physical contact should be gentle—and minimal. Touch is often the culmination of the energetic healing process.

For instance, a child holding the hand of a Representative of his or her parent, or a grandmother placing her hand on a child's shoulder connects their two Individual Energy Fields. It may also be appropriate for partners to hold hands in silence when facing their future; or, as in the ways of the ancient traditions, participants may touch foreheads or use another gesture that is mindful and respectful.

Physical contact can complete a ritual, so the movement of releasing should be slow and graceful. Any sudden movements are to be avoided as they are jarring to the Individual and Family Energy Fields.

Wordless Representation

Representatives do not need to speak to be effective in their role. With practice we can learn to be fully present and of service to the Client without saying a word. Wordless representation is an essential part of learning how to fully embody the spirit of the person we are representing and transmit their consciousness. As a Representative or Facilitator, the practice of silence helps carefully attune to shifts in consciousness during a Constellation.

A seasoned Representative often repeats silently to himself or herself, like a mantra, the Words of Empowerment that come organically. At a certain point, he or she releases any attachment to the words or language and simply allows the consciousness moving through them to be expressed. This alchemical blend of the Representative's energy and the Client's within the Vesica Pisces transforms the consciousness of both, and is not dependent in any way on an exchange of words.

A Constellation Journeyer
Richard — Returning

It was time for me to meet my "father." We began, standing maybe twelve-fifteen feet apart, just looking at each other. Not saying anything, the Representative for my father looked into my eyes with such love, the ice that had enveloped my heart for so many years started to melt, and my tears began to flow. I slowly stepped toward my "father," and the closer I got the more the emotions I had never allowed myself to feel started coming up. I said, "You are my father, and I am your son." My "father" simply held me. "I love you, Daddy," was all I could say. The years, decades really, of denial, sadness, and self-hatred drained away. It was the first time in seventy-one years that I allowed myself to feel love for my father.

Representation in Spirit-Mind Constellations

A Spirit-Mind Constellation is a practice of slowly engaging energy bodies, using nonverbal communication, and moving through the Four Levels of Consciousness to the Soul Level. These are the most advanced form of Constellations in the Constellation Approach. They are non-directed and mostly wordless.

Following the Natural Movement guidelines and the physical practices of resolution (such as bowing, touching, embracing and releasing, foreheads meeting, leaning into one another, and reconciling), Representatives are guided by their intuition. To be a reliable Representative in a Spirit-Mind Constellations, please remember these guidelines:

1. In all likelihood, you will have had previous experience in Movements of the Soul Constellations and Wordless representation; and participated as a Client in Spirit-Mind Constellations.
2. Consciously, empty yourself of your own desires and needs.
3. Allow the energies of reconciliation and peace to transmit through each of your chakras and your Individual Energy Field without reservation.

A Spirit-Mind Constellation resembles the delicate unfolding of a flower, formerly hidden—but beautiful—truths revealed for all to see. We strongly encourage you to seek TCA guidance if you're contemplating a Spirit-Mind Constellation for the first time.

Self-Selecting as a Representative

Representatives enter a Constellation in one of three ways: they are selected by the Facilitator, chosen by the Client, or **Self-Select**. In Self-Selection, the Client calls the name of the person or Meta-influence they would like represented and waits for someone to stand in response. This manner of being of service offers a unique opportunity to become attuned to the Ancestral Energy Field.

When one self-selects as a Representative, it is imperative to release any personal attachments or needs, such as desiring to help or wanting to belong or be recognized. First, we sit in stillness and wait for the Ancestral Field to select us (or not). Sometimes the feeling that the Ancestral Field is selecting us manifests as a gut sense or intuition that we are meant to represent a specific person or Meta-influence. At other times, the Spirits of the ancestors will literally compel us—perhaps with the sensation of pounding heart or a strong urge to stand without knowing why. The more experienced we become as a Representative in Movements of the Soul and Spirit-Mind Constellations, the easier it is to be guided by the Ancestral Energy Field.

But when we're called or guided by the Ancestral Field to be a Representative, our participation always has significance for our own evolution of consciousness. More often than not, the insights, understanding and healing we receive arise during the fourth phase of the Constellation. This is when the powerful energy of Spirit-Mind consciousness sweeps through the entire Family Energy Field, affecting each one of us individually and collectively.

Appendix C

The Constellation Approach Immersion Program

I believe that to have world peace we must first have inner peace. Those who are naturally at peace with themselves will be open towards others. I think this is where the very foundation of universal peace lies.

—Tenzin Gyatso, 14th Dalai Lama

The Constellation Approach Immersion Program offers intensive journeys of exploration through your family lineage. The Program is a one-, two-, or three-year internal expedition into the on-going evolution of consciousness, both personal and collective. The process can be likened to an upward spiraling staircase, winding in an ever-widening arc that will expand virtually every aspect of your life and enhance your experience of peace. Each class will guide you further upward, while also helping to ground you powerfully in the here and now.

In Year One, you will begin the process of finding peace by focusing primarily on personal Constellations as a Client. This first year's work is about healing the self. You will read, study, learn new Constellation Approach concepts and experience the many different ways Constellations are practiced—through direct participation in each class.

During Year Two, you will deepen your understanding of the collective family consciousness, including the complexities and nuances of your family lineage, and the role of your ancestors. Healing and learning will emerge from repeated practical experience in the dual roles of Client and Representative, working on a wide range of issues. In order to fully grasp the dynamics of the Constellation Approach process, it's essential to experience both of these roles in the sacred circle so that complete healing can occur.

By Year Three, your knowledge of healing through the Constellation Approach will have expanded and broadened beyond the individual and familial levels to encompass humanity itself—and the role each of us is called to play. We will explore the societal implications of the Meta energies that influence every family and all of civilization. The shifts that happen during this time of mastery correspond to the Soul level of consciousness. Third-year students gain a comprehensive understanding of interconnected journeys of the individual Soul, family and ancestral lineage, and how the evolution of human consciousness occurs through many, many generations.

While developing the Constellation Approach over a number of years, we've come to believe that learning happens in a circular fashion. Everyone is equal, everyone is included, and everyone is a teacher in his/her own way. We also believe in the benefit of having different levels of experience within the same group. Beginning students not only learn from us as teachers and facilitators, but they also observe and learn from fellow students who have advanced to the second and third years of the Program. In this way, a model of courage and trust is created.

It's important to remember that no two Constellations are alike. They may be similar in method, but each person, each Constellation, offers new threads of healing, understanding, and learning for everyone participating—including us. Our goal always is to create an atmosphere of shared knowledge and wisdom that will support—much as how learning is transmitted in ancestral traditions. The older, more experienced members of the circle are not separated from, but rather available and of service to, the younger generation. Each person is on their own journey, yet still very much a part of the group, progressing together on the path of conscious evolution.

Acknowledgements

There are many people we want to acknowledge and thank, for without them, this book would have never come into being.

We bow to our Immersion Program students, seminar participants and private clients who trusted us to facilitate their Constellations over the past fourteen years. Without their willingness to open themselves to the unknown, we could never have experienced or understood the power and grace of the Family Energy Field.

We could not have honed the 'art and craft' of the Constellation Approach without the benefit of learning from some of the senior European facilitators of Family Constellations, first and foremost, Bert Hellinger; Hunter Beaumont, Stephan Hausner, Harold Hohnen, Judith Hemming, Claudia Mengel, Bella Roth, and Gunthard Weber.

We are indebted to the Tracking Wonder Consultancy, specifically our editors Jeffrey Davis and Tanya Robie, for their determined care and enthusiasm throughout. We also want to thank Holly Moxley, our main illustrator and book designer for all her creative effort and talent. Together they brought our dream to reality.

We feel sincere gratitude to the following people: Stephen Jimenez—a true Godsend, for his guiding words and gentle hand; Sandra Mayo for her fitting yet timeless art that graces our cover; Julia Cameron for inspiring our book cover; Mark Weiman of Regent Press for publishing our material; Jessica Eisner, our behind-the-scenes coordinator, for seamlessly assisting us with the office administration during this project.

We appreciate the continuous support of our colleagues from the Barbara Brennan healing community and those from the Metzner Alchemical Divination training for being an important part of the network of this sacred path.

Our dear friends—Joanna Seere, Craig Kay, Briege Farrelly, Karl Direske, Eyal Buchler, Myrna Finn, Clive Russ, and Carolyn Darling — we are deeply grateful to each of you for standing by us through the chaotic birthing process of writing. Michael Mervosh and The Hero's Journey Foundation, thank you for your generosity. Karin and Ron Aarons, and Ricci and Jack Coddington, we appreciate your steady support, clarity and kindness. Susan Ulfelder and Suzi Tucker, your initial encouragement has changed our lives completely, for the better.

A special note of appreciation goes to the Faust and Williams families, particularly our siblings—Linda, Corinne, Robert, Scott, Bonnie, Julie, Kenneth and Chris—for without you, we could have never been inspired to learn this work. We love you all so very much.

Glossary

Acknowledging, Accepting, and Agreeing: foundational concepts of TCA; corresponds to the Mental, Emotional and Spiritual Levels of Consciousness.

Acknowledging What Is: coined by Bert Hellinger; an invitation to objectively observe what has occurred in our lineages and our lives without rejection, blame, or judgment.

Act of Bowing: a way of showing respect or gratitude to someone who is honored; in TCA bowing is enacted in three ways: head, waist and full prostration; used particularly in relation to parents.

Alchemy: a power or process that changes or transforms something in a mysterious or special way.

Ancestral Blessing: feeling that is bestowed by Representative of ancestor while Client is enacting the bow of full prostration (Deep Bow) or in state of deep surrender.

Ancestral Energy Field: the unseen, guiding force attributed to the members of a Family Lineage that have gone before us; familial forbearers.

Ancestral Lineage Healing: (*i.e.* Family Lineage Healing), a path to explore our Family Lineage, to find peace, to evolve and to experience our Soul nature; the basis of TCA.

Auric Field: (*i.e.* the Individual Energy Field), formed by the emanation of the seven chakras; extends approximately the arm's length of our body in 360° or greater.

Awakened Consciousness: unhindered perception, a way of perceiving that is non-dualistic, unifying, and mindful.

Balance: the family system's state of equilibrium maintained trans-generationally.

Bond of Joy: the Soul Bond of creating life through birth connecting four family lines—paternal and maternal lineages of each of one's parents.

Bond of Sorrow: the Soul Bond that occurs when the life of another person is taken; connects both the perpetrator and the victim's Family Lineages.

Chakra System: Sanskrit for 'wheel;' part of the subtle body made up of seven or more important energy vortices that emanate from the front, back, top of head and bottom of torso of the physical body; corresponds to the major organs through which life force moves; creates the Individual Energy Field or aura.

Client: the person actively working on a stated issue within a Constellation.

Collective/Societal Conscience: the set of shared beliefs, ideas, and moral attitudes that operate as a unifying force within society; has continual effect on people; includes Family Conscience.

Congenital Essence: all the energetic qualities that are inherited from our parents that become the basis for a person's individual energy signature.

Constellation: (see also Family Constellation); any brilliant cluster, gathering or collection; the placement of people or place-markers that depicts a relationship and/or situation in one's life; reflects inner feelings and images which are unknowingly carried, bringing new and different perspectives to light.

Cord of Our Being: symbolic representation of a person and each of his/her parents; three cords that create the Rope of Time.

Country of Origin: the country/countries where ancestors originate that link each descendant to the energies of those homelands; the traits and qualities of the land and its people; where bloodlines began.

Desire: the essential requirement for the forward progression of Soul's evolution.

Destiny: what each person creates from her/ his fate.

Doorway of Existence: TCA concept; made up of two halves—one half, father; the other half, mother; from which one's unique entrance into life began; shared with biological siblings.

Energy Medicine: the belief and practice that consciousness resides in fields of energy that surround as well as permeate the body; a healing technique or modality.

Enlightened Love: profound love and understanding, once recognized is unforgettable.

Entanglement: attitudes, feelings, and particular fates that belong to others that one may unconsciously believe are their own; when involved unconsciously in another Soul's affairs.

Facilitator: guide or director of a Constellation.

Familial Archetype: a role that a male or female may inhabit within their family system.

Family Conscience: holds every family member's personal histories, different fates, and important life events; originates within the system and safeguards the right of membership for all who belong to the family, protecting and bonding them.

Family Constellation: created by Bert Hellinger; the placement of people or place-markers that depicts a relationship and/or situation in one's life; reflects inner feelings and images which are unknowingly carried, bringing new and different perspectives to light.

Family Energy Field : TCA concept; subtle body of consciousness created by a Family Constellation specific to the Client working that depicts a unique representation of their family; *a.k.a.* Family Soul.

Family Lineage: a line of descendants from one's biological father or mother.

Family Soul: the combined consciousness that is made up of each family member's individual Soul; *a.k.a.* Family Energy Field.

Fate: inherited strengths/weaknesses a person uses to create one's destiny.

Four Phases of a Constellation: step-by-step process of unfolding through the four Levels of Consciousness that include conceptual thinking, physical sensation, emotional response, and time.

Greater Conscience: beyond the personality and egoic levels; that which draws a person forward into life; Spirit-Mind.

Guilt: emotional experience that occurs when a person, accurately or not, has deviated from the order of the group (family); when our belonging is endangered.

Guilty Feelings: a repetitive cycle of emotional entanglement based upon the fear of experiencing the consequences of deviation from or not belonging to the group (family).

Inclusion: each member belongs equally to the family; similarly respected regardless of personal qualities or particular action or behavior; encompasses both the living and the departed.

Individual Conscience: inner sense of right and wrong; unconsciously directed by the Family and Collective/Societal Conscience.

Individual Energy Field: the subtle body that surrounds the physical body formed by the seven major chakras; also called the aura, auric field, and Human Energy Field.

Inner Feminine: receptive and magnetic; emotional, sensory, perceptual, nurturing, and caregiving.

Inner Masculine: generative and expressive; investigating, probing, searching, and penetrating.

Innocence: a feeling that exists while no deviation from the order of the group (family) exists.

Levels of Consciousness: four aspects that intersect, permeate, and affect all aspects of our being; Mental, Physical, Emotional, and Spiritual.

Love and Loyalty: an individual's deep commitment to the family; potentially becomes distorted through entanglement with another family member's difficult fate or issue.

Meta-representative: a participant (or figurine) that stands in for a Phenomenological Influence or non-personal energy, such as illness, war, family religion, or ancestral homeland.

Movements of the Soul Constellations: non-Facilitator directed; Representatives move (walk from position to position) guided by sensations felt within the Family Energy Field; "invisible conductor" offering the Client a different perspective on their presenting issue.

Natural Movements (of Representatives): guided by the Orders of Love; the manner in which specific Representatives step toward one another and into the Vesica Pisces in a Constellation.

Orders of Love: patterns observed by Bert Hellinger; when in alignment, offer harmony and peace within the family; when out of alignment, create Entanglements; in TCA are named Precedence, Balance, and Inclusion.

Participant Energy Field: group of individuals in attendance at a Constellation seminar or program that support the process occurring between a Client and Representative(s) within a Constellation.

Perpetrator: a person who commits, or is responsible for, wrongdoing; something illegal, criminal, morally wrong.

Phenomenon(a): any incident(s) deserving inquiry and investigation; event that is particularly unusual or of distinctive importance.

Phenomenological Constellation: non-systemic, i.e. includes Representative(s) not part of the family system (called Meta-representative); ex. country of origin, war, congenital illness.

Precedence: a person or persons who were chronologically the first to enter the hierarchy of the family; ex. 1) sibling birth order; 2) first marriage is first, second marriage is next.

Rings of Influence: similar to magnetic fields; shapes and affects the family conscience by conscious and unconscious means; ex. congenital illness, religious belief, ethnicity, political affiliation, gender, nationality.

Representative: a group participant, place-marker or figurine that stands in for a family member or important person to the Client working and is placed in a Constellation.

Round: when each person in the group is given the opportunity to speak briefly, either about a current issue or their present feelings.

Samskaras: impressions or traces of past deeds; the imprints left within the subconscious mind by experiences that a person has brought into this incarnation from previous lifetimes.

Soul: consciousness residing within the physical body.

Soul Agreements: contracts that we have to support each other in this lifetime.

Soul Bond: strongest bond among individuals, families, and groups via birth and death; ex. the birth of a child; taking the life of another.

Soul Field: includes all relations—the entirety of one's Family Lineages; those who are living and those departed; may include ancient ancestors, spiritual teachers, elders and guides.

Soul-Level Awareness: occurs upon pursuit of a path of awakening; in TCA through Soul Agreements and agreeing to our Soul nature.

Source: consciousness that exists outside of time and space.

Spirit: consciousness that resides outside of our physical body; i.e. animal spirits, ancestor spirits, spirits of place, plant spirits.

Spirit-Mind: ineffable; the ultimate flow that carries life forward; guides the Soul beyond the egoic levels of personality, gender, ethnicity, nationality, religion and more.

Spirit-Mind Constellations: advanced; Representatives walk slowly, interact wordlessly, and move continually until resolution of the Constellation occurs.

Strands of Awareness: *i.e.* Ten Universal Themes of TCA; components include the Threads of Consciousness.

Suspending Moral Judgment: to pause, postpone, or interrupt one's usual way of perceiving a situation and open to greater levels of awareness and understanding.

Systemic Constellation: includes members of the Family Lineages (parents, their siblings, grandparents, great grandparents, our siblings), current family (partner, children, grandchildren, step or adoptive children) or relationships (past, current).

Systemic Approach: a Systemic Constellation that is resolved via a step-by-step process moving trans-generationally from the oldest generation toward the current.

The Constellation Approach (TCA): a method of Family Lineage Healing practiced through the lens of three modalities: Family Constellations, energy healing; and conscious awakening to our Soul.

Tears of Regret: tears released when a person encounters a loss; connects with a deep longing, or faces responsibility for one's actions.

Tears of Relief: tears released after a breakthrough of resistance; feeling love within the depths of one's heart and Soul.

Ten Universal Themes: (*i.e.* Strands of Awareness) Family of Origin, Father's Lineage, Mother's Lineage, Sibling Relationships, Disease—Illness, Death, War—Conflict, Immigration—Migration, Religion, Relationships.

The 3 R's: the three purposes of the Words of Empowerment; to state reality, to reinforce, to reconcile.

Threads of Consciousness: non-personal manifestations that arise in human nature; have ability to connect one another, particularly family members both positively and negatively.

Three-Day Guideline: suggested timeline for integrating a Constellation before sharing or processing it with others.

Three Healing Words: "please," "thank you," "yes;" simple yet powerful words used within a Constellation for reconciliation, resolution, and Soul recognition.

True Guilt: aids one in breaking away from restriction in one's life; necessary in order to progress; instills character strength.

Veil of Forgetting: considered as the separation between heaven and earth, spirit and matter, pre- and post-birth; thought to erase conscious memory of one's incarnational choices.

Vesica Pisces: the joining of two fields to create a third; source of immense energy and power. In TCA, sacred intersection that occurs between two Representatives in a Constellation that can open a connection to the Soul nature of each.

Victim: a person who has suffered, been harmed, injured, or killed as a result of the actions or negative attitudes of someone else or of a people.

Words of Empowerment: particular words spoken by the Client and/or Representative(s) to one or more Representatives in a Constellation in a succinct and respectful manner.

World Work Pathways: *i.e.* Metzner's Six Life Pathways of Destiny; based on six vocational ways of being in the world: warrior, teacher, healer, visionary, builder, explorer.

Select Bibliography

Arrien, Ph.D Angeles. *The Four-Fold Way: Walking the Paths of the Warrior, Teacher, Healer and Visionary.* New York: HarperCollins, 1993.

Aum. Vol. II, in *Encyclopedia of Hinduism,* edited by K. L. Seshagiri Rao and Kapil Kapoor, 35-36. San Rafael: Mandala Publishing, 2013.

Aurobindo, Sri. *The Psychic Being: Soul: Its Nature, Mission and Evolution.* Twin Lakes: Lotus Press, 1990.

Barnstone, Willis, ed. *The Other Bible: Ancient Alternative Scriptures.* New York: HarperCollins, 1984.

Boring, Francesca Mason. *Connecting to Our Ancestral Path: Healing through Family Constellations, Ceremony, and Ritual: A Native American Perspective.* Berkeley: North Atlantic Books, 2012.

Boszormenyi-Nagy, Ivan and Geraldine Spark. *Invisible Loyalties: Reciprocity in Intergenerational Family Therapy.* New York: Harper & Row, 1973.

Brennan, Barbara Ann. *Hands of Light: A Guide to Healing Through the Human Energy Field: A New Paradigm for the Human Being in Health, Relationship, and Disease.* New York: Pleiades Books, 1987.

—. *Light Emerging: The Journey of Personal Healing.* New York: Bantam Books, 1993.

Bryson, Thomas, and Dr. Ursula Franke-Bryson. *Encounters with Death.* Munich: Night Sky Productions, 2012.

Campbell, Joseph. *The Power of Myth.* New York: MJF Books, 1988.

Cohen, Dan B. *I Carry Your Heart in My Heart: Family Constellations in Prison.* Heidelberg: Carl-Auer-Systeme Verlag, 2009.

Colum, Padraic. *Nordic Gods and Heroes.* New York: Dover Publications, Inc., 1996.

Condron, Daniel. *Dreams of the Soul: The Yogi Sutras of Patanjali.* Windyville: SOM Publishing, 1991.

Davidson, H.R. Ellis. *Gods and Myths of Northern Europe.* New York: Penguin Books, 1964.

Edinger, Edward F. *Ego and Archetype: Individuation and the Religious Function of the Psyche.* Boston: Shambhala, 1992.

Faust, J., and P. Faust. "The Role of Energy and Intuition in the Constellation Approach." In *Messengers of Healing: The Family Constellations of Bert Hellinger Through the Eyes of a New Generation of Practitioners,* edited by J. Edward Lynch and Suzi Tucker, 58-82. Phoenix: Zeig, Tucker & Theisen, Inc., 2005.

Franke, Ursula. *In My Mind's Eye: Family Constellations in Individual Therapy and Counseling.* Translated by Colleen Beaumont. Heidelberg: Carl-Auer-Systeme Verlag, 2003.

—. *The River Never Looks Back: Historical and Practical Foundations of Bert Hellinger's Family Constellations.* Translated by Karen Leube. Heidelberg: Carl-Auer-Systeme Verlag, 2003.

Gerber, Richard. *Vibrational Medicine: New Choices For Healing Ourselves*. Santa Fe: Bear & Company, 1988.

Grigg, Ray. *The Tao of Relationships: Lao Tzu's Tao Te Ching Adapted for a New Age*. Atlanta: Humanics Limited, 1988.

Hammer, Leon. *Dragon Rises, Red Bird Flies: Psychology & Chinese Medicine*. Barrytown: Station Hill Press, 1990.

Hausner, Stephan. *Even If It Costs Me My Life: Systemic Constellations and Serious Illness*. Translated by Colleen Beaumont. New York: Routledge, Taylor & Francis Group, 2011.

Hellinger, Bert and Ten Hövel, Gabriele. *Acknowledging What Is: Conversations with Bert Hellinger*. Translated by Colleen Beaumont. Phoenix: Zeig, Tucker & Co., Inc., 1999.

Hellinger, Bert. *Farewell: Family Constellations with Descendants of Victims and Perpetrators*. Translated by Colleen Beaumont. Heidelberg: Carl-Auer-Systeme Verlag, 2003.

—. *Insights: Lectures and Stories*. Translated by Jutta ten Herkel. Heidelberg: Carl-Auer-Systeme Verlag, 2002.

—. *Love's Own Truths: Bonding and Balancing in Close Relationships*. Translated by Maureen Oberli-Turner and Hunter Beaumont. Phoenix: Zeig, Tucker & Theisen, Inc., 2001.

—. *No Waves Without the Ocean: Experiences and Thoughts*. Translated by Jutta ten Herkel and Sally Tombleson. Heidelberg: Carl-Auer-Systeme Verlag, 2006.

—. *On Life & Other Paradoxes; Aphorisms and Little Stories from Bert Hellinger*. Translated by Ralph Metzner. Phoenix: Zeig, Tucker & Theisen, Inc., 2002.

—. *Peace Begins in the Soul: Family Constellations in the Service of Reconciliation*. Translated by Colleen Beaumont. Heidelberg: Carl-Auer-Systeme Verlag, 2003.

—. *Rachel Weeping for Her Children: Family Constellations in Israel*. Heidelberg: Carl-Auer-Systeme Verlag, 2003.

—. *To the Heart of the Matter: Brief Therapies*. Translated by Colleen Beaumont. Heidelberg: Carl-Auer-Systeme Verlag, 2003.

—. *With God in Mind—Our Thinking About God: Where It Comes From and Where It Leads*. Translated by Ludwig Fischer. Bischofswiesen: Hellinger Publications, 2007.

Hellinger, Bert with Gunthard Weber and Hunter Beaumont. *Love's Hidden Symmetry: What Makes Love Work in Relationships*. Translated by Zweierlei Glück. Phoenix: Zeig, Tucker & Co., Inc., 1998.

Hillman, James. *Re-Visioning Psychology*. Paperback, Reissue Edition. New York: HarperPerennial, 1997.

—. *The Soul's Code: In Search of Character and Calling*. New York: Grand Central Publishing, 1996.

Holmes, Dr Paul, Marcia Karp, and Michael Watson. *Psychodrama Since Moreno: Innovations in Theory and Practice*. London: Routledge, 1994.

Hurley, Dan. "Grandmother's Experiences Leave a Mark in Your Genes." *Discover Magazine*, May 2013.

Huxley, Aldous. *The Perennial Philosophy*. HarperPerennial Modern Classics Edition. New York: HarperPerennial Modern Classics, 2009.

Ingerman, Sandra. *Soul Retrieval: Mending the Fragmented Self*. Revised & Updated. New York: HarperOne, 1991.

Iverson, Lisa B. *Ancestral Blueprints: Revealing Invisible Truths in America's Soul*. Bellingham: Family Constellations West Publishing, 2009.

Judith, Anodea. *Eastern Body, Western Mind: Psychology and the Chakra System as a Path to the Self*. Berkeley: Celestial Arts, 1996.

—. *Wheels of Life: A User's Guide to the Chakra System*. St. Paul: Llewellyn Publications, 1987.

Kaplan, Connie. *The Invisible Garment: 30 Spiritual Principles that Weave the Fabric of Human Life*. San Diego: Jodere Group, 2004.

Kaptchuk, Ted J. *The Web That Has No Weaver: Understanding Chinese Medicine*. New York: Congdon & Weed, Inc., 1983.

Kerner, Jerome. *Be It Ever So Humble: A dialogue at the threshold of Family, Ancestors, Culture and Home*. United States of America: Booksurge.com, 2009.

King, Serge. *Kahuna Healing*. Wheaton: The Theosophical Publishing House, 1983.

Kluger, Jeffrey. *The Sibling Effect: What the Bonds Among Brothers and Sisters Reveal About Us*. New York: Riverhead Books, 2011.

Leland, Kurt. *Otherwhere: A Field Guide to Nonphysical Reality for the Out-of-Body Traveler*. Paperback. Newburyport: Hampton Roads Publishing, 2002.

—. *The Unanswered Question: Death, Near-Death, and the Afterlife*. Newburyport: Hampton Roads Publishing, 2002.

Lipton, Bruce H., and Steve Bhaerman. *Spontaneous Evolution: Our Positive Future and a Way to Get There From Here*. Carlsbad: Hay House, Inc., 2010.

Lynch, J. Edward, and Suzi Tucker. *Messengers of Healing: The Family Constellations of Bert Hellinger Through the Eyes of a New Generation of Practitioners*. Phoenix: Zeig, Tucker & Theisen, Inc., 2005.

Maciocia, Giovanni. *The Foundations of Chinese Medicine: A Comprehensive Text for Acupuncturists and Herbalists*. Edinburgh: Churchill Livingstone, 1989.

Madelung, Eva, and Barbara Innecken. *Entering Inner Images: A Creative Use of Constellations in Individual Therapy, Counseling, Groups and Self-Help*. Translated by Colleen Beaumont. Heidelberg: Carl-Auer-Systeme Verlag, 2004.

McCoy, Daniel. *The Love of Destiny: The Sacred and the Profane in Germanic Polytheism*. Nashville: McCoy Publishing, 2013.

McGoldrick, Monica and Randy Gerson. *Genograms in Family Assessment.* New York: Norton Professional Books, 1985.

McGoldrick, Monica. *Genograms: Assessment and Intervention.* Third Edition. New York: Norton Professional Books, 2008.

Meade, Michael. *Fate and Destiny: The Two Agreements of the Soul.* Seattle: GreenFire Press, 2010.

Metzner, Ralph. *Diving for Treasures: Poems and Epilogs.* Berkeley: Regent Press for the Green Earth Foundation, 2015.

—. *Eyes of the Seeress—Voices of the Poet.* Berkeley: Regent Press for the Green Earth Foundation, 2011.

—. *The Life Cycle of the Human Soul: Incarnation; Conception; Birth; Death; Hereafter; Reincarnation.* Berkeley: Regent Press for the Green Earth Foundation, 2011.

—. "The Psychology of Birth, the Prenatal Epoch and Incarnation: Ancient and Modern Perspectives." El Verano: Green Earth Foundation, 2004.

—. *The Six Pathways of Destiny.* Berkeley: Regent Press for the Green Earth Foundation, 2012.

—. *The Unfolding Self: Varieties of Transformative Experience.* Novato: Origin Press, 1998.

—. *The Well of Remembrance: Rediscovering the Earth Wisdom Myths of Northern Europe.* Boston: Shambhala, 1994.

Monroe, Robert. *Journeys Out of the Body.* Updated Edition. New York: Broadway Books, 2009.

Moore, Thomas. *Care of the Soul: A Guide for Cultivating Depth and Sacredness in Everyday Life.* New York: HarperPerennial, 1992.

Myss, Caroline. *Anatomy of the Spirit: The Seven Stages of Power and Healing.* New York: Harmony Books, 1996.

—. *Sacred Contracts: Awakening Your Divine Potential.* Berkeley: Harmony Books, 2003.

Neuhauser, Johannes, ed. *Supporting Love: How Love Works in Couple Relationships: Bert Hellinger's Work with Couples.* Translated by Colleen Beaumont. Phoenix: Zeig, Tucker & Theisen, Inc., 2001.

Newton, Michael. *Destiny of Souls: New Case Studies of Life Between Lives.* St. Paul: Llewellyn Publications, 2000.

—. *Journey of Souls: Case Studies of Life Between Lives.* St. Paul: Llewellyn Publications, 1994.

Palmer, Louise Danielle. "How to Heal Your Family: Family Constellations-a mystically effective way to heal the present by changing the past." *Spirituality & Health*, 2006 Nov/Dec.

Petridis, Chrysovalantis. *Plato's Mythologizing of the Myth of Er.* Portland: Inkwater Press, 2009.

Pierrakos, Eva. *Guide Lectures for Self-Transformation.* Phoenicia: Center for the Living Force, Inc., 1984.

Plotkin, Bill. *Soulcraft: Crossing into the Mysteries of Nature and Psyche.* Novato: New World Library, 2003.

Reddy, Michael. *Health, Happiness, & Family Constellations: How Ancestors, Family Systems, and Hidden Loyalties Shape Your Life-and What YOU Can Do About It.* Kimberton: ReddyWorks Press, 2012.

Rogers, D.D., Ph.D., Peter C. *Ultimate Truth: Book 1.* Bloomington: AuthorHouse, 2009.

Ruhl, Michaelene R. "Clients' Experiences of Family Constellations in Psychological Healing." PhD diss., Michigan School of Professional Psychology, 2013.

Samskāra. Vol. IX, in *Encyclopedia of Hinduism,* edited by K. L. Seshsagiri Rao and Kapil Kapoor, 149-152. San Rafael: Mandala Publishing, 2013.

Schwartz, Howard. *Before You Were Born.* Brookfield: Roaring Book Press, 2005.

Sheldrake, Rupert. *Morphic Resonance: The Nature of Formative Causation.* Paperback, Revised and Expanded Edition of A New Science of Life. Rochester: Park Street Press, 2009.

—. *The Presence of the Past: Morphic Resonance and the Memory of Nature.* Revised and Expanded Edition. Rochester: Park Street Press, 2012.

Singer, June. *Boundaries of the Soul: The Practice of Jung's Psychology.* New York: Anchor Books, 1972.

Singer, Michael A. *The Untethered Soul: The Journey Beyond Yourself.* Oakland: New Harbinger Publications, Inc., 2007.

Ulsamer, Bertold. *The Art and Practice of Family Constellations: Leading Family Constellations as Developed by Bert Hellinger.* Translated by Colleen Beaumont. Heidelberg: Carl-Auer-Systeme Verlag, 2003.

—. *The Healing Power of the Past: A New Approach to Healing Family Wounds.* Translated by Tom Breyfogle. Nevada City: Underwood Books, 2005.

Van Kampenhout, Daan. *Images of the Soul: The Workings of the Soul in Shamanic Rituals and Family Constellations.* Heidelberg: Carl-Auer-Systeme Verlag, 2001.

—. *The Tears of the Ancestors: Victims and Perpetrators in the Tribal Soul.* Phoenix: Zeig, Tucker & Theisen, Inc., 2008.

von Franz, Marie-Louise. *An Introduction to the Symbolism and the Psychology.* Toronto: Inner City Books, 1980.

Worland, Justin. "The Bill Could Help Veterans and Mental Health." *Time Magazine,* February, 2013.

Zukav, Gary. *The Seat of the Soul.* New York: Fireside, 1989.

Resources

Educational

The Constellation Approach (TCA)
For information of the authors' Immersion Program, seminars, and private sessions.
www.constellationapproach.com

Bert Hellinger
For information about Bert and Sophie Hellinger's offerings in Europe.
www.hellinger.com

Barbara Brennan School of Healing
For information on becoming a Brennan Healing Science Practitioner.
www.barbarabrennan.com

Ralph Metzner
For information on Ralph Metzner's offerings and the Ecology of Consciousness book series.
www.greenearthfound.org

Family Lineage

Ancestry.com
Family history website designed "to help everyone discover, preserve and share their family history."
www.ancestry.com

23andme.com
Genetic research site, offers purchase of saliva testing to "discover your ancestral origins and trace your lineage with a personalized analysis of your DNA."
www.23andme.com

Family Tree Builder
Free, downloadable software application from MyHeritage.com
www.myheritage.com/family-tree-builder

Photo: Ana M. Reyes

About the Authors

Jamy and Peter Faust have been studying, practicing and teaching the Healing Arts for over twenty-five years.

Jamy holds a Master of Arts degree in Holistic Counseling and Psychology, and is a graduate of the Barbara Brennan School of Healing, where she formerly taught. She has taught LichtArbeit (LightWork) seminars with Integra Institute, Germany; is trained in Metzner Alchemical Divination practices; and is certified in Japanese Shiatsu. Jamy is also the founder of Amethyst Opening, a depth-work process that combines sacred ceremony, neo-shamanic journeying and awakening practices. She attended the University of Hawaii, Manoa, where she received her Bachelor's degree in Health Education. While residing in the Hawaiian Islands, she began practicing Tibetan Buddhism and took refuge with the 16th Karmapa of the Kagyü Lineage.

Peter's first career was in Culinary Arts. At age thirty-three he began his studies in Eastern Medicine and Spiritual Healing, attending the New England School of Acupuncture and the Barbara Brennan School of Healing, where he also taught for many years. He holds a Master's degree in Japanese and Chinese Acupuncture, and is licensed to practice Herbal Medicine. Peter also leads men's workshops through the Hero's Journey Foundation. He received his Bachelor's degree from Pennsylvania State University, and met Jamy while working in Hawaii.

Both Jamy and Peter have private practices near Boston, and lead seminars and trainings together in the Constellation Approach. They have been married for thirty years and have a lifetime commitment to helping others find peace through their family lineage.

They can be reached at: faust@constellationapproach.com

Believe nothing, no matter where you read it,
or who has said it, even if I have said it,
unless it agrees with your own reason
and your own common sense.

—Gautama Buddha

CPSIA information can be obtained
at www.ICGtesting.com
Printed in the USA
FSOW03n1610250917
39157FS